COMMITMENTS AND FLEXIBILITIES IN THE WTO AGREEMENT ON SUBSIDIES AND COUNTERVAILING MEASURES

The ability of countries to promote and protect their domestic industries in the face of stiff global competition is an important consideration in any trading agreement. Member states of the World Trade Organization are expected to adhere to the WTO Agreement on Subsidies and Countervailing Measures, but to what extent do the WTO Members have policy space to subsidize their industries? Using an economically informed framework, Caiado examines the flexibilities countries may find at the WTO to grant subsidies and impose tariffs to protect designated industries. By testing the Treaty system of entitlements and enforcement mechanisms against the theory of incomplete contract, this work offers a comprehensive analysis of the capacity of the SCM Agreement to achieve its goal: the concomitant regulation of opportunistic behavior and assurance of ex post flexibility.

José Guilherme Moreno Caiado concluded his PhD at the DFG Graduate School "The Economics of the Internationalization of the Law" at the University of Hamburg. He held a Marie Curie Fellowship for the DISSETTLE project and is the co-organizer of the PEPA/SIEL Conference Series. His research and publications focus on public and private issues of compliance with international economic law.

CAMBRIDGE INTERNATIONAL TRADE AND ECONOMIC LAW

Series editors

Dr Lorand Bartels, *University of Cambridge*
Professor Thomas Cottier, *University of Berne*
Professor William Davey, *University of Illinois*

As the processes of regionalisation and globalisation have intensified, there have been accompanying increases in the regulations of international trade and economic law at the levels of international, regional and national laws.

The subject matter of this series is international economic law. Its core is the regulation of international trade, investment and cognate areas such as intellectual property and competition policy. The series publishes books on related regulatory areas, in particular human rights, labour, environment and culture, as well as sustainable development. These areas are vertically linked at the international, regional and national level, and the series extends to the implementation of these rules at these different levels. The series also includes works on governance, dealing with the structure and operation of related international organisations in the field of international economic law, and the way they interact with other subjects of international and national law.

Books in the series

The Return of the Home State to Investor-State Disputes: Bringing Back Diplomatic Protection?
Rodrigo Polanco

The Public International Law of Trade in Legal Services
David Collins

Industrial Policy and the World Trade Organization: Between Legal Constraints and Flexibilities
Sherzod Shadikhodjaev

The Prudential Carve-Out for Financial Services: Rationale and Practice in the GATS and Preferential Trade Agreements
Carlo Maria Cantore

Judicial Acts and Investment Treaty Arbitration
Berk Demirkol

Distributive Justice and World Trade Law: A Political Theory of International Trade Regulation
Oisin Suttle

Freedom of Transit and Access to Gas Pipeline Networks under WTO Law
Vitalily Pogoretskyy

Reclaiming Development in the World Trading System, 2nd Edition
Yong-Shik Lee

COMMITMENTS AND FLEXIBILITIES IN THE WTO AGREEMENT ON SUBSIDIES AND COUNTERVAILING MEASURES

An Economically Informed Analysis

JOSÉ GUILHERME MORENO CAIADO

University of Hamburg

CAMBRIDGE
UNIVERSITY PRESS

CAMBRIDGE
UNIVERSITY PRESS

University Printing House, Cambridge CB2 8BS, United Kingdom

One Liberty Plaza, 20th Floor, New York, NY 10006, USA

477 Williamstown Road, Port Melbourne, VIC 3207, Australia

314–321, 3rd Floor, Plot 3, Splendor Forum, Jasola District Centre,
New Delhi – 110025, India

79 Anson Road, #06–04/06, Singapore 079906

Cambridge University Press is part of the University of Cambridge.

It furthers the University's mission by disseminating knowledge in the pursuit of
education, learning, and research at the highest international levels of excellence.

www.cambridge.org
Information on this title: www.cambridge.org/9781108474320
DOI: 10.1017/9781108565158

First published 2019

Printed and bound in Great Britain by Clays Ltd, Elcograf S.p.A.

A catalogue record for this publication is available from the British Library.

Library of Congress Cataloging-in-Publication Data
Names: Caiado, Jose Guilherme Moreno, author.
Title: Commitments and flexibilities in the WTO agreement on subsidies and countervailing
measures : an economically informed analysis / Jose Guilherme Moreno Caiado, University
of Hamburg.
Description: Cambridge, United Kingdom ; New York, NY, USA : Cambridge University
Press, 2019. | Series: Cambridge international trade and economic law | Based on author's
thesis (doctoral – Universitat Hamburg, 2016). | Includes bibliographical references and index.
Identifiers: LCCN 2019008385 | ISBN 9781108474320 (hardback)
Subjects: LCSH: Antidumping duties – Law and legislation. | Subsidies – Law and legislation.
Classification: LCC K4635 .C35 2019 | DDC 382/.63–dc23
LC record available at https://lccn.loc.gov/2019008385

ISBN 978-1-108-47432-0 Hardback

To my parents, for their unconditional support, and to
Friederike who, as a result of me tying myself to this mast, has
at times had to steer our ship by herself.

CONTENTS

ix

FIGURES

TABLES

BOXES

FOREWORD

At the time of this writing, the multilateral trading system, and with it, the WTO, is under considerable stress, both institutionally and in light of outside pressure caused by an increasing retreat into protectionism, nationalism, and bilateralism. However, to paraphrase Mark Twain, reports of the death of the multilateral trading order are greatly exaggerated. Anyone who may wish to ring the death knell of the WTO is reminded that there are issue areas that can only be sensibly addressed in a multilateral context.

Take subsidies, the policy tool at the heart of this book, as an example: subsidies, while politically expedient in a domestic context, can cause negative international externalities. Once granted, subsidies can distort the international conditions of competition, and thus cause economic harm (or "serious prejudice" in WTO parlance) to the interests of other countries. To prevent a downward spiral of harmful "beggar-thy-neighbor" policies imposed by subsidizing countries onto each other, a contract between countries suggests itself. Yet, any agreement on curbing the use of subsidies by nature ought to be multilateral. There is no efficient bilateral treaty that regulates the use of subsidies between two (or a number of) signatories but leaves policy discretion *vis-à-vis* non-signatory third parties. Bilateralism may work in the context of, say, tariffs, but it fails in the context of subsidies. In that sense, if it didn't exist already, sovereign countries would have to invent the multilateral WTO Agreement on Subsidies and Countervailing Duties (the *SCM Agreement*) to address the problem of negative global spillovers from excessive subsidization.

It is thus no surprise that the *SCM Agreement* is considered a central pillar of the WTO framework. This is not only reflected in the number of high-profile WTO disputes over subsidies and countervailing measures, but also in considerable academic interest in the topic. However, the literature on the *SCM Agreement* is largely impressionistic. Commentators either limit themselves to criticizing decisions by WTO panels or the Appellate Body, or to providing a description of problems of and loopholes in the agreement and offering a catalogue of quick-fix solutions.

The present book by José Caiado stands out in an important respect: it does not content itself with the "What?" of describing the extant WTO rules on subsidies, or the "how to" of fixing problems with the agreement. Instead, Caiado first delves into the "Why?" behind the *SCM Agreement*, before explaining how insights from this analysis inform the substance and architecture of the agreement, and before engaging in recommendations for reform.

More specifically, this book constitutes the first – and long overdue – comprehensive contract-theoretical analysis of the *SCM Agreement*. Applying a Law and Economics toolkit, Caiado assesses the relevant actors, their preferences, incentives, limitations (be they limits of rationality, limits of capability, or resource limitations), and option spaces and strategies. This enables the author to provide answers to a series of key institutional questions including: What motivated WTO Members to conclude an agreement on subsidies in the first place? What were the basic contractual commitments exchanged between signatories, and how did contracting parties deal with the inevitable incompleteness of the contract, particularly the inability of contracting parties to foresee future events? Why did the drafters of the *SCM Agreement* include a set of opt-out rules permitting *ex post* flexibility, and is the price-tag for exercising such opt-outs sufficient to curb opportunistic behavior? Why did the contracting parties decide to delegate gap-filling responsibility to courts, rather than attempting to fill such gaps themselves at the conclusion of the contract? How did contractual rules of flexibility (and contractual loopholes) determine Members' depths and breadth of cooperation *ex ante*, that is, at the time of concluding the contract? What motivates Members to flout the rules, rather than sticking with contract-consistent flexibility tools?

The *SCM Agreement*, like many other WTO Agreements, is in need of improvement. However, without an understanding of the relevant actors, their preferences, incentives, limitations, options, and strategies, *any* recipe for improvement and reform of the *SCM Agreement* risks being ineffectual at best, and counter-productive at worst. It is meticulously researched and well-argued books like Caiado's that are able to inform good policymaking. Books like this are uniquely suited to form the foundation for a feasible reform agenda, and to guide the way towards making the WTO a better and more effective organization – and this book offers significant contributions in this respect.

Simon Schropp
Managing Economist at Sidley Austin LLP

PREFACE

This work examines the international legal rules governing use of non-agricultural subsidies, as established by the WTO Agreement on Subsidies and Countervailing Measures (SCM Agreement, or Treaty) and interpreted by relevant case law. Its hypothesis is that explanation for the design of the current Treaty lies in the desire of rational policymakers to regulate subsidy use in such a way as to ensure provision of flexibility, while at the same time avoiding the erosion of tariff cuts and distortions to competition. The question, therefore, is whether the current Treaty mechanisms designed to promote flexibility are adequate to meet this objective. This question is addressed through use of an analytical framework based in "incomplete contract," and methods involving deductive reasoning and legal doctrinal analysis and interpretation. The analysis of the SCM Agreement indicates that despite the many criticisms identified in legal and economic scholarship, drafters have created a complex system of interplay between commitments and flexibilities, reflecting a great deal of economic insight. It is asserted, however, that the flexibility in the system requires improvement due to the high level of uncertainty to which agreements on subsidies are subject. The development of this thesis begins with an introduction to basic economic analyses of governmental use of subsidies, and generation of an economically informed description of the SCM Agreement. By testing the Treaty system of entitlements and enforcement mechanisms against the theory of incomplete contract, the work offers a comprehensive analysis of the capacity of the SCM Agreement to achieve its goal: the concomitant regulation of opportunistic behavior and assurance of *ex post* flexibility. Its conclusions offer insights that will enable policymakers and adjudicators to better understand and interpret the SCM Agreement, and provide a basis for future research.

ACKNOWLEDGMENTS

This book is the result of my doctoral studies at the DFG International Graduate College "The Economics of the Internationalisation of the Law."

As my PhD supervisor, professor Anne van Aaken has from the beginning challenged, supported, and guided me with a trust that has persisted despite my many missed deadlines and moments of silence. It was Anne who introduced me to professor Hans-Bernd Schäfer, who through his introduction to the vast world of economics has repeatedly proven his generosity and patience. Simon Schropp, who completes my supervisory board, has been decisive in shaping the structure of this thesis.

I have been privileged to work at the Institute of Law and Economics of Hamburg University under the leadership of professors Thomas Eger, Stefan Voigt, and Patrick Lyons. I am especially thankful for the support of David Börn and Christiane Ney-Schönig, and the friendship of Luis, Thomas, Daragh, Christoph, Joseb, and all the others sharing offices in the Wiwi Bunker.

My research stays in St. Gallen, Sao Paulo, and Geneva have also been crucial to the development of this work. I am grateful to Katrin Krehan, Paulo Casella, José Augusto Fontoura Costa, Gabrielle Marceau, Maria Pereyra, and Graham Cook for making these possible.

The colleagues from the Marie Curie Network DISSETTLE (Dispute Settlement in Trade: Training in Law and Economics) have also had a great influence on this work. My thanks go to all of them, as represented in particular by Theresa Carpenter and Angelica Zanninelli.

Alongside these projects, SIEL (the Society of International Economic Law) and its PEPA Network have provided important academic support in international economic law. Since Colin Picker first recruited me at a conference in Sydney, I have had the pleasure to work closely with him, Meredith Kolsky Lewis, Gabrielle Marceau, Freya Baetens, Holger Hestermeyer, and many others.

To conclude, a special acknowledgment to my colleagues who have, one way or another, contributed to this work, either by reading early drafts and discussing WTO law, or supporting me in times when I needed motivation: Thomas Berghaus, Vera Thorstensen, Anna Micara, Cedric Bär, Diego Kosbiau, Geraldo Vidigal, David De'Remmer, Jelena Baumler, Michelle Ratton Sanchez Badin, Carlo de Stefano, Marios Iacovides, Daniel Ari Baker, Rodd Izadnia, Giovanna Adinolfi, Roberto Kanitz, Carolina Saldanha Ures, Marina Takitani, Stephan Wittig, Edwin Vermulst, Jeremie Charles, Dominic Coppens, Geraldo Vidigal, Ada Siqueira, and Yuri Szabo Yamashita.

AB	Appellate Body
Anti-Dumping Agreement	Agreement on Implementation of Article VI of the Agreement General Agreement on Tariffs and Trade, 1994
Covered agreements	The agreements listed in Appendix 1 to the Understanding on Rules and Procedures Governing the Settlement of Disputes
DSB	Dispute Settlement Body
DSU	Understanding on Rules and Procedures Governing the Settlement of Disputes (Dispute Settlement Understanding)
GATS	General Agreement on Trade in Services
GATT 1947	General Agreement on Tariffs and Trade, 1947
GATT 1994	General Agreement on Tariffs and Trade, 1994
GPA	Agreement on Government Procurement
ICJ	International Court of Justice
IMF	International Monetary Fund
ITO	International Trade Organization
MERCOSUR	Southern Cone Common Market, Treaty of Asuncion, done at Asuncion, March 26, 1991, 30 ILM 1041
MFN	Most-favored-nation
NTBs	Non-tariff barriers
OECD	Organisation for Economic Cooperation and Development
Plurilateral Trade Agreements	The agreements and associated legal instruments included in Annex 4 to the Agreement Establishing the World Trade Organization
SCM Agreement, or Treaty	Agreement on Subsidies and Countervailing Measures
SCM Committee	WTO Committee on Subsidies and Countervailing Measures
Secretariat	Secretariat of the World Trade Organization

SPS Agreement	Agreement on the Application of Sanitary and Phytosanitary Measures
TBT Agreement	Agreement on Technical Barriers to Trade
TPR	Trade Policy Review
TPRM	Trade Policy Review Mechanism
TRIMS Agreement	Agreement on Trade-Related Investment Measures
TRIPS Agreement	Agreement on Trade-Related Aspects of Intellectual Property Rights
UNCTAD	United Nations Conference on Trade and Development
VCLT	Vienna Convention on the Law of Treaties between States and International Organizations or between International Organizations, 1986, Doc A/CONF.129/15; 25 ILM 543
WCO	World Customs Organization
WHO	World Health Organization
WTO	World Trade Organization
WTO Agreement	Marrakesh Agreement Establishing the World Trade Organization, done at Marrakesh, April 15, 1994, 1867 UNTS 154; 33 ILM 1144

WTO DISPUTE SETTLEMENT REPORTS

(cont.)

(*cont.*)

Short Title	Full Case Title and Citation
	in Large Civil Aircraft, WT/DS316/AB/R, adopted 1 June 2011, DSR 2011:I, p. 7
EC and Certain Member States – Large Civil Aircraft	Panel Report, European Communities and Certain Member States – Measures Affecting Trade in Large Civil Aircraft, WT/DS316/R, adopted 1 June 2011, as modified by Appellate Body Report, WT/DS316/AB/R, DSR 2011:II, p. 685
India – Autos	Appellate Body Report, India – Measures Affecting the Automotive Sector, WT/DS146/AB/R, WT/DS175/AB/R, adopted 5 April 2002, DSR 2002:V, p. 1821
India – Autos	Panel Report, India – Measures Affecting the Automotive Sector, WT/DS146/R, WT/DS175/R, and Corr.1, adopted 5 April 2002, DSR 2002:V, p. 1827
Indonesia – Autos	Panel Report, Indonesia – Certain Measures Affecting the Automobile Industry, WT/DS54/R, WT/DS55/R, WT/DS59/R, WT/DS64/R, Corr.1 and Corr.2, adopted 23 July 1998, and Corr.3 and Corr.4, DSR 1998:VI, p. 2201
Japan – DRAMS (Korea)	Appellate Body Report, Japan – Countervailing Duties on Dynamic Random Access Memories from Korea, WT/DS336/AB/R and Corr.1, adopted 17 December 2007, DSR 2007:VII, p. 2703
Japan – DRAMS (Korea)	Panel Report, Japan – Countervailing Duties on Dynamic Random Access Memories from Korea, WT/DS336/R, adopted 17 December 2007, as modified by Appellate Body Report WT/DS336/AB/R, DSR 2007:VII, p. 2805
Japan – Film	Panel Report, Japan – Measures Affecting Consumer Photographic Film and Paper, WT/DS44/R, adopted April 22, 1998, DSR 1998:IV, p. 1179
Korea – Various Measures on Beef	Appellate Body Report, Korea – Measures Affecting Imports of Fresh, Chilled and Frozen Beef, WT/

(cont.)

(cont.)

(cont.)

Short Title	Full Case Title and Citation
	2012, as modified by Appellate Body Report WT/DS353/AB/R, DSR 2012:II, p. 649
US – Lead and Bismuth II	Appellate Body Report, United States – Imposition of Countervailing Duties on Certain Hot-Rolled Lead and Bismuth Carbon Steel Products Originating in the United Kingdom, WT/DS138/AB/R, adopted 7 June 2000, DSR 2000:V, p. 2595
US – Lead and Bismuth II	Panel Report, United States – Imposition of Countervailing Duties on Certain Hot-Rolled Lead and Bismuth Carbon Steel Products Originating in the United Kingdom, WT/DS138/R and Corr.2, adopted 7 June 2000, upheld by Appellate Body Report WT/DS138/AB/R, DSR 2000:VI, p. 2623
US – Shrimp	Appellate Body Report, United States – Import Prohibition of Certain Shrimp and Shrimp Products, WT/DS58/AB/R, adopted 6 November 1998, DSR 1998:VII, p. 2755
US – Shrimp	Panel Report, United States – Import Prohibition of Certain Shrimp and Shrimp Products, WT/DS58/R and Corr.1, adopted 6 November 1998, as modified by Appellate Body Report WT/DS58/AB/R, DSR 1998:VII, p. 2821
US – Softwood Lumber III	Panel Report, United States – Preliminary Determinations with Respect to Certain Softwood Lumber from Canada, WT/DS236/R, adopted 1 November 2002, DSR 2002:IX, p. 3597
US – Softwood Lumber IV	Appellate Body Report, United States – Final Countervailing Duty Determination with Respect to Certain Softwood Lumber from Canada, WT/DS257/AB/R, adopted 17 February 2004, DSR 2004:II, p. 571
US – Softwood Lumber IV	Panel Report, United States – Final Countervailing Duty Determination with Respect to Certain Softwood Lumber from Canada, WT/DS257/R and Corr.1, adopted 17 February 2004, as modified by Appellate Body Report WT/DS257/AB/R, DSR 2004:II, p. 641

(cont.)

1

Introduction

In the first quarters of 2016, milk prices in Germany fell to historic lows. The fall was due, among other things, to intensified competition in the EU agricultural market, and to a drop in demand caused by unilateral Russian trade sanctions against certain EU products. A corresponding fall in the income of farmers, while consumers benefited from the lower prices, gave rise to antagonistic reactions by certain societal groups, and triggered discussions about the fairness of market mechanisms and the need for governmental intervention in certain economic sectors. In the words of an editor of a respected German newspaper:

> When regarding the decline in milk prices, one could give the cold look, as cold as a milk tank in the dairy, and say: That is what happens in the market economy. Supply and demand determine price. Who cannot beat the cheaper competition, must look for another occupation [...] and don 't consumers benefit by the price war in the refrigerated section of supermarkets? [...] But the preservation of family agriculture in Germany might for several reasons be in the general interest. Farmers cultivate the cultural landscape. The family businesses are often the last economic, social and political stabilizer in structurally weak areas.[1]

A commentator in the same paper, addressing the role played by the German government in such a moment of sectoral crisis, noted, not

---

[1] Berthold Kohler, "Das Schicksal der Bauern" *Frankfurter Allgemeine Zeitung* (Frankfurt 05.18.2016) p. 1: "Auf den Verfall der Milchpreise kann mann mit der Kälte eines Milchtanks in der Molkerei schauen und sagen: So ist das in the Markwirtschaft. Angebot und Nachfrage betimmen den Preis. Wer die billigere Konkurrenz nich schlagen kann, muss sich eben eine andere Beschäftitung suchen [...] Und profitieren nicht die Verbraucher vom Preiskammpf in den Kühlregalen der Supermärkte? [...] Aber auch noch aus anderen Gründen liegt die Erhaltung der bäuerlichen Landwirtschaft in Deutschland im Gemeininteresse. Die Bauern pflegen die Kulturlandschaft. Die Familienbetriebe sind oft die letzten ökonomischen, sozialen und auch politischen Stabilisatoren in strukturschwachen Gebiete." Translation by the author.

without irony, that politics usually solves such issues by directing public money to the sector that is in difficulty.

> And the politics? It has undertaken the first best option in a crises situation: make millions of government money available. It started with an EU decision last year under the impact of the first price change. This was blamed on the fall of Russian demand as a result of the import boycott from Moscow, but also on the abolition of the milk quota last March. Now, the plan is to pay, through the federal governments, millions to decelerate the exodus of farmers. The word on the streets is of an amount between 60 to 100 million EUR.[2]

The milk price "crisis" illustrates one characteristic of a market-based economy: its facility for distribution of income within a society due to changes in supply and demand and corresponding variation in prices. Although most economists will agree that this process leads to an efficient result overall, some of the affected groups will receive direct benefit, whereas others will lose income. The losers are, however, unlikely to give up without a struggle to obtain public support. If a government values a specific group or economic activity, it would be usual for the state to intervene in the market, often through the use of subsidies.

The governmental use of subsidies to foster domestic economic groups and sectors is as old as it is controversial. In economic theory, there are two major issues regarding the subsidization. The first is that governments might fail to correctly define the problem because of incomplete information about whom, and to what extent, to subsidize. Even when acting on goodwill to address, through subsidy, a legitimate economic problem in their domestic market (like, in the view of some, the survival of milk farmers), such a failure will result in less than optimal investment of resources and losses in overall welfare.

This potential for domestic misallocation of resources might call for domestic regulation demanding, for instance, that careful consideration be undertaken prior to implementation of government intervention. In EU regulation for state aid, for instance, member states are required

---

[2] Jan Grossarth, "Die Milch macht die müden Bauern nicht mehr munter" Frankfurter Allgemeine Zeitung (05.18.2016): "Und die Politik? Sie hat zunhächst das Erstbeste unternommen, was sich in einer sochen Notlage anbietet: Millionen Staatsgeld zur Verfügung gestellt. Den Anfang machte ein Beschluss der EU im vergangenen Jahr unter dem Eindruck des esrten Preisknicks. Der wurde erklärt mit dem Wegbrechen der russischen Nachfrage infolge des Importboykotts Moskaus, aber auch mit dem Wegfall der Milchquote im Määrz, die europaweit die Menge begrenzt hatte. Jetzt sollen Millionen vom Bund folgen, ausgezalt, um den Exitus der bäuerlichen Milchwirtschaft abzubremsen. Von 60 bis 100 Millionen Euro ist die Rede." Translated by the author.

to notify state aid measures and to secure prior approval by the Commission,[3] thus reducing possible distortions and ensuring that the subsidy is an adequate instrument to achieve its objective.[4]

Another issue in regard to subsidization of domestic groups is the problem of agency accountability.[5] Public resources are scarce, and there is a constant dispute at the domestic level regarding their distribution.[6] Governments inevitably have to choose certain groups over others, thus promoting a redistribution of wealth within the population.

Even with authority to implement redistributive policies, domestic governments may run into issues of accountability[7] related to the tendency of general voters to be disorganized and uninformed. Governments will arguably therefore promote the interests of organized groups, and thus their own, over the interests of the general population.[8]

---

[3] OECD, Competition, State Aids and Subsidies (Policy Roundtables, 2010) p. 105–07.

[4] Luca Rubini, *The Definition of Subsidy and State Aid: WTO and EC Law in Comparative Perspective* (Oxford University Press 2009) p. 59–62.

[5] Although this is certainly a relevant issue in a domestic context, it is not clear whether they would also solve the international problems, as there might be subsidies that are overall welfare-increasing for a state, and thus possibly desired by rational voters, and still harm producers and exporters in other states. Besides, the focus of the WTO agreements are international problems by nature, and the transparency and monitoring instruments we see in the SCM Agreement should be better understood as a control mechanism to other states or to foreign players, and thus addressing the international problem, rather than the domestic issues raised by subsidies, even though the WTO instruments might contribute to mitigate domestic problems as well. This, however, will not be the focus of this research, which rather emphasizes the contractual elements of the SCM Agreement, as will be detailed below. See Chapter 2.

[6] For instance, domestic groups lobby either not to pay taxes or to be the beneficiary of a governmental policy implemented with public resources.

[7] There are different types of principal agent problems involving the government and different results thereof. Przeworski, for instance, works with three classes of principal agent relations (i) the regulation class, which involves cases between the government and private economic agents; (ii) the oversight class, composed of relations between bureaucrats and politicians; and (iii) accountability class, formed by relations between citizens and governments. Overall, he concludes that public officials, subjected to the pressure of interest groups, "may not know how to or may not want to engage in actions that promote the general welfare rather than their own or that of their private allies" Adam Przeworski, "On the Design of the State: A Principal-Agent Perspective" in Luiz Carlos Bresser Pereira and Peter Spink (eds), *Reforming the State: Managerial Public Administration in Latin America* (Reforming the State: Managerial Public Administration in Latin America, Lynne Rienner Publishers 1999) p. 15–17. Political economic theory, however, recognizes that certain groups are in a better position than others to extract resources from the government budget. Farmers may, for instance, be well organized and politically influential, to the detriment of the welfare of the consumer or general public.

[8] Recall that the welfare of the general voter is also an element of the policymaker's political function. Therefore, policymakers have to take at least parts of the interest of disorganized voters into consideration when designing a domestic policy. See Section 3.3.4.

Several instruments aim to overcome this problem by encouraging policymakers to consider the interests of disorganized voters. Regulatory measures might, for instance, increase the informed-ness of the general public by requiring transparency, effective monitoring, and mandatory guidelines for the concession of subsidies. Raising the level of information available to interested voters:[9] (i) enables better assessment of the adequacy and efficiency of the subsidy as a means of achieving a determined policy objective; and (ii) increases the cost of an irresponsible action by the policymaker.[10]

National subsidization of domestic groups or sectors also has wider implications for international trade. By giving a competitive advantage to local firms, domestic subsidies often induce changes in corporate behavior that create cross-border spillovers affecting international trade partners.[11] An influential publication recently posed the following questions related to the role of the German government in fostering international business:

---

[9] Several civil organizations have a goal to raise the information level of voters and the general public. For instance, in the United States, a movement named Good Jobs First attempts to promote accountability by tracking subsidies given to corporations in an attempt to pressure the companies to offer jobs that meet certain quality standards. "Good Jobs First" <http://www.goodjobsfirst.org> accessed 29.07.2016. Other similar initiatives with focus on international trade include "Global Subsidies Initiative" <http://www.iisd.org/gsi/> accessed 29.07.2016, and "Global Trade Alert" <http://www.globaltradealert.org/> accessed 29.07.2016.

[10] For a general overview of the relation of transparency and subsidies, see Andre de Moor, *Key Issues in Subsidy Policies and Strategies for Reform* (Economic Commission for Latin America and the Caribbean 1997) p. 19–20. On the impact of transparency in specific sectors, see, for instance, Doug Koplow and John Dernbach, "Federal Fossil Fuel Subsidies and Greenhouse Gas Emissions: A Case Study of Increasing Transparency for Fiscal Policy" (2001) 26 *Annual Review of Energy and the Environment* p. 361–89; Tracey M Price, "Negotiating WTO Fisheries Subsidy Disciplines: Can Subsidy Transparency and Classification Provide the Means towards an End to the Race for Fish" (2005) 13 *Tulane Journal of International and Comparative Law* 141 p. 165–66; and Tara Laan, "Gaining Traction: The Importance of Transparency in Accelerating the Reform of Fossil-Fuel Subsidies" in Global Subsidies Initiative (ed), *Untold Billions: Fossil-Fuel Subsidies, Their Impacts and the Path to Reform* (Untold Billions: Fossil-Fuel Subsidies, Their Impacts and the Path to Reform, International Institute for Sustainable Development and United Nations Environment Programme 2010) p. 12–14.

[11] The "cross border" effect of governmental measures is not an exclusivity of subsidies. In the milk example above, much of the fall in prices was attributed to a Russian boycott that resulted in a closure of the Russian market to milk produced in Germany. But measures do not need to have the direct objective of disrupting trade in order to spill over in trade partners. Trade-promoting mechanisms may have similar effects.

The main question: How strategically does Germany want to operate its foreign policy? Should the federal government, like the French State, offer direct guarantees for companies to take risks abroad? Should Berlin offer companies favorable loans by state banks (KfW) to compete for large projects, as it does Beijing?[12]

The concern of this business-oriented publication was that German companies were losing opportunities, not because of the superior market competitiveness of their foreign contenders, but due to interventions by foreign governments in favor of their domestic firms. The article asserts that by granting export guarantees or credit at lower than market prices, foreign governments were subsidizing their companies to enable the foreign products to be offered more competitively abroad, thus giving the foreign firms opportunity to gain market share and reduce profits by German competitors.

Subsidization of exports, a typical mechanism for fostering domestic production, causes negative externalities to trade partners. Export subsidies are however, only one part of the problem, as subsidization of products intended for the domestic market might also cause cross-border spillovers.

The problem of the impact of domestic subsidies on international trade has been subjected to imposition of regulatory parameters on various fronts. The OECD was probably the central place for regulation of industrial trade in the 1970s. As noted in the article referred to above, the hands of the German government were rather tied by OECD rules on export subsidies:

> Now, if the federal government participate through Hermes guarantees, these should comply with OECD consensus on export credit rules. The consensus is from 1978, from a time when most Asian countries were aid recipients, not competitors. The rules determine in detail how small interest on government loans can be, how big government guarantees should be, and at what level of debt a country is expelled. The agreement, to which officials of member countries should comply, aims at "substantially eliminating" the state export support.[13]

---

[12] Editorial, Bedingt bereit zum Export (2016) p. 26. In German: "Die Grundstzfragen lauten: Wie strategisch will Deutchsland die Außenwirschaftpolitk betreiben? Soll der Bund wie der französische Staat direkt für Unternehmen bürgen, damit sie im Ausland Risiken eingehen? Soll Berlin die Unternehmen über günstige Kredite staatlicher Banken (KfW) ins Rennen um große Projekte schicken, wie es Peking tut?" Translated by the author.

[13] Editorial, *Bedingt bereit zum Export* (2016) p. 26. In German: "Nun, falls sich der Bund über Hermes-Bürgschaften beteilige, geschehe das nach dem OECD-Konsens über Exportkreditbestimmungen. Der Konsens stammt aus dem Jahr 1978, aus einer Zeit, als

With a further 50 years of global economic development, however, and the rise of several economically powerful nations that are not bound by the OECD, has come a need for broader rules, both in terms of substance and reach. The regime and form of oversight chosen by states for the regulation of subsidies is a series of treaties under the World Trade Organization.

In law and economics theory, an international treaty is a legal instrument used by a group of states to (re)allocate authority among themselves in order to overcome problems preventing cooperation and to regulate excessive unilateralism.[14] Like a contract, a treaty is used to generate mutual benefits to those who are party to it, through the regulation of future behavior.[15] In a trade agreement, for instance, parties exchange market access concessions through tariff cuts, in order to improve the welfare of certain economic sectors by fostering exports and reducing the prices of imports.

The parties to a trade agreement are expected to reach a mutual increase in welfare[16] through the process of negotiation of tariff reductions. The aim is to balance the positive and negative effects of tariff

---

die meisten Länder Asiens noch Empfänger von Entwicklungshilfe waren, keine Wettbewerber. Darin ist bis ins Detail geregelt, wie klein Zinsen für staatliche Kredite, wie groß Staatsgarantien sein dürften und ab welcher Schuldenhöhe ein Land ausfeschlossen wird. Der Vertrag, den Beamte der Mitgliedsländer regelmäßig anpassen, soll den 'Konditionenwettlauf' bei staatlicher Exportunterstützung 'weitgehend eliminieren.'" Translated by the author.

[14] States are the subject of international law *per excellence*, but other subjects also have competence to enter into treaties, such as international organizations, certain territories, etc.

[15] Under the contractual theory of law and economics, parties thus trade a portion of their sovereignty in order to obtain an expected benefit in the future. The economic study of contracts has long been object of law and economic theory. See, for instance, Robert Cooter and Thomas Ulen, *Law and Economics* (International Edition, New York: Pearson Addison Wesley 2008). For a discussion about the analogy about contracts and treaties, see Joel P Trachtman, *The Economic Structure of International Law* (Cambridge University Press 2008) p. 120–22.

[16] As it will be discussed in the appropriate section, the concept of welfare increase supports different views. Part of the literature focuses on net global welfare, other scholars argue that policymakers prioritize domestic net welfare, and a third school of thought defends that policymakers strive to increase the welfare of domestic politically organized groups as a means to gain political support. The decision to adopt one or the other view has impacts on how commitments are designed. For instance, if we assume that governments are benevolent at a global level, we would expect a treaty to lower tariffs to zero. However, if we assume that governments respond to political economy incentives, it seems more plausible that trade agreements reduce certain tariffs while keeping certain markets protected.

reductions—increases in the welfare of exporters and consumers and decreases in welfare of domestic producers—across all parties in order to achieve a set of tariff cuts that ensures mutually beneficial results to negotiators.

An international agreement regulating subsidies, such as the Agreement on Subsidies and Countervailing Measures (SCM Agreement) may be similarly understood as an instrument to guarantee mutual benefits to participants by overcoming unjustified unilateralism. In relation to subsidies, this can be achieved, for instance, by tackling protectionist policy substitution, or in other words the opportunistic use of subsidies as a means of bypassing tariff reductions. A subsidies agreement might also prevent states from engaging in strategic actions, such as profit shifting, that lead to externalities for trade partners. It could also create monitoring mechanisms to better inform parties about the behavior of others, facilitating the identification and prevention of opportunistic uses of subsidies.

By regulating the unilateral use of subsidies, WTO Members thus ideally promise to make use of subsidies in such a way that they (i) preserve the balance of concessions negotiated under the GATT, and (ii) avoid strategic behaviors that result in imposition of negative externalities on trade partners. The SCM Agreement ensures that WTO Members realize the gains expected from tariff reductions and, at the same time, benefit from less distorted competition in the world trading system.[17]

Commitments that restrict the discretion of governments to act unilaterally are the cornerstone of any international agreement. In the GATT, such commitments comprise explicit rules governing market access, as in Article II (restrictions on unilateral increase in tariffs), qualified by rules requiring homogeneity in the competitive conditions afforded all parties to the agreement (non-discrimination and most favored nation clauses). In the SCM, commitments entail the agreement of Member States to prohibitions and restrictions on the use of certain subsidies, as determined by Articles 3 and 4.

Such commitments are, however, only one aspect of an international agreement. Treaty negotiators must also strike an appropriate balance between commitments, which generally restrict unilateral action, and flexibility, which is necessary to adjust the limitations

---

[17] Through the SCM Agreement, WTO Members trade market access guarantees (and expected increased trade flows in certain economic areas) for sovereignty by committing to restrict their regulatory discretion.

reflected in such commitments to exceptional and unforeseen circumstances.

Flexibility is a concept drawn from contract theory to designate the possibility, in a narrow sense, of acting within a range of legality without breaching the treaty.[18] In a broader sense, flexibility also includes the option of breaching the commitment and paying compensation, usually at a level at which the other party remains indifferent toward performance or compensation.[19] The various legal and economic arguments for the introduction of flexibility into a treaty all aim for similar results: to allow for *ex post* adjustment of commitments in order to, in good faith, customize the application of the treaty to unforeseen or ambiguously regulated situations, while controlling for opportunistic behaviors.[20]

The question that arises is therefore how strict or flexible rules should be. How are commitments and flexibilities to be combined in order to achieve the purposes of an agreement? How, for example, should activities be regulated to overcome externality problems and promote joint welfare, while appropriately separating good faith measures from opportunistic behavior?[21]

---

[18] The concept has been recently applied to subfields of international economic law, such as WTO and investment law. See, respectively, Simon Schropp, *Trade Policy Flexibility and Enforcement in the WTO: A Law and Economic Analysis* (Cambridge International Trade and Economic Law, Cambridge University Press 2009) p. 101–23; and Anne van Aaken, "Opportunities and the Limits of an Economic Analysis in International Law" (2011) 3 *Transnational Corporations Review* p. 27–46. This perception of flexibilities as a permitted action within a legal range is found in Anne van Aaken, "Smart Flexibility Clauses in International Investment Treaties and Sustainable Development" (2014) 15 *The Journal of World Investment & Trade* p. 827–61.

[19] This is commonly termed "efficient breach" and is understood as a flexibility mechanism because it allows parties to make *ex post* adjustments. If attached to an appropriate level of compensation, these mechanisms may lead to efficient outcomes. See, for instance, Cooter and Ulen, *Law and Economics* p. 307–41. For an application and criticisms on its use in international law, see Trachtman, *The Economic Structure of International Law* p. 142–44; and also Joost Pauwelyn, *Optimal Protection of International Law* (Cambridge University Press 2008) p. 66–74.

[20] From a legal theory viewpoint, flexibilities are necessary because treaties are incomplete, meaning that negotiators cannot fully predict all future states of the world and have issues in translating their will into the contract. Economically, they are necessary because subsidies, as well as other instruments of state intervention in the economy, can be used for legitimate purposes such as overcoming market failures and protecting health, environmental and social values.

[21] Opportunistic behavior in a subsidies agreement works twofold. At the commitment level, subsidies agreements are designed to avoid that subsidies be opportunistically used

In recent years, scholars of international trade law have examined, through economically informed analysis, how the rules of the world trading system have dealt with issues related to treaty design and the balancing of commitments and flexibility: how treaties might control for opportunistic behavior while granting states enough space to implement legitimate policy objectives. While much attention has been placed on the GATT, however, only recently has the scholarship approached other substantive areas of WTO law such as technical barriers to trade or intellectual property. The SCM Agreement, a treaty that contains rules regulating industrial subsidies, has also been overlooked.

The outstanding issue of flexibility in the SCM regulation of subsidies is important, because the use of subsidies is on the rise in several economic sectors,[22] as are WTO disputes over this issue.[23] According to the World Bank, there has been a steady increase in governmental spending classified as subsidies in virtually all G20 Members between 2006 and 2010. This is especially true for emerging economies such as Brazil, India, South Africa, Korea, and Russia, but is also valid for major economies such as France, Germany, Japan, Canada, the UK, and the USA. Of the developed countries, only Italy showed a slight decrease in levels of subsidization between 2010 and 2012.[24]

---

to circumvent tariff commitments and to strategically shift profits from foreign to domestic firms. On the enforcement level, once the contract is already in place, parties might opportunistically use poorly or ambiguously drafted commitments to prevent a WTO Member from making use of good faith subsidies. Treaties should, therefore, strive to identify and strictly regulate opportunistic behavior (both at the commitment and enforcement level) while allowing for good faith subsidies either because they respond to a legitimate economic need, such as a subsidy used to tackle a market failure, or because they are a good faith response to unforeseen contingencies.

[22] There are different datasets suggesting this, such as "Global Trade Alert."

[23] This is particularly true after 2008, as governments made use of several measures to mitigate the impacts of the crises in their territories. Moreover, with international rules already restricting the use of several subsidies, states have made use of more elaborated measures to implement public policies in several areas, such as environment, posing a challenge on those responsible for judging their consistency.

[24] Data on subsidies and other transfers (current LCU) retrieved on 25.11.2015 <http://data.worldbank.org/indicator>. There was no data for Argentina, China, Mexico, and Saudi Arabia. As will be discussed, subsidies are an object of difficult definition and this fact poses a problem on measuring the amount of subsidies given by governments. For instance, the World Bank dataset includes social expenses that would, normally, not fall under the SCM Agreement.

Table 1: *Subsidies given by G20 members between 2006 and 2012.*

	2006	2010	2012
Australia	173,315,000,000	240,944,000,000	263,998,000,000
Brazil	324,537,752,576	509,729,304,777	597,340,933,432
Canada	160,574,000,000	209,175,000,000	219,689,000,000[25]
France	416,440,670,000	492,316,000,000	521,706,000,000
Germany	560,970,000,000	622,440,000,000	625,200,000,000
India	3,485,140,000,000	7,905,000,000,000	9,938,860,000,000
Indonesia	334,028,993,820,455	472,684,961,057,015[26]	n.a.[27]
Italy	359,123,000,000	429,055,000,000	425,176,000,000
Japan	52,090,600,000,000	58,567,800,000,000	62,241,000,000,000
Korea	98,284,800,000,000	135,399,621,000,000	147,577,560,000,000[28]
Russia	2,886,900,000,000	7,671,200,000,000	9,701,300,000,000
South Africa	317,630,000,000	543,234,467,528	675,103,005,616
Turkey	139,462,495,225[29]	186,659,799,807	239,315,752,212
UK	277,048,000,000	352,755,000,000	373,058,000,000
US	1,678,200,000,000	2,409,400,000,000	2,473,300,000,000[30]

Source: The World Bank

The data suggests that subsidies are still a commonly used instrument for the implementation of public policy. Along with the level of "general" subsidies, the number of subsidizing measures that have a potentially harmful and discriminatory impact on international trade has also increased.[31] The number of bailout and domestic subsidization programs has been particularly high. The Global Trade Alert dataset registered over 1200 of such measures between 2009 and 2015.[32]

---

[25] Data for the year 2013.
[26] Data for the year 2009.
[27] Not available.
[28] Data for the year 2011.
[29] Data for the year 2008.
[30] Data for the year 2013.
[31] It would require studies beyond this research to test for a clear connection between the rise of such more "general" subsidies, as provided by the World Bank, and the increase in protectionist subsidies, as captured by the Global Trade Alert data. The fact, however, is that according to the data available, both general subsidies and protectionist measures have increased in the period.
[32] In the present research it was used to establish the data of the measure the publishing date indicated at the Global Trade Alert. Since the website shows both "publishing date" and

Table 2: *Number of subsiding measures by year and type.*

	2010	2011	2012	2013	2014
Total number of bailout and state aid in the year.	108	63	139	189	261
Total number of export subsidy in the year.	15	18	7	60	44
Total number of local content requirement in the year.	29	12	11	118	151
Total	152	93	157	367	456

Source: Global Trade Alert

Subsidies related to export and import substitution reached a total of 177 and 317 measures, respectively, since June 4th of 2009, from which most have been classified as "red impact," suggesting a high likelihood of discrimination against the commercial interests of foreign companies and states.

This growth in subsidization seems to have fostered the use of countervailing measures in international trade. Countervailing measures are unilateral trade restrictive measures applied by one state to offset the cross-border effects of a subsidy granted by a foreign state.[33] The number of investigations into the use of "countervailing duties" (CVDs) has been back on the rise since 2005, but initiations in the period between 2011 and 2017 are clearly higher than in previous years. While numbers show an average annual initiation of 15 investigations between 1995 and 2010, there were on average 33 investigations initiated each year during the period from 2008 to 2014.[34]

---

the "inception date," a choice needed to be done. However, the "inception date" is not always present. So, in order to be able to catalogue all data, the publishing date was elected to mark the measure in time.

[33] At the WTO website the data regarding the number of compensatory measures is divided between countervailing initiations and countervailing measures. In both cases, the reports cover the period between January 1995 and June 2014. The information provided on the website is based on information delivered by Members that submitted semi-annual reports for the relevant periods. A relevant observation is made by the WTO on that section of the website, stating that the data might be incomplete to the extent Members have not submitted reports or have submitted incomplete reports.

[34] Since 1995, a total of 486 countervailing duties investigations were initiated.

Initiated CVDs investigations

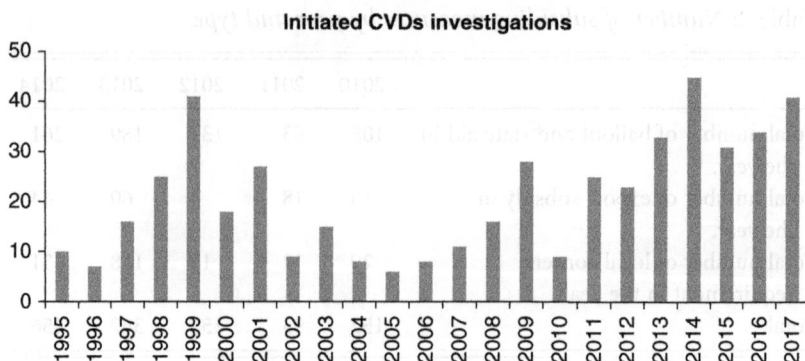

Figure 1:   Initiated CVDs investigations by year.
Source: WTO

The number of multilateral disputes brought to the WTO has also been significant, despite a small decrease in the past years. Between 1995 and 2017, a total of 118[35] disputes have referred specifically to the Agreement on Subsidies and Countervailing Measures,[36] with recent peaks in 2012 and 2013.[37] Relevant disputes over highly complex measures involving major WTO Members have, moreover, been recently settled or initiated. New disputes pertaining to the energy and aircraft sectors were initiated in 2014, and in 2015 an important incentive program by a WTO Member was challenged for allegedly constituting an import substitution subsidy, thus raising important questions about the flexibility of the SCM Agreement.

This rise in the use of subsidies, and in subsidies-related disputes, sparked an important debate about the boundary between the international regulation of subsidies and the discretion of states to use subsidies as a means to implement public policies. In the recent Canada Renewable Energy dispute, for instance, Japan and the EU challenged a Canadian measure, arguing that the measure constituted a subsidy prohibited under

---

[35] Until the last day seen, that is May 20 of 2015.

[36] WTO, "Dispute Settlement: Disputes by Agreement" (2016) <https://www.wto.org/> accessed 09.19.2018.

[37] The complaints are submitted as a request for consultation, by which the member government explains its belief on how other member state has breached the agreement. As it can be noticed in the following graphic, the number of disputes brought to WTO referring to the Agreement on Subsidies and Countervailing Measures has generally declined, having its peak in the years between 1996 to 1998.

Number of WTO disputes per year

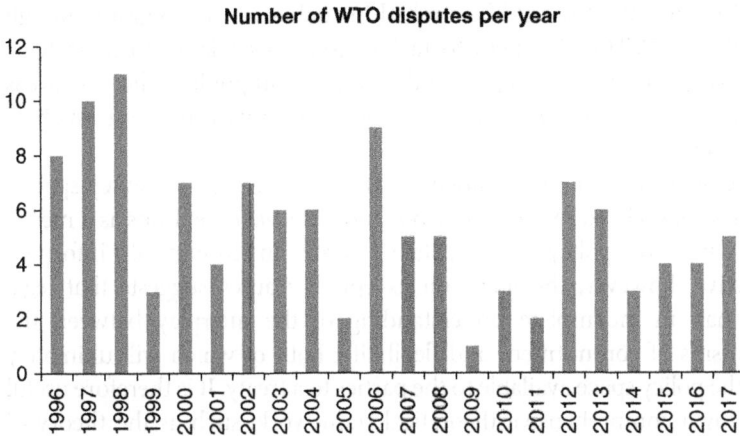

Figure 2: Initiated WTO disputes, by year, with SCM Agreement claims.
Source: WTO[38]

WTO law.[39] Canada, arguing in favor of its measure, stated that not only
are policies to foster the renewable energy industry crucial to "secure the
supply of electricity" but that they are also necessary to "protect the
environment."[40] In Canada's view, therefore, the commitments set out in

<hr/>

[38] WTO, "Dispute Settlement: Disputes by Agreement" (2016) <https://www.wto.org/>
accessed 09.01.2018.

[39] Annex 1, First Written Submission by Canada, Panel Reports, Canada – Certain Measures
Affecting the Renewable Energy Generation Sector / Canada – Measures Relating to the
Feed-in Tariff Program, WT/DS412/R and Add.1 / WT/DS426/R and Add.1 (Canada –
Renewable Energy), adopted May 24, 2013, as modified by Appellate Body Reports WT/
DS412/AB/R / WT/DS426/AB/R, DSR 2013:I, p. 237, para 3. Controversially, the measure
also determined that, in order to be eligible to enter the scheme, producers should make
use of a minimum amount of Canadian produced equipment, such as solar cells and
turbines, thus imposing a limit on the use of foreign produced equipment. The Canadian
government conditioned the participation in the scheme to sources previously approved,
manly solar and wind. There is an interesting literature about which sources should be
considered as renewable. See Luca Rubini, "Ain't Wastin' Time No More: Subsidies for
Renewable Energy, The SCM Agreement, Policy Space, and Law Reform" (2012) 15
Journal of International Economic Law p. 525–79.

[40] Canada argued that private markets would not always be in a position to provide for all
the goods necessary to a modern economy and society (such as a society that highly values
the protection of the environment) and that subsidies would be legitimate measures to
achieve these values by fostering the production of related goods. In other words, Canada
argued that subsidies were necessary to foster the production of renewable energy due to
a failure in the energy market. This failure would take place because private players in the
energy market perceive energy as a commodity and therefore do not differentiate between
the different sources, thus preferring the cheapest product available in the market. As the

the SCM Agreement should be applied in such a way as to grant enough flexibility for WTO Members to tackle situations related to a strategic economic sector (energy supply), and to implement public policies in areas in which the market does not have proper incentives to invest (such as environment).

The case generated a great doctrinal debate on issues of "policy space," most of which related to the (re)introduction of legal exceptions as a means of providing more policy space for states.[41] From an economically informed perspective, however, the focus on exception clauses suggests that legal theory has an incomplete understanding of the interplay between the mechanisms of commitment and flexibility, both of which will ultimately define the policy space available to the parties to a treaty. It is therefore useful to employ a comprehensive theoretical framework, such as the theory of incomplete contract developed in law and economics, to analyze the SCM Agreement and to contribute to the discussion related to policy space.

The next chapter discusses the theoretical framework used by law and economics (L&E) to explain the existence of international treaties and analyzes their formation and design. It argues that, despite the complexities of L&E analysis, a simple model for international legal analysis may be established to understand (i) the behavior of states, based on the concept of rationality; and (ii) their approach to (a) costs and benefits, such as externalities and transaction costs, and (b) strategic cooperation, which varies depending on whether the strategy encourages opportunistic behavior (collaboration games) or not (coordination games). The chapter first provides an overview of the core concepts of international law and economics and a description of the situations in which states, understood as rational entities, might resort to cooperation. It then focuses on cooperation through treaties as a means of overcoming costs associated with

---

production of renewable energy tends to be more expensive than that originating of well-established sources, such as coal and nuclear, governmental intervention would be necessary to reduce barriers to entry and to create a market for renewable energy.

[41] Several authors suggested that exceptions should be (re)introduced in the agreement, to which others responded that the text of the SCM Agreement clearly revoked previously stated exceptions and would not allow for the application of GATT Article XX. For a great part of the legal scholarship, therefore, the issue of broadening the flexibility in the SCM Agreement required the renegotiation of current rules, a power only invested in WTO Members, leaving therefore little margin for WTO courts to tackle this problem through interpretation. Moreover, the commitments in the SCM Agreement, especially those related to prohibited subsidies, are commonly viewed as too strict, leaving little room for interpretation by panels and the AB.

externalities and issues of cooperation, such as strategic behavior. To conclude, the chapter focuses on the transaction costs associated with contracting, proposes a theory of incompleteness[42] of treaties, and argues that there is a need for inclusion of contractual flexibility to permit the *ex post* completion of international agreements.

The third chapter introduces basic economic analyses of the use of subsidies by governments. It addresses the impact that subsidies have on governments, firms, and consumers, and discusses the cross-border effects of subsidies on foreign governments. Having examined the complexity of the design and effects of subsidizing measures, the chapter concludes that there may be incentive for governments to internationally regulate the use of subsidies. It also, however, suggests that states are exposed to a series of uncertainties in relation to the use of subsidies as a policy tool. As suggested by contract theory, these uncertainties should affect how treaties are drafted, requiring negotiators to make use of different legal mechanisms to ensure the efficient *ex post* application of rules drafted *ex ante*.

The fourth chapter then applies this economically informed framework to describe the SCM Agreement. It pays special attention to the development of the rules regulating industrial subsidies and the Treaty currently in force. By testing the system of entitlements and enforcement

---

[42] In international L&E, parties would, if possible, draft complete contracts. Complete contract is an ideal-type of contract in which rational parties have the ability to perfectly allocate rights and obligations so that the contract provides for legal consequences and describes the corresponding welfare maximizing behavior due by the parties under every possible future scenario. Due to uncertainties caused by transaction costs and limitations to negotiators' rationality, treaties (as well as contracts) are in fact incomplete, requiring the introduction of legal mechanisms to allow parties to complete the contract. After a brief discussion of the classification of such mechanisms, we take the position that flexibility mechanisms are *par excellence* the legal instruments that allow parties, through explicit contract language or through contractual remedies, to fill the gaps in a contract or at least induce parties to mimic, *ex post*, the behavior they would have assigned each other *ex ante*, should they had been in a position to write a complete contract. The terms *ex post* and *ex ante*, when referencing a chronological moment in contract formation, are commonly used in law and economics to refer to a moment before the signature or the entering into force of a contract (*ex ante*) and the moment, following the signature or entering into force, in which parties would like to deviate from foreseen commitments (*ex post*). See, for instance, Robert E Scott and George G Triantis, "Incomplete Contracts and the Theory of Contract Design" (2005) 56 Case W Res L Rev p. 187–201; Schropp, *Trade Policy Flexibility and Enforcement in the WTO: A Law and Economic Analysis* p. 27–29; and Anne van Aaken, "Delegating Interpretative Authority in Investment Treaties: The Case of Joint Commissions" (2014) 11 *Transnational Dispute Management* p. 21–47.

mechanisms of the SCM Agreement against the contract theory framework, this work offers a comprehensive analysis of the limits of the Treaty
in its goal to regulate opportunistic behavior while ensuring *ex post*
flexibility.

Chapter Five then analyzes in more detail the rules of the SCM
Agreement as a means of tackling the main uncertainties in contract
theory: absence of forseeability, ambiguity, and information asymmetry.

Chapter Six provides conclusions, and proposes recommendations to
policymakers and adjudicators. It also discusses the limitations of the
work and offers insights for future research.

2

Contractual Aspects of Treaties

This chapter presents and critically analyzes the theoretical framework adopted by law and economics (L&E) to explain the existence of international treaties and examine their formation and design. Making use of contract theory, it (i) proposes a concept of rationality as a basis for understanding the behavior of states; and (ii) examines government attitudes to (a) costs and benefits, such as externalities and transaction costs; and (b) strategic cooperation, which varies depending on whether the endeavor encourages opportunistic behavior (collaboration games) or not (coordination games).[1]

The chapter first provides an overview of the core concepts of international law and economics, and a description of the situations in which states, understood as rational entities, could conceivably resort to

---

[1] The problem of cooperation is complex and not an obvious one, as states have different possible courses of action to deal with international issues. Once a problem has been identified as the result of another state's action, nations might choose to take unilateral measures, sometimes even resorting to military action, or they might cooperate. If cooperation is the preferred measure, representatives of the states will meet, with more or less formalities, in an attempt to find a mutually agreed solution, among which we then have agreements/treaties/contracts. Such contracts might be more or less complex, but they will invariably involve negotiators who must, through legal language, regulate state behavior in order to overcome the problem or to at least make it tolerable to the parties. Negotiators will have a reasonable understanding of the problem, prescribe certain actions, restrict other actions, and carve out exceptions in light of the information available regarding the problem at hand and reasonably anticipated controversies that its regulation might entail. For instance, trade regulators decided to regulate trade by establishing a cap to tariffs and a ban on quotas, but also anticipated that this could drive to tensions with other societal values, such as human health and environmental protection, thus introducing exceptions in the GATT to that purpose. Negotiators, however, have limited capacity to regulate issues and treaties will be necessarily incomplete and filled with gaps. Once a situation falls into a gap, treaties will call for re-negotiations and/or interpretation by third parties, preferably with competence/authority to impose a decision on the signatories of the treaty.

cooperation. It then focuses on cooperation through treaties as a means of overcoming costs associated with externalities and issues of cooperation, such as strategic behavior. To conclude, the chapter focuses on the transaction costs involved in contracting, argues in favor of a theory of incompleteness of treaties, and the use of contractual mechanisms capable of facilitating flexibility in order to allow for the *ex post* completion of international agreements.

2.1 International Law and Economics and Rational Choice

Economic analysis of law is relatively new to international legal research but has been applied in the study of other fields of law, both generally and in specific substantive areas.[2] It seeks to explain the effects of international rules on the behavior of those who are subject to them, and evaluates the factors influencing creation of the rules. Economic analysis therefore provides both internal and external perspectives: the internal one a commonly used legal method of rule interpretation, and an external or objective view of the law that is characteristic of the social sciences.[3]

In law and economics theory, international norms, including treaties, are legal instruments used by states[4] to (re)allocate authority by regulating excessive unilateralism.[5] By making international rules, states "sacrifice" portions of their sovereignty to regulate their own unilateralism,

---

[2] Law and economics, or economic analysis of law, can be defined as "the application of economic theory . . . to examine the formation, structure, processes and impact of law and legal institutions," Charles K Rowley, "Public Choice and the Economic Analysis of Law" in Nicholas Mercuro (ed), Law and Economics (Springer 1989) p. 125. For a historical overview of the law and economics school, as well as its several areas of application, see Ejan Mackaay, 'History of law and economics' in Boudewijn Bouckaert and Gerrit De Geest (eds), Encyclopedia of law and economics, vol I The History and Methodology of Law and Economics (Encyclopedia of law and economics, Edward Elgar 2000).

[3] See van Aaken, "Opportunities and the Limits of an Economic Analysis in International Law" p. 27–30.

[4] States are the subject of international law *par excellence*, but other subjects also have competence to enter into treaties, such as international organizations, certain territories, etc. See Christian Kirchner, "The Power of Rational Choice Methodology in Guiding the Analysis and the Design of Public International Law Institutions—Concluding Remarks" (2008) U Ill L Rev p. 419–28, 421.

[5] Allocation of authority is commonly named "jurisdiction" in the legal jargon as in Trachtman, *The Economic Structure of International Law* p. 119, or simply "rights and obligations" or "entitlements." Common to all three concepts is the idea that authority is explicitly assigned to a state, so that this state has the right or the obligation (also the authority) to do something, that is to say the state is entitled to a certain conduct or result by his or the other party's action or inaction. We will use the three terms as synonyms.

while taking advantage of the opportunity for receipt of consideration from the counterpart state, which in turn regulates the authority of that foreign party in a certain area of law. Treaties, like contracts, are thus used to generate mutual benefits to the parties through the mutual regulation of future behavior.[6]

For purposes of analysis of the regulatory decision-making process (as to form and extent of regulation), states are, in L&E theory, perceived as actors capable of rational behavior. Such behavior is commonly defined as that which is conditioned by "preferences (rankings of objects of choice)"[7] that are "complete and transitive,"[8] that is to say "the agent does not prefer any feasible alternative to what he or she chooses."[9] Simply put, the concept of rationality assumes that parties have preferences, and that they act to maximize them.

Rational choice theory permits extrapolation in public international law from classic doctrinal analysis involving application and interpretation of legal norms to analysis of legal institutions, subjects of law, and the processes of legal creation. This is an innovative departure from approaches used in other legal fields and deserves further methodological development in order to achieve more consistent application in the analysis of certain aspects of the law.

Recognition of rational choice theory is not universal: it has faced skepticism, especially in countries with an "absolutist" tradition in international legal analysis.[10] It has been said that rationalism abstracts from many intra-state relations and disregards the role of non-state actors and individuals in the creation and enforcement of international law.[11] It does, however, permit analysis of the behavior of domestic groups such as NGOs, in addition to the analysis of states and international organizations that one would expect of public international law.

---

[6] Under the contractual theory of law and economics, parties thus trade a portion of their sovereignty in order to obtain an expected benefit in the future. The economic study of contracts has long been object of law and economic theory. See, for instance, Cooter and Ulen, *Law and Economics* p. 276. For a discussion about the analogy about contracts and treaties, see Trachtman, *The Economic Structure of International Law* p. 120–2.

[7] Daniel M Hausman, "Philosophy of Economics" in Edward N Zalta (ed), *The Stanford Encyclopedia of Philosophy*, vol Winter 2013 (The Stanford Encyclopedia of Philosophy, Stanford University 2013).

[8] Ibid.

[9] Ibid.

[10] For an overview, see Pauwelyn, *Optimal Protection of International Law* p. 16–25.

[11] See, for instance, Larry A DiMatteo and others, *Visions of Contract Theory: Rationality, Bargaining, and Interpretation* (Carolina Academic Press 2007) p. 35–47.

Another criticism is that rational choice theory does not have adequate tools to deal with state preferences that cannot be monetized, such as national security.[12] While some rationalist scholars do work with the monetization of preferences, others prefer instead to apply a cost and benefit analysis that encompasses the interests of a wide range of domestic groups, thus taking into consideration concerns other than purely "monetized" values.[13]

Finally, rationalist approaches arguably suffer from a certain ambiguity regarding how they deal with the preferences of decision-makers who, although they might be concerned with overall welfare, could also be interested in increasing the welfare of the leaders of their home state, or even fostering their own interests.[14] The development of public choice analysis in international legal research, however, increasingly offers tools that can be used to understand and address the roles of domestic interest groups and the influence that they exercise over policymakers.

These criticisms, while relevant, seem somewhat exaggerated and the use of rationality has proven so far to be a valuable tool for legal scholars.[15] In rational analysis, legal theory draws upon the social sciences, becoming better equipped to understand the processes of lawmaking and the consequences of legal norms for the behavior of individuals.[16]

This analysis is, moreover, especially helpful for disentangling various uses of theoretical economic tools in relation to the law. It views economics as a methodological approach to solution of legal problems, as distinct from other possible economic applications aimed at the formulation or interpretation of law.

---

[12] See Jeffrey L Dunoff and Joel P Trachtman, "Economic Analysis of International Law" (1999) 24 *Yale J Int'l L* 1 p. 15. See also DiMatteo and others, *Visions of Contract Theory: Rationality, Bargaining, and Interpretation* p. 35–8.

[13] See the discussion on political economy, Section 3.3.4.

[14] See DiMatteo and others, *Visions of Contract Theory: Rationality, Bargaining, and Interpretation* p. 35–47.

[15] Kirchner notes that a rational choice-based theory may contribute to the study of international public law in two main ways. First, it could "provide positive analyses of alternative legal solutions and thus clarify the expected outcomes of lawmaking and the application of legal rules in public international law." Second, it could "shed light on normative propositions from a perspective of normative individualism." Kirchner, "The Power of Rational Choice Methodology in Guiding the Analysis and the Design of Public International Law Institutions—Concluding Remarks" p. 426.

[16] See, for instance, ibid. p. 419–20; and van Aaken, "Opportunities and the Limits of an Economic Analysis in International Law" p. 28–30.

There are at least two common misconceptions relating to the L&E approach. The first is the misunderstanding that this method relates solely to the use of economic, statistical, or mathematical tools in the application of a legal rule. Such tools are useful wherever the law requires a practical calculation that is beyond the capacity of its normal analytical instruments. Think, for example, of the calculations required to determine the retirement benefit of a United Nations employee, or the damage that a subsidies program might cause to a domestic industry of various countries. In such situations, economics is asked to solve a specific problem in order to give effect to the legal system on the ground. Economic tools or calculations are not, however, the essence of the L&E theory involving rational choice.

A second misconception of the L&E approach arises out of a narrow perception of economic analysis as equivalent to the discipline of international economic law (IEL) or trade, investment, and international finance. Although the IEL discipline and its sub-fields are certainly fertile ground for the economic analysis of law, IEL as an object of research can be subjected to various analytical methods such as dogmatic, historical, or sociological analysis. The object of research (the IEL discipline) should not be confused with the research methodology (the economic analysis of law).

The L&E theory of rational choice is neither a set of economic tools for the implementation of law, nor the discipline of IEL, but a broader methodology for economic analysis of international rules. It encompasses a conception of behavior, and the underlying motivations for action or inaction of actors and subjects of international law. It enables assessment of the role of rules in creating incentives and driving behavior of international and domestic actors. As an analytical method, therefore, rational choice enables researchers to evaluate state behavior as formulators and subjects of international law, in ways that doctrinal theory is not equipped to do. Instead of a competing analytical method to be feared, rational choice should be seen as a complementary tool that can enable scholars of international issues to better understand legal phenomena in dimensions beyond legal doctrine.[17] In this spirit, this work first presents underlying rationales for the introduction of

---

[17] In previous work, the author has made a broader introduction of the linkage between rationality and international law. See Gustavo Ferreira Ribeiro and José Guilherme Moreno Caiado, "Why an Economic Analysis of International Public Law: Challenges and Perspectives in Brazil" (2015) 12 *Braz J Int'l L* p. 246.

mechanisms capable of facilitating flexibility in treaties, and then, drawing on economic (or rationalist) theory, focuses on the SCM Agreement.

2.1.1   Preferences in International Law

Rational choice assumes that individuals behave to maximize their preferences. International law, however, is usually concerned with the behavior of the state, rather than that of individuals. Throughout this work, therefore, references to international law and the international trading system[18] will imply a theoretical analogy between individuals and states.

The literature on international relations offers a variety of views on this issue. The Realist School understands the state as the central unitary rational actor that seeks to maximize, for example, its power at the international level. Similarly, but with a focus on elements other than power, Institutionalism also sees the state as a "black box," placing little emphasis on the influence of domestic political groups.[19]

The influence of domestic groups on state behavior is better captured by discourse related to political economy, in which the preferences of states are commonly identified as the preferences of a policy-maker of a democratic country.[20] As elections are used by democracies to select high-level policymakers, it is often assumed that election or reelection is

[18] This assumption poses an initial problem because states are composed by an amalgam of different societal groups, which creates difficulty in establishing the preferences of states. As noted by Kirchner, there are "long agency chains between the ultimate principal the citizen of a nation state participating in lawmaking, and the agent, the actual persons engaged in lawmaking" Kirchner, "The Power of Rational Choice Methodology in Guiding the Analysis and the Design of Public International Law Institutions—Concluding Remarks" p. 421. There are, however, at least two reasons that support this analogy. "Rhetorically, the analogy is an accepted practice in mainstream international relations discourse, and since this article is an immanent rather than external critique, it should follow the practice. Substantively, states are collectivities of individuals that through their practices constitute each other as 'persons' having interests, fears, and so on. A full theory of state identity- and interest-formation would nevertheless need to draw insights from the social psychology of groups and organizational theory, and for that reason my anthropomorphism is merely suggestive." Alexander Wendt, "Anarchy Is What States Make of It: The Social Construction of Power Politics" (1992) 46 *International Organization* p. 391–425, 397.

[19] For an overview of the different schools of thought and their application to international law, see Barbara Koremenos, "Institutionalism and International Law" in Jeffrey L Dunoff and Mark A Pollack (eds), *Interdisciplinary Perspectives on International Law and International Relations: The State of the Art* (Interdisciplinary Perspectives on International Law and International Relations: The State of the Art, Cambridge University Press 2013).

[20] See Section 3.3.4.

the highest ranked preference of a policymaker. In democracies, there-fore, any state action (such as signing an international treaty) needs to strike a delicate balance between the preferences of the various domestic constituencies responsible for votes and campaign contributions.

In international treaty negotiations, policymakers aim to restrict the unilateral actions of foreign states in a manner that will increase their own national welfare or economy as a whole, as well as that of relevant domestic groups. This balancing exercise should grant the policymaker more popular and/or financial support in their efforts to maximize their electoral preferences.

At the same time, however, policymakers are asked to restrict their own unilateralism in favor of the foreign counterpart, which will argu-ably have a negative effect on the welfare of certain domestic constitu-encies. States (policymakers) can agree to a treaty only when it is perceived to result in a net increase to their own welfare.[21]

States will, for instance, agree to tariff restrictions through a trade agreement as long as the "political loss of doing so (in terms of foregone terms-of-trade gains and political support losses of import competing lobbies) is outweighed by positive externalities (political support gain and general trade efficiencies)."[22] Through the negotiation of the GATT, for example, states agreed to limit their unilateral competence to raise tariffs in order to gain market access to other contracting parties that bound their tariff levels to an equal extent. These other parties did so because they determined, by weighing welfare gains and losses within their jurisdictions,[23] that the agreement would allow them to reach a mutual increase in welfare.

---

[21] For Scott, the economic approach to contracts assumes that "parties act rationality, within the constraints of their environment, in the sense that the wish to contract if they believe the arrangement will make them better off and not otherwise" Robert E Scott, "The Law and Economics of Incomplete Contracts" (2006) 2 *Annu Rev Law Soc Sci* p. 279-97, 280.

[22] Schropp, *Trade Policy Flexibility and Enforcement in the WTO: A Law and Economic Analysis* p. 186.

[23] When asking what governments gain from a trade agreement, Bagwell and Staiger conclude that "a trade agreement is appealing to governments if it offers them greater welfare than they would receive in the absence of the agreement. If in the absence of an agreement, governments set trade policies in a unilateral fashion, then a trade agreement is appealing provided that an inefficiency (relative to governments preferences) exists under unilateral tariff setting. Viewed from this perspective, the role of a trade agreement is then to remove the inefficiency, so that member governments can enjoy higher welfare" Kyle Bagwell and Robert W Staiger, "An Economic Theory of GATT" (1999) 89 *The American Economic Review* p. 215-48, 215.

Policymakers are familiar with this balancing exercise, which is present in all international negotiations, but legal scholars do not usually address it fully. As mentioned previously, legal methods are state-of-the-art tools for the application of existing law to concrete cases and disputes, but have limited analytical power in relation to the elements that states ought to consider when making the law. Development of the law requires methods for identification and assessment of the factors that influence the decision-making process of policymakers. One of these methods is cost and benefits analysis, which is discussed in the section below.

2.1.2   Balancing Costs and Benefits

The concept of rationality encourages interpretation of the behavior of agents through the identification and ranking of their preferences. The use of this concept reaches a roadblock, however, when the importance of different preferences is not easily identifiable. A common assumption defines this shortcoming: economic analysis *cannot* tell the researcher which preferences to maximize. This implies that it may be problematic to wander into deductive terrain regarding whether, for example, a particular state values environmental protection more than it values economic growth. So how can we explain a behavior in the absence of clear preferences? Economics deals with this question by offering models that explain "how to maximize the things we value"[24] irrespective of what it is that states value. The most basic of these is known as a "price theory" model or a "costs and benefits" model.

In a price theory model, all other things being equal, individuals will prefer cheaper goods over more expensive products. They will also prefer more efficient means of achieving a goal to less efficient ways of accomplishing the same objective.[25] In the international setting, this means that states react to costs and benefits that affect their preferences.[26] With the

---

[24] Trachtman, *The Economic Structure of International Law* p. 2–3.

[25] Ibid.

[26] In the domestic level, the manner in which individuals maximize their preferences, either by eliminating a cost or by getting a direct benefit, is through exchanges in the market (if I value a certain good more than its owner, I can purchase that good from her or him). Thus, the assumption is that a plurality of rational agents exercising free decision power will reach an agreement if each agent is better off with the final result. One way to transfer this domestic market analogy to international law is to consider that the transactions in the international market do not involve goods or services, but jurisdiction or, simply put, power. In this setting, states make exchanges of jurisdiction in order to maximize their preferences by reducing costs associated to the power that the other party has to act in

creation of the WTO and the abandonment of the old GATT dispute resolution system, for example, member states lost their power to veto dispute settlement reports and saw an increase in the likelihood of being sanctioned for breaches of international commitments. A rationalist would argue that WTO Members are therefore likely to be more cautious about breaching, which might improve their compliance with WTO law. Similarly, the SCM Agreement can be perceived as a treaty that leads to mutual benefits to its contracting parties by eliminating or attenuating harmful cross border effects. This is true in relation to subsidies used as an alternative to tariffs, to circumvent tariff commitments, as well as those used to divert trade and shift profit from international competitors to domestic firms.

An important insight of economic theory, given the aim to maximize preferences through action based on cost and benefit considerations, is that individuals, and therefore states, may choose to transact with each other in a way that is efficient in terms of both price and means of achieving a goal.[27]

At the individual level, a person might, for example, prefer a car over a vacation abroad, and will transact their possessions (often labor) accordingly. Similarly, if states prefer to foster the welfare of exporters over that of importers they will, under certain conditions addressed below, negotiate with other states the removal of foreign barriers to allow their exports to grow.[28] In both the individual and state scenarios is the idea that by having a common denominator for exchanges (costs and benefits), parties will engage more efficiently in transactions to achieve their goals. The currency of exchange, however, differs. Individuals often transact in goods: one individual has a car and the other has money. If they value these goods differently, they might engage in an exchange.

As an economic player, states also engage in the exchange of goods and services with private parties and other states. However, these are not the

---

certain legal areas, or by expanding the benefits it might get by gaining authority over such an area.

[27] The balancing process proposed by the price theory model also means that states will constantly weigh pros and cons between resorting to unilateral measures and engaging with international rules. In cases where the cons of the international rules outweigh the pros of unilateral action, unilateralism becomes a completely justifiable choice under rational theory. Despite this conclusion, the growing amount of international regulation suggests that states perceive that the benefits of international law offset its costs in several areas, and they are willing to engage in exchanges that maximize their preferences.

[28] See Section 3.3.4.

relevant transactions from a viewpoint of understanding how international law is essentially shaped. The common denominator of international law transactions, rather than goods or services, is the power to sovereignly and unilaterally dictate rules within the state's domain. In other words, when making exchanges with its sovereign peers, a state is making exchanges in jurisdiction.[29] In the case of an international treaty, one or more parties commonly surrender their authority over a certain issue (geographic area or substantive legal issue), expecting to receive a benefit in the form of a similar jurisdictional consideration.[30]

So, what is the jurisdictional consideration that one state might offer another in the process of cooperation? The answer to this question is simple: promotion of positive actions or minimization of negative measures.[31] The action of one state may have positive or negative impacts on others, and gains may be achieved by either fostering the positive benefits and effects of actions or limiting those that are adverse. In other words, state actions produce externalities, and it is the regulation of such externalities that constitutes the basic rationale of international cooperation.

This understanding of external effect, in which domestic action, and even inaction, might have negative repercussions for the preferences and interests of another state, supports the assertion that the international market is characterized by transactions in jurisdiction. If a negative externality has sufficient impact on the preferences of another state, the affected state might resort to transactions in jurisdiction to persuade the other to change its harmful measure. On the assumption that states are free and rational agents, such exchanges will occur only if jurisdiction "is more valuable to one state than to another."[32]

The next section analyzes the concept of externality and discusses the challenges for cooperation posed by incentives for states to behave unilaterally.

---

[29] See Trachtman, *The Economic Structure of International Law* p. 26–28.
[30] See ibid.
[31] This difference between measures with positive and negative effects in the welfare of states will be discussed in more details in Section 2.1.3.
[32] While many international treaties deal with reciprocal exchanges of jurisdiction, it is reasonable to assume that certain treaties in which jurisdiction of one of the parties is reallocated have, in fact, counterparts other than reciprocal transference of power, but that are valued by the parties, such as transfers of technology, security, or even direct financial contributions.

2.1.3   Externalities

The engine of international rule-making is thus the maximization of state preferences: preferences that are affected by externalities imposed by actions of other states. As discussed, states have the opportunity to overcome certain international problems of jurisdictional transactions by giving up authority to act in a unilateral fashion in a certain legal domain.[33]

If states are rational and free actors, as they are considered to be, exchanges that address such externalities through reallocation of jurisdiction will occur only when that jurisdiction "is more valuable to one state than to another."[34]

This is evident in various regulatory regimes. In environmental law, for instance, there is a state preference to protect the health of its domestic population from the adverse effects, or cross-border externalities, caused by pollution generated by factories in neighboring countries. Similarly, in trade law, the state preference to maximize domestic welfare can be harmed by cross-border externalities resulting from imposition of trade-restrictive measures abroad.

In the presence of an externality, states may have an opportunity to negotiate limits to unilateral powers, and generate gains, through cooperative action. Legal measures, such as soft law, treaties, and international organizations that are available for this purpose give states a range of

---

[33] Trachtman considers that these transactions might occur in the spot market or in the wholesale market. In a spot market, the first considers that transactions occur either by unilateral or bilateral persuasion, such as the use of economic sanctions or military force to pressure for a change, or use of a means of exchange or reciprocity in attempt to convince another party by means of an exchange or reciprocity. The wholesale market latter assumes that transactions occur through institutionalization: i.e. a reallocation of power by means of a more formal legal instrument such as a treaty, or through an international organization. Further references to jurisdictional transactions in this work will imply wholesale market transactions. There are two reasons for this. The first, as noted by Trachtman, is that the concept of wholesale is more appropriate than that of the spot market for understanding complex systems of rules such as treaties and organizations. Secondly, the rational choice analysis conducted throughout this thesis will not explicitly deal with issues of power asymmetry, which would be more suitably addressed in an analysis of spot market transactions. The transaction and allocation of jurisdiction might occur at the negotiation level, by means of explicit treaty clauses, or also by recourse to adjudicatory bodies. See Joel P Trachtman, "Regulatory Jurisdiction and the WTO" (2007) 10 *Journal of International Economic Law* p. 631–51, 634–40.

[34] While many international treaties deal with reciprocal exchanges of jurisdiction, it is reasonable to assume that in certain treaties in which jurisdiction of one of the parties is reallocated, the parties value considerations other than reciprocal transference of power, such as transfers of technology, security, or even direct financial contributions.

choices. Externalities offer a powerful explanation as to why states engage in cooperative behavior, but are less indicative as to which cooperative mechanisms should be used by states in the context of jurisdictional transaction.

An assumption of rationality in the study of international cooperation helps us to understand the strategic responses of individuals—through action or inaction—in response to the action or inaction of others. Given that different vehicles, such as customs rules, treaties, or soft law[35] may have distinct advantages for the respective regulation of different types or aspects of cooperative enterprise, the rationality of states is likely to influence their choice of a form of cooperation: whether they should, for instance, establish an international organization, or regulate a matter through non-binding soft law.[36]

It is particularly important, for an understanding of strategic interactions between states, to pay attention to the nature of the incentives that exist for parties to defect from a cooperative solution. The significance of incentives is that a cooperation is likely to be very unstable if, by unilateral defection, a party is able to appropriate the gains of the cooperative activity. The literature suggests that international trade is particularly prone to this: that its regulation is difficult because there are many incentives for states to defect from rules in order to individually appropriate the benefits of cooperation.[37]

2.1.4 Cooperation Problems[38]

The "law and economics" analysis of international law predicts that states will react to negative externalities caused by foreign measures by engaging in international legal negotiations to exchange jurisdiction. L&E advises that states should, in this process, take into consideration the behavioral pattern (whether a coordination or a collaboration game)[39]

---

[35] Trachtman, *The Economic Structure of International Law* p. 72–195.

[36] Guzman and Meyer, "Explaining Soft Law" (2010).

[37] See Schropp, Trade Policy Flexibility and Enforcement in the WTO: A Law and Economic Analysis p. 27–29.

[38] This section draws on previous work of the author. See José Caiado, "From Coordination to Collaboration: Explaining International Disputes over Tariff Classification" (2012) 3 *Economic Analysis of Law Review* p. 95–108.

[39] The literature on international relations considers the strategic structure of the decision problem faced by states when cooperating to influence their policy choices and to have consequences for the likelihood of international cooperation. See, for instance Duncan Snidal, "Coordination versus Prisoners' Dilemma: Implications for International Cooperation and Regimes" (1985) 79 *The American Political Science*

dictated by the cooperation framework in which they find themselves. The significance of this is that the international legal instruments adopted by states' parties should vary in response to the externalities in question, and to the problems particular to the type of international cooperation among them.

Taking the rationalist approach, international cooperation can be understood in terms of game theory, and, according to Martin, may be represented as either collaboration or coordination.[40]

Coordination games result in two equilibria reflecting the different preferences of each of the players, and a dilemma as to which ought to prevail. Bargaining will be intense, as the result has a direct impact on the distribution of the element under negotiation, but the importance of the resulting equilibrium is that, once decided, there are no incentives to defect. Coordination games do not, therefore, require strong surveillance and enforcement mechanisms, but rather instruments that are able to facilitate bargaining.

Oeter, in his economic analysis of customary international law, argues that matters regulated by custom can be characterized as coordination problems,[41] in which cooperation is only possible if the actors have available to them information about the prior behavior of states. From this hypothesis, he conjectures that precedents established by national common law jurisprudence could provide access to such information, enabling each actor to observe and record the behavior of others in the international community.

Concepts key to the system of customary international law are: (i) the mutual observation of the behavior of states; and (ii) the expectation of a specific government behavior in response to a particular situation. These elements reduce the costs to states of information and decision-making, and minimize the risks associated with cooperation. Still, why

Review p. 923–42; and Arthur Stein, "Coordination and Collaboration: Regimes in an Anarchic World" (1982) 36 *International Organization* p. 299–324. For a critical overview of this literature and an alternative perspective focusing on monitoring and enforcement issues, see James D Fearon, "Bargaining, Enforcement, and International Cooperation" (1998) 52 *International Organization* p. 269–305, 271.

[40] Lisa Martin, "The Rational State Choice of Multilateralism" in John Gerard Ruggie (ed), *Multilateralism Matters: The Theory and Praxis of an Institutional Form* (Multilateralism Matters: The Theory and Praxis of an Institutional Form, Columbia University Press 1993) p. 91–93.

[41] See Stefan Oeter, "Legitimacy of Customary International Law" in Thomas Eger, Stefan Oeter, and Stefan Voigt (eds), *Economic Analysis of International Law* (Economic Analysis of International Law, Mohr Siebeck 2014).

would states observe customary international law? Following Guzman, it is arguable that greatest compliance occurs in matters related to the reputation of the state. If a state invests in the building of social capital, for example, it is likely to have a tendency to avoid actions that affect such capital. It would be extremely expensive, however, to investigate the reputation of a particular state on the basis of its past behavior, and reference to legal rules provides a cheaper means of identifying these patterns. Customary international law can therefore be described as a tool that facilitates coordination among states.[42]

This thinking can be applied to international trade law to understand the common system of nomenclatures for the trade of products (Harmonized Code). The system was arguably created to avoid the costs of trade associated with a multiplicity of country-based classifications, which required the active pursuit, by importers and exporters, of specific information related to the classification of each product and each state related to cross-border transfer. An international agreement on a harmonized list of product classifications largely eliminates these costs and facilitates exchange among private parties. Negotiation of a common list can be a difficult task, with states unwilling to accept potentially costly changes to classification, but once there is agreement on the system, there seems to be little incentive for deviation.

In collaboration (as opposed to coordination) games, however, the resulting equilibria are suboptimal and both players must agree to move towards the optimal outcome. Instruments for cooperation include "extending the shadow of the future" and relying on international organizations. As these games provide strong incentives for defection, mechanisms to preserve cooperation focus on maintenance of the optimal equilibrium, usually by (i) extensive monitoring of compliance; and (ii) extending the shadow of the future, to ensure that long term benefits are higher than short term costs. As maintenance often assumes a centralized form, there is a significant role for organizations.

In international economics, tariffs, which are set by unilateral state action, are a good example of a public measure that gives rise to collaboration games. Countries have an incentive to use them opportunistically as a means of grasping a higher payoff to the detriment of a foreign trade partner. States are able to regulate tariffs by treaty, thus extending

---

[42] See ibid. and Andrew T Guzman, *How International Law Works: A Rational Choice Theory* (Oxford University Press 2008); and also Andrew Guzman and Timothy L Meyer, "Explaining Soft Law" (2010) *Berkeley Program in Law & Economics* p. 1–45.

the shadow of the future, and by creation of courts and review mechanisms to assure compliance and monitoring.

This understanding of tariffs explains the emergence of the WTO and its sophisticated system of enforcement which comprises, among other things, the Trade Review Mechanism and the Dispute Settlement Understanding. These instruments create, respectively, an international system for monitoring trade measures imposed by member states, and a compulsory mechanism for the resolution of trade disputes, both of which help to ensure WTO compliance.

As discussed in Chapter 3, because subsidies, like tariffs, can be used as a protectionist tool, it is necessary to ensure that states adhere to certain rules designed to tackle the externalities produced by unilateral subsidization. Regulation by treaty seems consistent with the cooperation theory described above, and capable of addressing the level of complexity of these regulatory and enforcement mechanisms. The next section analyzes this, therefore, in more detail.

2.2 Treaty as Contracts

The L&E analysis of international law predicts that states might respond to the negative externalities of other states[43] by transactions in jurisdiction through international law. Due to the cooperative nature of international regulation, however, parties need to consider that there may be incentives for states to behave opportunistically.

As defined by Cohen, "opportunism is broadly understood as deliberate contractual conduct by one party contrary to the other party's reasonable expectations based on the parties' agreement, contractual norms, or conventional morality."[44] Opportunistic conduct is thus an "attempted

---

[43] In this process, L&E advises that states should take the behavioral pattern dictated by the cooperation framework in which they find themselves into (whether a coordination or a collaboration game). This is important because the structure of the legal instruments should vary to respond to the externalities and to the type of cooperation problem addressed by the international law. In the situations in which parties decide to regulate through treaties, L&E also recommends that parties take into account the several transaction costs associated to the drafting and enforcing of different kinds of international agreements. In doing so, parties should give preference to a legal tool that allows for *ex post* completion of contracts.

[44] George M Cohen, "The Negligence-Opportunism Tradeoff in Contract Law" (1992) 20 *Hofstra Law Review* p. 941–1016, 957.

redistribution" of contractual gains that have already been determined by negotiation and agreement.[45]

In the context of trade agreements, opportunism suggests that parties might attempt to appropriate the largest possible portion of cooperation gains. This assumption is reinforced by the cooperative nature of international trade relations, which facilitates creation of incentives for such behaviour.[46] This field of substantive law is accordingly defined largely by treaty, a binding legal instrument that offers stable and enforceable rules to control for opportunistic behavior.

In international L&E, contract theory is a common analytical framework for the study of treaties.[47] Scholars view treaties as analogous to domestic contracts because like contracts, treaties comprise an exchange of rights and obligations between rational parties for the modeling of future behavior, with the intention of creating a legally binding and enforceable document.[48]

---

[45] See George M Cohen, "Implied Terms and Interpretation in Contract Law" in Boudewijn Bouckaert and Gerrit De Geest (eds), *Encyclopedia of Law and Economics, vol III The Regulation of Contracts* (Encyclopedia of Law and Economics, Edward Elgar 2000) p. 90; and compare with Timothy J Muris, "Opportunistic Behavior and the Law of Contracts" (1980) 65 *Minn L Rev* p. 521; and Steven J Burton, "Breach of Contract and the Common Law Duty to Perform in Good Faith" (1980) 94 *Harvard Law Review* p. 369–404, 103–04.

[46] See discussion in Section 2.2.2, on cooperation problems.

[47] See, for instance, Eric A Posner and Alan O Sykes (eds), *Economic Foundations of International Law* (Harvard University Press 2013) p. 63–78; and Trachtman, *The Economic Structure of International Law* p. 119–49. Also, for Trachtman, the methodologies of law and economics, which has been much developed on contract law, can reinvigorate the analysis of treaty law. The author recognizes that this is a well-recognized analogy in international law, i.e. that treaties are analogous to contracts. Similarities include the agreement of the parties and the intention to create a legally binding document with rights and obligations, modeling future behavior of the parties. However, dissimilarities between the domestic and the international order negatively affect this analogy. Doctrinal differences might, as well, pose difficulties, as doctrines such as "consideration" find no perfect match in treaty law, although the distinction of binding and non-binding agreements might be very close. Such dissimilarities, however, do not prevent an analysis of treaties based on contractual law. In fact, the employment of rational choice theory to the studies of treaties open an important field of investigation and should be encouraged.

[48] Theory assumes that parties are free to enter into an agreement, and that rational parties will only sign a treaty when they perceive that this will increase their individual welfare. As correctly put forward by Pauwelyn, the term "welfare" is not used in law and economics as a synonym of monetary welfare, but rather refers to "the maximization of an individual's or state's preferences, whatever these preferences may be (financial, moral, religious, geopolitical, etc.). The totality of these preferences is what is included in the so-called 'utility function' of each actor." Pauwelyn, *Optimal Protection of*

The generally accepted definition of contract as "an enforceable mutual commitment over time" focuses on three elements.[49] The first is the temporal dimension. Unlike other exchanges, which must happen simultaneously, a contract foresees promise of future delivery: a commitment.[50] The second element of contract is the content of the commitment: the substantive rules or contractual terms, which in the treaty analogy are devised to enable a transaction in jurisdiction to overcome a cooperation problem caused by externalities arising from unilateral actions. The third characteristic of contract is enforcement: rules that give effect to mutual contractual commitments and deter defection.

A contract is the result of a process of negotiation, through which the parties establish basic commitments by assigning each other rights and obligations (entitlements[51]) and define rules for protection and enforcement. Entitlement protection rules concern the rights of the parties to make decisions regarding their *ex post* behavior at the performance stage of the contract. Such protection is provided mainly through liability or property rules, which determine whether performance of contractual commitments is required, or whether a party may, with payment of compensation, unilaterally appropriate the rights of the other. Enforcement rules back up entitlement protection by providing mechanisms and procedures for use in case of infringement, to ensure that "the protection of rights is enforceable, and that punishment is not an empty threat."[52]

International Law p. 28–29. See also Scott, "The Law and Economics of Incomplete Contracts" p. 280.

[49] Richard Craswell, "Contract Law: General Theories" in Boudewijn Bouckaert and Gerrit De Geest (eds), *Encyclopedia of Law and Economics, vol III The Regulation of Contracts* (Encyclopedia of Law and Economics, Edward Elgar 2000) p. 18; and Dunoff and Trachtman, "Economic Analysis of International Law" p. 30. See also Scott and Triantis, "Incomplete Contracts and the Theory of Contract Design" p. 187. The framework adopted in this thesis mainly focuses on commitment and enforcement aspects of contracts, which encompass the main aspects of contractual theory and thus offer a powerful analytical instrument to understand international treaties.

[50] This is compatible with the discussion on transaction in jurisdiction. See Section 2.1.3 regarding the discussion of transactions on the spot or wholesale market.

[51] The term "entitlement" is used in law and economics to describe an issue of conflicting interests in which the state or the parties at cause make a decision to assign rights and obligations so that one party "will be entitled to prevail." This entitlement problem is seminal in the law and economics literature of tort and contract law. See Guido Calabresi and A Douglas Melamed, "Property Rules, Liability Rules, and Inalienability: One View of the Cathedral" (1972) 85 *Harvard Law Review* p. 1089–128, 1090.

[52] Schropp, *Trade Policy Flexibility and Enforcement in the WTO: A Law and Economic Analysis* p. 49.

Rationalist approaches to contract generally assume that parties would write a "complete contract": as if there are and will be no contractual imperfections, no limits to rationality or enforceability, no transaction costs, and no enforcement costs.[53] As discussed in detail below, however, imperfections exist, and the complete contract is no more than an ideal benchmark.

This is problematic, particularly for long-term contracts, such as trade agreements, because longevity leaves the agreement open to potentially severe uncertainties. Thus, in trade agreements, as in other contracts, "a trade-off arises between *ex ante* strong commitment devices on the one hand and flexibility *ex post* in order to uphold the efficiency of the contract on the other hand."[54] The next section discusses the main elements and implications of the ideal of complete contract, which has an important function as the rational benchmark for analysis of incomplete contract. This in turn lays the groundwork for analysis of the impact of uncertainty on the capacity for negotiation and enforcement of trade agreements.

2.2.1   The Complete Contract Benchmark

Use of the concept of "complete contract" has a strong tradition in domestic law in the rational analysis of contract.[55] A complete contract is entered into by entirely informed and perfectly rational parties, in the absence of imperfections such as the information costs associated with contractual transaction, and in the presence of optimal enforcement capacity.[56] It provides for a "complete description of every possible present and future state of the world, no matter how small the probability of the contingency."[57]

In his study on international trade law, Schropp identifies the following aspects of the complete contract. First, it is efficient in its enhancement of the welfare of the parties in every possible future scenario. It also has perfect foresight, and can therefore avoid or hinder any attempt at opportunistic

---

[53] van Aaken, "Delegating Interpretative Authority in Investment Treaties: The Case of Joint Commissions" p. 23–24.

[54] Ibid.

[55] Steven Shavell, "Damage Measures for Breach of Contract" (1980) 11 *The Bell Journal of Economics* p. 466–90.

[56] Ibid.

[57] Schropp, *Trade Policy Flexibility and Enforcement in the WTO: A Law and Economic Analysis* p. 58.

behavior. Such a contract, moreover, prescribes a course of action to address every possible future situation; it is therefore "renegotiation-proof," in the sense that performance must always be preferred and supported.

Finally, a complete contract provides for such detailed primary rules of entitlement that no default rules in the form of property or liability rules are necessary. A complete contract perfectly distinguishes forbidden from permitted behavior by exhaustive description of all possible actions and inactions of parties under all possible future scenarios relevant to the agreement.[58] Consequently, there is no need to add to the contract any *ex post* legal instrument to evaluate or model unregulated, or ambiguously regulated, behavior.

To summarize, a complete contract maximizes joint welfare—no other contract can do better—while preventing opportunism, assigning rights in relation to every potential scenario, and releasing parties of obligations under very specific contractual conditions.

Ideally, therefore, states, understood as rational actors, will strive to have an "agreement that specifies the obligations of the contracting parties and the payments to be made under each conceivable circumstance,"[59] otherwise known as a complete contract.

Assuming that all actors are free to enter into an agreement, and that rational parties will only sign a treaty that they perceive to increase their individual welfare, it may be concluded that a treaty increases the welfare of each party to it. Because rational parties would only enter an agreement that makes them better off, a complete contract is commonly referred to as "Pareto efficient."[60] In L&E economic jargon, a Pareto

---

[58] Contracts are usually signed to allow parties to reap gains from trade, but contracts can also have other important functions such as minimize transaction costs and transfer risks between the parties. For an overview of the literature of these contractual functions, see Schropp, *Trade Policy Flexibility and Enforcement in the WTO: A Law and Economic Analysis* p. 31.

[59] Shavell, "Damage Measures for Breach of Contract" p. 466. Within the international law framework, one could read the term "payment" used by Shavell as meaning "behavior" or "action." This seems to be appropriate because Shavell's work dealt manly with domestic buy/sell or services contracts in which a product or service is transferred or executed upon a monetary consideration, thus the "payment" term used by Shavell. In international law, however, most treaties are concerned with the exchange of authorities and an action or inaction usually does not foresee a monetary consideration but a similar action or inaction by the other state. Also, the contract theory literature "assumes that the private goal of contracting parties is to maximize the shared value created by a contract," Scott and Triantis, "Incomplete Contracts and the Theory of Contract Design" p. 2.

[60] Pareto efficiency, named after Vilfredo Pareto, related to the "satisfaction of individual preferences" in situations in which it is "impossible to change it so as to make at least one

efficient agreement maximizes the joint welfare of all parties to an extent that cannot be exceeded by any other contract. The contract is complete in this sense if there are no "mutually beneficial changes that the parties can make" to it.[61]

An individual party, however, under certain conditions, might accomplish a higher individual welfare if, having received the expected benefit of the regulated behavior, it then defects, thus appropriating the gains of the contract without performing its obligation. In short, it fails to comply with the contract or treaty. Contracts must accordingly contain enforcement provisions to ensure compliance.

In practice, the price of violation or non-compliance is: (i) the damages payable by a state in the event of breach; and (ii) the likelihood of punishment, determined by the ability of the system to (a) identify unlawful conduct, and (b) prove its existence before a competent court.

In a world of full information, all potential welfare-maximizing behaviors and non-compliance scenarios would be described in the contract, making any breach of contract a form of opportunistic behavior subject to enforcement procedures. The existence of opportunistic behavior requires that even complete contracts are backed up by enforcement mechanisms which, for rational parties, is a simple matter of raising the costs of defection to ensure compliance with the joint welfare-maximizing behavior anticipated in the contract.[62]

Within the analytical framework of complete contract, scholars presume that it is feasible for the preferences of the parties to be fully expressed in writing, and that written expressions of intent should be favored when confronted with potential gaps in agreement between the parties. The presumption further informs the rules for interpretation of contract, such that "the absence of a written term is taken to imply that the parties reached no agreement over some contingency, and the contract [should be] enforced accordingly."[63]

The presumption of feasibility of a complete contract rests, however, on specific determinations concerning the availability of information at

---

person better off (in his own estimation) without making another person worse off (again, in his own estimation)," Cooter and Ulen, *Law and Economics* p. 14.

[61] Shavell, "Damage Measures for Breach of Contract" p. 467.

[62] As noted by Cohen, economic analyses "generally conclude that if a contract is complete, there is no beneficial role for a court other than to enforce the contract according to the term," Cohen, "Implied Terms and Interpretation in Contract Law" p. 80.

[63] Gillian K Hadfield, "Judicial Competence and the Interpretation of Incomplete Contracts" (1994) 23 *The Journal of Legal Studies* p. 159–84, 161.

the negotiation stage, and on the effectiveness of enforcement. Should any of these assumptions fail, behavior that the parties might have preferred to regulate could remain unregulated. The contract would in fact be incomplete.

2.2.2 Contracting in the Presence of Uncertainty

The ideal of "complete contract" rests on assumptions of full information and perfect enforcement. In reality, however, parties do not have access to all available information, as necessary for regulation of complex issues, and may find it difficult to translate their common will into clauses that assign identifiable and unambiguous commitments *ex post*. The assumptions underlying complete contract, including the presence of fully informed rational parties contracting in the absence of transaction costs,[64] are, in real life, rarely verifiable.

In real life, uncertainty, which arises from conditions affecting rational actors during decision-making,[65] may pose a threat to the successful conclusion of a contract.[66] Even if, for example, parties are convinced that a treaty is the most efficient means of regulation in relation to a particular issue of international trade, the drafting of a treaty, like tariff negotiation, might be so costly that it never in fact takes place. Interaction resulting in engagement in strategic action between the parties might also raise costs that prevent the conclusion of transactions, as in a situation in which a negotiator to a trade agreement thinks that the other party is withholding essential information about the subject under discussion.[67]

Uncertainty is an unavoidable element of the processes of negotiation and enforcement. Specific uncertainties will necessarily lead to contractual gaps, such as the absence of contractual language or a particular mechanism, which will ultimately prevent efficient *ex post* implementation of the

---

[64] This does not imply that complete contracts are not useful for an economically informed analysis. As noted by Cohen, the concept can function as a "useful benchmark, similar to perfect competition" and, in this sense, "just as some markets are close enough to being perfectly competitive . . . so some contracts may be complete enough" so that completion mechanisms are more or less useful or suitable to address incompleteness. Cohen, "Implied Terms and Interpretation in Contract Law" p. 80.

[65] Simon Schropp, Trade Policy Flexibility and Enforcement in the WTO: A Law and Economic Analysis (Cambridge International Trade and Economic Law, Cambridge University Press 2009) p. 65.

[66] Scott and Triantis, "Incomplete Contracts and the Theory of Contract Design" p. 3–4.

[67] Trachtman, The Economic Structure of International Law p. 4–5.

contract.[68] To foster efficient transactions, therefore, parties need to come up with instruments that are capable of dealing with uncertainty.

In response to such potential inefficiencies, the theory of contract identifies different types of uncertainty that originate, respectively, in the presence of (a) transaction costs and (b) the bounded rationality of the signatories.[69]

2.2.2.1 Transaction Costs in Contracting

Uncertainty results, to a large extent, from the costs associated with contractual transactions.[70] In general terms, there are "costs to engaging in transactions"[71] and such "transaction costs are the costs of exchange."[72] More specifically, transaction costs fall into distinct categories of which the cost of information is significant in a contractual relationship.[73] In contract theory, information cost is frequently divided into the costs of negotiation (front-end stage) and of enforcement (back-end stage).[74]

Negotiation costs, which are incurred before the signing of a treaty (*ex ante*), include those related to information collection, bargaining, drafting, and legal fees. They also include potential costs associated with strategic action by other parties, especially the withholding of information relevant

[68] Hadfield, "Judicial Competence and the Interpretation of Incomplete Contracts" p. 161.

[69] See Katz, who stresses that the more problematic reasons for contract incompleteness arise from bounded rationality and (asymmetrical) information problems. See Avery W Katz, "Contractual Incompleteness: A Transactional Perspective" (2005) 56 *Case W Res L Rev* p. 169, 172.

[70] There seems to be a great deal of controversy about the origin of the term and its most appropriate use. On the one hand, there is a definition that focuses on costs of trading something, and on the other there is a group that focuses on costs associated to the establishment and enforcement of property rights. For a detailed analysis of the term, see Douglas Allen, "Transaction Costs" (1999) 14 *Research in Law and Economics* p. 893–913. A more suitable definition, which narrows transaction costs to information costs, is commonly employed in the analysis of contracts and will thus serve as reference for this work. See, for instance, Scott and Triantis, "Incomplete Contracts and the Theory of Contract Design" p. 190.

[71] Trachtman, *The Economic Structure of International Law* p. 4.

[72] Cooter and Ulen, *Law and Economics* p. 88.

[73] Scott and Triantis, "Incomplete Contracts and the Theory of Contract Design" p. 3–4. When dealing with property law, Cooter and Ulen also mention costs associated to searching an adequate product, but such costs seem less appropriate to the study of contracts, and even if relevant, they could be accommodated in a broader definition of negotiation costs. Cooter and Ulen, *Law and Economics* p. 88–91.

[74] Robert E Scott and George G Triantis, "Anticipating Litigation in Contract Design" (2006) *The Yale Law Journal* p. 814–79, 822–23; and Scott and Triantis, "Incomplete Contracts and the Theory of Contract Design" p. 191–92.

to the contract.[75] The costs at this "front-end stage" of the contracting process are thus incurred by the parties in "anticipating future contingencies and writing a contract that specifies an outcome for each one."[76]

At the "back-end stage" of contracting, or *ex post* enforcement, costs are incurred by parties to monitor, renegotiate, or litigate disputed provisions or actions pursuant to the treaty.[77] Costs associated with judicial errors or limitations also raise concerns about "observing and proving the existence (or non-existence) of any relevant fact."[78] In the evaluation of both front- and back-end transaction costs, parties must be aware of the potential for strategic action by other parties, as asymmetric information may impair recognition of a breach of contract.

The threat of future opportunistic behavior raises the complexity of treaty preparation significantly. During *ex ante* negotiations, "parties might not foresee all possible contingencies or they would have to incur prohibitively high negotiation and drafting costs . . . to provide for an efficient obligation in each case."[79] *Ex post*, even "contracts that provide optimal obligations for all contingencies may be too costly to enforce" as enforcement could require information "known to the parties but not to the court."[80]

Transaction costs can therefore affect a contract with respect to the extent of both the commitments of the parties and its enforceability. Information is key, enabling parties at the outset to "observe and identify contingencies and to provide for the optimal trade obligations in each."[81] It also plays a crucial role in the identification and verification of such contingencies *ex post*. If *ex post* costs of adjudication are significantly high, it might not "pay to undertake the costs of contract completion ex ante."[82] Information costs can therefore "prevent otherwise efficient

---

[75] See Scott and Triantis, "Anticipating Litigation in Contract Design," who focus on the first set of costs. For a focus on asymmetric information problems, see Katz, "Contractual Incompleteness: A Transactional Perspective" p. 174.

[76] Scott and Triantis, "Incomplete Contracts and the Theory of Contract Design" p. 190.

[77] Ibid.

[78] Ibid. p. 4. See also Katz, for whom "because the parties have better information about the contract than courts or third party enforcers do, it may not be possible for an adjudicating tribunal to determine, at a reasonable cost, what the contract provided, whether the parties complied with their duties, or what the resulting damages might be," Katz, "Contractual Incompleteness: A Transactional Perspective" p. 174.

[79] Scott and Triantis, "Incomplete Contracts and the Theory of Contract Design" p. 5. On issues of information costs on negotiations, see also Scott and Triantis, "Anticipating Litigation in Contract Design" p. 823–24.

[80] Scott and Triantis, "Incomplete Contracts and the Theory of Contract Design" p. 5.

[81] Ibid.

[82] Katz, "Contractual Incompleteness: A Transactional Perspective" p. 174.

transactions"[83] from occurring, unless legal mechanisms are used to overcome them.

2.2.2.2 Bounded Rationality in Contracting

Uncertainty might also be the result of "bounded rationality."[84] Bounded rationality is a concept used in behavioral and psychological studies to define the limits of the concept of rationality.[85] In contract theory, the limits of rationality are also an important source of contractual uncertainty.[86] The theory of deviation from

---

[83] Trachtman, *The Economic Structure of International Law* p. 4.

[84] The idea of full rationality, despite its central role in economic legal analysis, is now criticized in the L&E literature of behavioral and psychological studies. This movement, already common in studies on domestic law, is now also gaining ground in the study of international law. According to Broude, the behaviorist approach differs from classical economic analysis for it acknowledges the limitations of the concept of rationality and for incorporates concepts backed by empirical research. Broude makes the case that the idea of rationality is so fragile that the behaviorist analysis should be considered to be closer to sociology than to rational choice. This sociological behaviorism, according to Broude, could open new areas of research in the study of international law, and can be applied to understand the behavior of three types of actors: (i) the state as a unitary actor; (ii) collective decision-making bodies at the international level; and (iii) the individual as a decision maker of international nature. Tomer Broude, "Behavioral International Law" (2013) *U Pa L Rev* p. 1099–2131.

[85] Another trend is the use of experiments that simulate in the laboratory or in the field the behavior and choices of different actors. However, even if these methods can be valuable for studying the behavior of, for example, international negotiators during the talks for signing of an agreement, its application to more complex ones, such as the state and international organizations, collides with the difficulty to compare the action of such entity to the "failures" commonly observed in the conduct of the individual. One of the proposed solutions, to individualize the behavior of states, can be found in the work of Hafner-Burton and others, analyzing a possible correlation between the choice of enforcement mechanisms of international treaties and the level of seniority of American negotiators. According to the authors, the more senior a negotiator is, the less she is concerned about such mechanisms. See Emilie M Hafner-Burton, D Alex Hughes, and David G Victor, "The Cognitive Revolution and the Political Psychology of Elite Decision Making" (2013) 11 *Perspectives on Politics* p. 368–86.

[86] The issue of rationality in contract theory has already been subjected to critics in the domestic law context, as in Richard H Thaler and Cass R Sunstein, *Nudge: Improving Decisions about Health, Wealth, and Happiness* (Yale University Press 2008), and criticized as a too rigid pattern that does not fully conform with reality of international negotiations, as in Broude, "Behavioral International Law" p. 1099; and Anne van Aaken, "Towards Behavioral International Law and Economics: A Comment on Enriching Rational Choice Institutionalism for the Study of International Law" (2008) *U Ill L Rev* p. 47–59, who further analyzed the issue under the concepts of bounded rationality, bounded willpower, and bounded self-interest. For a detailed overview on incompleteness due to bounded rationality when applied to contract theory in international trade

expected utility[87] suggests that no matter how well-informed and advised a treaty negotiator may be, he or she is always subject to bias or errors of judgment.

Biases, as errors of judgment, can be divided into three types: an availability or heuristic bias (drawing an incorrect inference of probability from a general perception); a bias of hindsight (the tendency to "attach excessively high probabilities to events that ended up occurring"); or an optimistic bias (the "tendency . . . to believe that the . . . probability of facing a bad outcome is lower than it actually is").[88]

Biases that depart from expected utility models amount essentially to loss aversion (by which losses are weighted more heavily than gains) and its correlative effects. The "endowment effect" suggests that the evaluation of an entitlement may turn on whether or not the agent has been assigned primary ownership. The "framing effect," on the other hand, describes the tendency of agents to respond to the same proposition in different ways, depending on how it is presented.[89]

Bounded rationality can have an impact at both the negotiation and enforcement phases of a contract. During negotiation, it can lead to human errors in assessment of the possibility or magnitude of an event and in the drafting of contradictory clauses. It can also have an effect at the enforcement stage. Van Aaken, on the basis of the behaviorist theory, suggests that to bind a variety of topics such as those covered by the WTO into a single negotiation or treaty can be an obstacle to the conclusion of negotiations, because parties tend to overvalue their concessions and underestimate those made by others. Similarly, at the enforcement stage, there is a tendency for parties to interpret clauses in their favor, which can lead to counterproductive behavior from the point of view of the value-creation of contracts.[90]

Cost-related uncertainty and bounded rationality are, in contract theory, *conditions* to which parties are exposed. Given such conditions, negotiators are not in a position to generate a contract that is "complete" as previously discussed, and the regulatory effect of the resulting

---

law, see Schropp, *Trade Policy Flexibility and Enforcement in the WTO: A Law and Economic Analysis* p. 64–65.

[87] Christine Jolls and Cass R Sunstein, "Debiasing through Law" (2006) 35 *The Journal of Legal Studies* p. 199–242, 202–03.

[88] Ibid. p. 202–03.

[89] Ibid.

[90] Anne van Aaken, "Behavioral International Law and Economics" (2014) 55 *Harvard International Law Journal* p. 421–83.

agreement will necessarily be incomplete. The contractual *outcome* of uncertainty is, therefore, incompleteness.

2.2.3 Contractual Incompleteness

Incompleteness might also be understood to be the rational choice of negotiators. Cohen notes that incompleteness tends to be efficient, and thus rational, in situations in which contracts are overly complex: that is, if negotiators are confronted with "a large number of low-probability contingencies that could affect the value of contractual performance, and the efficient responses to those contingencies vary greatly and so cannot easily be specified in advance."[91]

Incomplete, as opposed to complete, contracts will not perfectly determine the welfare-increasing behavior that should be undertaken in response to a particular contingency.[92] Parties to an incomplete contract might therefore regret, *ex post*, the manner in which they, through the treaty, assigned rights and obligations *ex ante*.[93] Contracts negotiated

[91] Cohen, "Implied Terms and Interpretation in Contract Law" p. 81. See also Warren F Schwartz and Alan O Sykes, "The Economic Structure of Renegotiation and Dispute Resolution in the World Trade Organization" (2002) 31 *The Journal of Legal Studies* p. 179–204, 183. For a discussion about differences in the use of the concept by lawyers and economists, see Scott and Triantis, "Incomplete Contracts and the Theory of Contract Design" p. 4.

[92] In certain situations, the offended party will not be able to point to a contractual provision that sufficiently prohibits the behavior of the offender, no matter how obviously opportunistic such behavior has been. In others, "the contingency is not sufficiently observable by the victim." It might also be the case that the offence is perceived and foreseen, but the damage cannot be easily assessed (the three mean that somehow, defection is imperfectly "detectable, verifiable, or quantifiable"). These three are a matter of enforceability. This matters because enforcement is a function of enforceability and enforcement capacity, and means that even if a party has enough enforcement capacity, it might be hesitant to cooperate if it perceives that enforceability is poor. From the injurer perspective, the problem is of overregulation, i.e. constraints are too rigid and impede "regret contingencies." These occur if the contract leaves gains from trade to be realized *ex post*. If the contract is rigid, and parties cannot properly see the occurrence or magnitude of events, this will reduce their *ex ante* willingness to cooperate. Schropp, *Trade Policy Flexibility and Enforcement in the WTO: A Law and Economic Analysis* p. 78. For a graphic description of this effect, see ibid. 80. At the enforcement level, situations might arise in which the contract allows for a behavior that parties would have preferred to prohibit or, on the opposite side, the contract might forbid a behavior that parties would have wanted to allow should they have had, *ex ante*, the information that has only been revealed to them *ex post*.

[93] A detailed overview of the impact of incompleteness in the contractual commitment of rational parties is made by Alexander Keck and Simon Schropp, "Indisputably Essential: The Economics of Dispute Settlement Institutions in Trade Agreements" (2008) 42 *Journal*

under uncertainty are necessarily incomplete, as the parties can neither foresee, nor prescribe, a due course of action for every *ex post* eventuality.

This is a particular problem for long-term contracts, such as trade agreements, which are valid indefinitely and thus subject to an escalation of uncertainty over time. Moreover, where decision-making involves sovereign states, access to information may be controlled, making it difficult for other parties to a treaty to assess the real impact of a potential contingency on a foreign trade partner. Finally, the nature of international agreements is characteristically complex, as they attempt to accommodate the conflicting interests of multiple states, which can significantly affect the precision of legal texts.

Contract theory categorizes these issues as "uncertainty about the future (unforeseeability), uncertainty about the actions of other players (asymmetrical information), and uncertainty about the meaning and scope of contractual provisions (e.g., textual ambiguity)."[94] The result is that contracts will necessarily suffer from either (a) insufficient language, involving contractual gaps and loopholes, or (b) contractual rigidity, in which the language of the contract is too strict.

Either way, the door is left open for opportunistic behavior, because the temptation to deviate from commitments, through the use of protectionist measures, for instance, is a constant element of contractual relations.[95]

On the one hand, poorly drafted commitments, or under-regulation, leave room for practices that contradict the object and purpose of the agreement and jeopardize the realization of expected contractual gains. On the other, over-regulation, or commitments that are overly strict,

of World Trade p. 785–812. Anticipating these problems, parties, who *ex ante* must assume that they might in the future be both in the position of injurer or victim, have incentives to be reluctant in committing themselves to the treaty. L&E theory advises that, should this regret have certain legal and/or economic foundations (good faith and/or efficiency), breach should be preferred over performance. This is commonly known as "efficient breach" of contracts. Nevertheless, if a contract under regulates, it might expose victims to bad faith/inefficient breaches, especially if the victims do not possess the means to correctly assess whether a breach has occurred and what the motives of the other party were.

[94] van Aaken, "Delegating Interpretative Authority in Investment Treaties: The Case of Joint Commissions" p. 26.

[95] See the discussion on cooperation under collaboration and coordination above. Also, see Martin, "The Rational State Choice of Multilateralism" p. 96. For a concrete application of this framework to the WTO rules, see Schropp, *Trade Policy Flexibility and Enforcement in the WTO: A Law and Economic Analysis* p. 54–56.

might allow parties to block good faith actions by the other party by holding them to a commitment.[96]

Opportunistic behavior is a serious threat to contracting. It "increases transaction costs because potential opportunists and victims expend resources perpetrating and protecting against opportunism."[97] In effect, "the more one contracting party is willing to contemplate the possible opportunistic behavior of his contracting partner, the less likely he will be to want to contract with that partner at all," so much so that it might hinder efficient cooperation from ever taking place.[98]

In contract theory, uncertainty related to treaty language or enforcement may reduce the willingness of parties to commit to the contract. In relation to the language of the treaty, issues will arise from (a) ambiguity and ambivalence; (b) insufficiency, which leads to gaps and possible harm to victims of *ex post* non-performance; and (c) rigidity, which prevents parties from allowing for regret, and potentially harming good faith breaches. Deficiencies in enforcement arise if a breach is not (a) detectable, (b) verifiable, or (c) quantifiable: errors that will affect the behavior of contracting parties and should be better understood.

The question therefore is how to facilitate the conclusion of contracts in the presence of uncertainty and incompleteness. The contract theory literature suggests that parties to an incomplete contract will typically use flexibility mechanisms, *ex post*, to address unforeseen contingencies, allowing them to separate opportunistic behavior from actions in good faith in order to penalize the first and foster the latter.

Whereas contractual language is the obvious mechanism for identification and control of behaviors that are welfare-decreasing and opportunistic, it is conceivable that these *ex ante* strong commitments will exceed their objective and become overly rigid in their regulation of the matter. Incomplete contracts, therefore, must provide a trade-off "between ex ante strong commitment devices on the one hand and flexibility ex post in order to uphold the efficiency of the contract on

---

[96] In the case of subsidies, for instance, a general prohibition on all subsidizing activities could, depending on the definition of the term subsidy, prevent WTO Members from investing in public education and health system. Assuming that WTO Members would like to preserve their regulatory competence in such areas, commitments therefore need to be tailored to give them discretion to legally act in such areas. In addition to the problem of opportunistic behavior, contract theory also foresees that an overly inflexible agreement creates incentives to exit, or not enter, the system, as explained by Pauwelyn, *Optimal Protection of International Law* p. 67.

[97] Muris, "Opportunistic Behavior and the Law of Contracts" p. 524.

[98] Cohen, "Implied Terms and Interpretation in Contract Law" p. 91.

the other hand."[99] If negotiators do not strike such a balance, they might defy mutually agreed constraints on participation, "prevent otherwise efficient transactions,"[100] and create incentives for parties to exit negotiations.

This issue is particularly important in international law, in which "the traditional starting point is the sovereignty of individual states and the rule that a state's full entitlement over its territory and people can only be altered by that state's consent."[101]

Attracting commitment and retaining state support for an international treaty is a major issue, simply because states are free to choose not only *what*, *if*, and *when* to negotiate in relation to a treaty, but also because they can in principle "unilaterally withdraw from most of their commitments."[102] If uncertainty gets too high, or incompleteness is not properly dealt with, therefore, conclusion of an international agreement may be impossible.[103]

As discussed in more detail in Chapter 3, the economic theory of subsidies reinforces the argument for flexibility[104] and demonstrates recognition of subsidization as a legitimate policy instrument with which to tackle market failures.[105] In markets permeated with imperfections,

[99] van Aaken, "Delegating Interpretative Authority in Investment Treaties: The Case of Joint Commissions" p. 26.

[100] Trachtman, *The Economic Structure of International Law* p. 4.

[101] Pauwelyn, *Optimal Protection of International Law* p. 31. He also notes that, in this sense, international law would be an archetype of a market-based regime with a property rule, in which entitlements can only be exchanged by negotiation and consent of parties.

[102] Ibid. p. 31.

[103] While non-cooperation might certainly be a rational choice, states have several legal options to deal with transaction costs and opportunistic behavior and thus to encourage efficient transactions to happen. International treaties and organizations are the most evident legal instrument available. Treaties and international organizations define and institutionalize the will of states and reduce transaction costs and the probability of opportunistic behavior by, for instance, improving enforcement of rules or monitoring domestic actions to make sure agreements are complied with. See Section 2.2.2.

[104] It seems important to present this argument at this stage, but this is simply an overview. A more detailed explanation on the economics of subsidies as a means to tackle market failures will be introduced in Chapter 3. In fact, the use of economic rationale as a justification for flexibility is also present in other areas of substantive international economic law, such as tariffs and international regulations and investments. This are policy areas in which trade restrictions can have positive impacts on employing social and environmental policies. The economic value of flexibilities in trade agreement is well described in Schropp, *Trade Policy Flexibility and Enforcement in the WTO: A Law and Economic Analysis* p. 101; and in investment policies in van Aaken, "Smart Flexibility Clauses in International Investment Treaties and Sustainable Development" p. 827.

[105] Economic justifications are commonly related to market failures such as imperfect competition and externalities as in WTO, *Exploring the Links between Subsidies, Trade and the WTO* (World Trade Report 2006) p. 58–62.

subsidies are a valuable mechanism with which to address issues of under-production and consumption of vital goods such as food, health, educa-tion, transport, innovation, and environmental goods, and other relevant social concerns[106].

The imposition of unduly restrictive commitments on the use of subsidies could, for these reasons, endanger the capacity of WTO Members to respond to social and economic needs within their jurisdictions.[107] Subsidies are, moreover, an efficient tool for govern-mental intervention in times of crisis, and policymakers might be reluc-tant to adhere to commitments that excessively restrict their ability to respond to exceptional conditions.[108]

The relationship between commitments and flexibility is therefore a relevant lens through which to address not only the incompleteness problems derived from transaction costs and bounded rationality (gen-eral contract theory), but also the non-trade concerns that coincide with use of subsidies as an economic instrument for tackling market failures (economic theory). As both over- and under-regulation leave room for opportunistic behavior, it is difficult for negotiators to strike a balance between commitments and flexibility that will both maximize joint wel-fare and regulate deviations from the treaty.[109] Contract theory suggests that the appropriate trade-off can be achieved by introducing legal mechanisms, commonly referred to as "flexibility mechanisms," into the contract to enable *ex post* tailoring of commitments negotiated *ex ante*. These mechanisms will be addressed in the Section 2.3.

---

[106] Non-trade goals are part of the negotiators decision-making process and need to be taken into consideration when designing flexibility mechanisms. This is due to the political function of the decision-making process to which policymakers are subjected and will be addressed in more detail, see Section 3.3.4.

[107] Commonly stated objectives for the use of subsidies related to policies to preserve cultural values of their societies, to expand access to common goods such as health, education and infrastructure, to foster transitions to a more environmentally friendly industry, and even to implement redistribution policies to fight poverty and income gaps in their own society. For a literature review on the subject, see WTO, *Exploring the Links between Subsidies, Trade and the WTO* p. 65–108.

[108] The Canadian case well represented these concerns when arguing that the policy was necessary not only to protect the environment (non-trade concern) but also to preserve Canada's energy security (an issue often linked to the risk of crisis).

[109] Applied to an agreement regulating subsidies, it could be said that if the contract is too strict, it might prevent a WTO Member from making use of good faith subsidies and, if too flexible, it might allow for the opportunistic use of subsidies as a means to circum-vent the commitments. Both situations are problematic as rigidity might harm injurers and flexibility victims.

2.3   Dealing with Incompleteness through Flexibility

A major issue for international regulation of excessive unilateralism is how to identify and control for opportunistic behavior under an incomplete treaty. Given that it is impossible to regulate, through commitments, all scenarios in which opportunism might occur *ex post*, states will resort to flexibility mechanisms to address the potential for opportunistic behavior by other contracting parties.

Different literatures take different approaches to the relationship between incompleteness and flexibility. Although flexibility is only one of various contractual means of dealing with incompleteness, legal scholars view it as the mechanism *par excellence*. Green, Trebilcock, and van Aaken, for example, adopt a broad concept of flexibility that encompasses treaty language, remedies and interpretation.[110] From an economics perspective, Schropp construes flexibility as just one narrowly defined instrument that may be augmented by others, such as comprehensive contracting and the principle of precaution[111] in order to address incompleteness.

Though they differ in terminology, each of the legal and economic perspectives uses contractual mechanisms to overcome treaty incompleteness. The approach adopted in this work is similar to that of the legal school in general, and the views of international trade lawyers in particular, focusing on specific flexibilities facilitated by language, third party interpretation, and contractual remedies. Analyzing the WTO as an incomplete contract, Mavroidis states that an "incomplete contract describes a contract that does not, in its original form, contain all information necessary for its operation,"[112] and "such contracts are usually completed either through subsequent re-negotiation of the

---

[110] See Andrew Green and Michael Trebilcock, "The Enduring Problem of World Trade Organization Export Subsidies Rules" in Kyle Bagwell, Gerorge Bermann, and Petros Mavroidis (eds), *Law and Economics of Contingent Protection in International Trade* (Cambridge University Press 2009) p. 126; and van Aaken, "Smart Flexibility Clauses in International Investment Treaties and Sustainable Development" p. 832–42, for a perspective of flexibility that also encompasses for instance the delegation of powers to adjudicators. In this regard, see also van Aaken, "Delegating Interpretative Authority in Investment Treaties: The Case of Joint Commissions" p. 23–29.

[111] See Schropp, *Trade Policy Flexibility and Enforcement in the WTO: A Law and Economic Analysis* p. 84–100.

[112] Petros C Mavroidis, "Licence to Adjudicate: A Critical Evaluation of the Work of the WTO Appellate Body So Far" in James C Hartigan (ed), *Trade Disputes and the Dispute Settlement Understanding of the WTO: An Interdisciplinary Assessment*, vol 6 (Emerald Group Publishing Limited 2009) p. 75.

contract, or by reference to other bodies of law (default rules), or through subsequent adjudication."[113]

As discussed, because of the inability to fully specify welfare-enhancing actions for every potential scenario, parties commonly use flexibility mechanisms[114] to tackle incompleteness. Importantly, the fact that legal flexibilities are embedded, *ex ante*, in the treaty, permits the parties to complete the contract, *ex post*, in a welfare-enhancing manner.[115] Policymakers can therefore, despite uncertainties and corresponding incompleteness, commit to an agreement by incorporating flexibility into its design: through rules that will identify and separate opportunistic behavior from good faith measures, and penalize the first while enabling the latter.

2.3.1 Flexibilities through Treaty Language

The first means of introducing flexibility into a treaty is simply its language. The parties, in designing the treaty, attempt to reallocate power among the contracting states through the use of clauses that delineate and define their rights and obligations. They might also draft exceptions and justification clauses and use preambular language and accessory instruments to clarify the rationale of the contract.

In the process of designing the rules that establish such rights and obligations, parties can choose between very specific or more generally articulated provisions: they might opt for precise terms, which permit or prohibit flexibility, or language that is imprecise and indeterminate.[116] The literature commonly frames this determination of the degree of

---

[113] Ibid.
[114] For an overview of other possible *ex ante* mechanisms available for parties to complete contracts such as record-keeping, systems of information, and improvement of incentives to agents who negotiate contracts, see Katz, "Contractual Incompleteness: A Transactional Perspective" p. 178.
[115] Thus avoiding opportunistic behavior while allowing for the exercise of good faith regret.
[116] While this framework might be useful for classification purposes, in reality agreements contain clauses that seem to combine terms of more or less precision. For instance, Article XX of the GATT explicitly allows for the justification of measures taken to protect public health, which could be understood as a specific term. In reality, however, there might be questions about what policy areas actually fall under the definition of public health, thus opening the term for interpretation. This is not meant as a general normative statement. The meaning here is based on the current exceptions foreseen in the multilateral trading system, especially the exception clauses foreseen in the GATT and the SCM Agreement.

completeness that a clause will have as a rational choice between rules, which are more specific, and standards, which are intentionally less precise about the performance required at a future point in time.[117]

Kaplow suggests that the choice between a very detailed clause (rule) and a broad clause (standard) turns on the costs associated with drafting and information at the moment of negotiation,[118] and that when there are low transaction costs parties will resort to detailed rules. If costs (and correspondingly uncertainties) are too high, parties will prefer to define rights and obligations more generally, thus postponing any specific issues that might arise to a later time. During the *ex post* stage of the contractual timeframe, parties might re-open negotiations or decide to litigate before a third party, such as a court, which will then complete the contract in a concrete set of circumstances.

There is, however, a trade-off between hard rules and less precise standards. In contract theory, "the advantage of writing a contract with hard and precise terms is to ensure credible commitments,"[119] because "precise hard terms are less open to interpretation and the uncertainty of risk-shifting to the injured party is thus diminished."[120] This strategy of "comprehensive contracting," which minimizes gaps, is aimed at "replicating the complete contract or, at least, relevant aspects thereof."[121] Through use of very detailed rules, parties attempt to assign a "course of action to every possible contingency,"[122] an approach which, in

---

[117] Although the distinction between rules and standards had already been applied to the legal analysis, as for instance in Pierre Schlag, "Rules and Standards" (1985) 33 *UCLA L Rev* p. 379, the economic legal analysis has been developed in the seminar paper by Kaplow: Louis Kaplow, "Rules versus Standards: An Economic Analysis" (1992) 42 *Duke Law Journal* p. 557–629.

[118] For the general framework for the use of rules or standards, see Kaplow, "Rules versus Standards: An Economic Analysis." For an application of this framework to an agreement that regulates export subsidies, see Green and Trebilcock, "The Enduring Problem of World Trade Organization Export Subsidies Rules" p. 126.

[119] Anne van Aaken, "Control Mechanisms in International Investment Law" in Zacharias Douglas, Joost Pauwelyn, and Jorge Vinuales (eds), *The Foundations of International Investment Law: Bringing Theory into Practice* (The Foundations of International Investment Law: Bringing Theory into Practice, Oxford University Press 2013) p. 412.

[120] Anne van Aaken, "International Investment Law between Commitment and Flexibility: A Contract Theory Analysis" (2009) 12 *Journal of International Economic Law* p. 507–38, 510.

[121] Schropp, *Trade Policy Flexibility and Enforcement in the WTO: A Law and Economic Analysis* p. 88.

[122] Ibid.

Kaplow's framework, would arguably be suitable for contracting under low transaction costs.

Given the complexity of international relations, however, it is not surprising that treaty negotiation is difficult and costly. Even the most detailed set of rules cannot cover every future situation and will require *ex post* interpretation: despite best efforts of the parties to describe the rationale of the treaty and regulate future behavior, certain contingencies will evade their due diligence. Even if a comprehensive contracting strategy were possible, therefore, a treaty will lack flexibility and yield suboptimal results in unforeseen and unpredictable situations. In other words, even a detailed contract is likely to be insufficient in the way it defines and allocates rights and obligations, thus leaving open the door for opportunistic behavior by the parties.

To address incompleteness, therefore, states might choose to add to the contract explicit flexibility mechanisms, such as general exceptions.[123] Whether these are used depends directly on the substance of the regulation at issue, because topics vary with regard to the extent of the uncertainty they are subject to and might call for specific flexibilities. Subsidies, for instance, can be used to tackle market failures, and this should be accounted for in a treaty.[124]

Instead of striving for complete contracts through substantive flexibility, states can choose to use more general language to convey obligations, and have the specificities determined by a third party at the enforcement stage.[125] As treaty language is closely related to its judicial interpretation, this is a two-fold strategy: having first chosen less precise over more detailed treaty language, states will delegate to third parties the power to interpret and apply these general terms. The complex topic of delegation of powers is addressed in more detail immediately below.

2.3.2 Flexibilities through Delegation

The use of less precise rules, or standards, creates the necessity of interpretation of a contract for the resolution of specific issues, and a strong

---

[123] For an overview of other, more technical, possible mechanisms that strive to reduce *ex ante* costs of contracting, see Katz, "Contractual Incompleteness: A Transactional Perspective" p. 177–80.

[124] As the substantive flexibilities depend largely on the matter of the regulation and the uncertainties to which they are subjected, they will be further addressed in the chapter dealing with the economics of subsidies.

[125] Scott and Triantis, "Incomplete Contracts and the Theory of Contract Design" p. 10.

association between the treaty terms and the authority responsible, *ex post*, for such interpretation.[126] In this sense, standards "shift authority from the law-maker to the judiciary."[127] In international law the judiciary, or courts, are bodies of adjudicators to which states delegate authority to "control the content" of treaties and their commitments.[128]

By delegating such powers of adjudication, parties expect that a court will, ideally, resolve an issue in the same way that they themselves would have done *ex ante*: that the court will construe their contractual commitments according to a Pareto efficient complete contract model.[129] By making use of standards, in other words, the parties defer to the enforcement stage the task of efficient regulation of all possible states of the world.[130]

In the contracts literature, such deferral is considered a rational decision for parties to take due to the potential superiority of information available to the courts upon enforcement over that which would have been available to the parties *ex ante*. Judicial decisions are, after all, made following the occurrence of an unexpected event, and the courts have the advantage therefore of being able to assess the implications of the contingency on contractual gains. In the presence of a contingency, therefore, if a party behaves in an opportunistic manner in order to appropriate a larger share of the contractual payoffs, the courts should be in a good position to observe this behavior and evaluate its consistency with the contract on the concrete facts of a particular case.[131] Courts are, in this sense, in a privileged position to limit *ex post* opportunistic behavior of parties.

---

[126] Treaty design thus becomes a complex task for policymakers. On the one hand, negotiators must attempt to the extensiveness of the definitions introduced in the agreement, and on the other, they must also calibrate the scope of review that will be granted to courts to review measures in different policy areas.

[127] van Aaken, "Delegating Interpretative Authority in Investment Treaties: The Case of Joint Commissions" p. 28.

[128] van Aaken, "International Investment Law between Commitment and Flexibility: A Contract Theory Analysis" p. 509. As noted by van Aaken, this delegation to courts has the effect of making commitments more credible.

[129] Schropp, *Trade Policy Flexibility and Enforcement in the WTO: A Law and Economic Analysis* p. 81, 109–15.

[130] Scott and Triantis, "Incomplete Contracts and the Theory of Contract Design" p. 11.

[131] In reality, courts "do not directly observe the materialization of contingencies or the performance of obligations, but instead rely on evidences or proxies," Scott and Triantis, "Anticipating Litigation in Contract Design" p. 837. This might affect choices related to the burden of proof and will be discussed in more details within the context of the WTO dispute settlement rules. See Section 3.3.4.

In reality, however, parties are often reluctant to delegate powers because courts are subject to errors in their analysis of facts and application of the law.[132] Judges, like other individuals, are also subject to bias in decision-making and could favor preferences other than those expressed by the parties. *Ex post* decisions do not necessarily, therefore, fully reflect the interests of the parties, and could lead to decisions that do not regulate behavior in an entirely welfare-enhancing way.[133]

Before analyzing the legal tests commonly used by the courts, it is helpful to understand how states resolve this trade-off between precision and delegation, and how it influences the capacity of courts to apply the rules in a welfare-enhancing way.

A variety of legal and institutional procedures are available to states for their delineation of the powers to be delegated to the courts. States can make use of substantive and procedural rules and their authoritative interpretations; they can set rules to govern selection of court members, create appeal mechanisms, and determine the relationship between international courts and domestic agencies; they can influence the interpretation of commitments and, ultimately, renegotiate or exit the treaty.[134] Common to these mechanisms of control is the notion that judges might not decide cases in the best interest of the parties (according to the object and purpose of the agreement) but rather be influenced by errors or external preferences.

Conceptualization of the trust that treaty parties place in the courts is closely related to one's comprehension of the nature of courts and needs to be addressed in more detail. In economic theory, the delegation of adjudicatory power is usually framed under a principal-agent framework, in which courts are perceived as agents of multiple principals.

In this conceptual framework, there is strategic interaction in the relationship between states and courts, in that the courts have "some discretion by delegation to deviate from the preferences of the principals,"[135] and the states may make use of control mechanisms to prevent decisions against their preferences. The issue for treaty makers is

---

[132] The issue of court limitation is present in a great number of legal economic analyses. Craswell even proposes that a certain stream of the incomplete contract literature be called "incomplete courts." For an overview of this literature, see Richard Craswell, "The Incomplete Contracts Literature and Efficient Precautions" (2005) 56 *Case W Res L Rev* p. 151, 157.

[133] Cohen notes that courts should, ideally, "follow the intentions of the parties." Cohen, "Implied Terms and Interpretation in Contract Law" p. 82.

[134] van Aaken, "Control Mechanisms in International Investment Law" p. 419–32.

[135] Ibid. p. 414.

thus the extent of the competence to be assigned to the courts for the review of state measures that might allegedly violate an agreement.[136] This is the dilemma that states face when deciding whether to delegate powers to a court.

On the one hand, states must decide "whether and to what extent" uncertainties can be foreseen *ex ante* and addressed in the agreement by means of detailed language, which in theory reduces the need for a court.[137] On the other, they must evaluate whether a third party can be trusted to complete the contract "*ex post* with the benefit (and bias) of hindsight."[138]

There are a variety of reasons why parties might doubt the ability of courts to adequately fulfil the role of interpretation according to a Pareto efficient complete contract model. Even with hindsight, courts might have difficulty with full detection of breaches (observability), identification of a breach within the provisions of the contract (verifiability), and calculation of resulting damages (quantifiability).[139] International law is, moreover, a complex system of rules and customs, and all potential interpretations of a legal provision might not be foreseen by the parties.

These issues could be dealt with by rules on monitoring and flag-raising, by requiring states to inform the court, and by equipping the court with competence to seek specialized opinions on areas outside its expertise.

Parties might also distrust courts because judges are susceptible to preferences other than those established by the parties in the treaty. One way in which parties could solve this problem is to shield judges and courts from external pressure by granting them independence.[140]

---

[136] This is assuming that parties will allow for adjudication. As the multilateral trading system counts with a well-established dispute settlement system, we will not enter into the discussion of costs and benefits associated to the decision of establishing courts or restricting flexibility to negotiation between the parties. *Ex post* interpretation is an important contractual flexibility mechanism. In fact, contract theory seems to only reinforce the importance of courts and other *ex post* interpreters due to the inevitable incompleteness of contracts. Considering that even the most detailed rule might not fully cover every possible future scenario, contractual terms might require *ex post* interpretation irrespective of their precision.

[137] van Aaken, "International Investment Law between Commitment and Flexibility: A Contract Theory Analysis" p. 512–13.

[138] Ibid.

[139] See Schropp, *Trade Policy Flexibility and Enforcement in the WTO: A Law and Economic Analysis* p. 67–69. For a discussion about the role of verification issues, Scott and Triantis, "Anticipating Litigation in Contract Design" p. 831–35.

[140] In other words, "[i]ndependence of the third party is a crucial factor for credibility of the commitment" van Aaken, "Delegating Interpretative Authority in Investment Treaties: The Case of Joint Commissions" 29.

2.3.2.1   Institutional Independence

In international relations theory, independence is defined as "the extent to which adjudicators for an international authority charged with dispute resolution are able to deliberate and reach legal judgments independently of national governments."[141] This definition is in line with legal scholarship on the concept of the independence of domestic law, which is largely concerned with the influence of the executive branch of government over adjudicators.

In international law, however, national governments are but one of several pressure groups that might influence the decision of courts. Special interest groups such as industry associations and NGOs also attempt to influence court decision-making according to their own interests. Consistency between the international and domestic concepts of legal independence would, it seems, require that international law allow global adjudicators to reach decisions unconstrained by external preferences, irrespective of whether they are exercised by governments or other interest groups.[142]

The issue of the independence of public bodies has recently attracted the attention of legal and economic scholarship[143] within a broader research agenda concerning the independence of governmental agencies and institutions and how competences should be allocated between politicians and bureaucrats.[144]

At the institutional level, independence is seen as the result of two main variables.[145] The first is the selection and tenure of staff, including judges. This is an important element because courts tend to be more independent if their employees are chosen on the basis of technical profile rather than political background and have stable working

---

[141] See KW Abbott and others, "The Concept of Legalization" (2000) 54 *International Organization* p. 401–19, 154.

[142] For a bibliographic survey on this issue, see José Caiado and Cedric Bär, "Die Rolle von nationalen Behörden im Subventionsregime des WTO-Rechts – wurde der Bock zum Gärtner gemacht?" in Sandra Brändli, Roman Schister, and Aurelia Tamò (eds), *Multinationale Unternehmen und Institutionen im Wandel – Herausforderungen für Wirtschaft, Recht und Gesellschaft Schriften der Assistierenden der Universität St Gallen (HSG)*, vol 8 (Bern Stämpfli 2013) p. 181.

[143] See, for instance, Bernd Hayo and Stefan Voigt, "Explaining De Facto Judicial Independence" (2007) 27 *International Review of Law and Economics* p. 269–90; and Lars P Feld and Stefan Voigt, "Economic Growth and Judicial Independence: Cross-Country Evidence Using a New Set of Indicators" (2003) 19 *European Journal of Political Economy* p. 497–527.

[144] See Abbott and others, "The Concept of Legalization" p. 154.

[145] See ibid.

contracts. The second important variable is control over material and human resources: a designated and periodic budget and permanent staff also tend to strengthen independence.[146]

A certain degree of independence seems to be proper of the role of judges.[147] Historically, in domestic legal systems, judges have been given a number of prerogatives to ensure their capacity to form their own convictions and determine the outcome of cases according to the law, regardless as to how unpopular such decision might appear in the eyes of the government or public opinion.[148] A similar system is in place in international law;[149] appropriately so, as international judges are also subject to governmental and public pressure. International courts are not, however, the only third parties responsible for the interpretation of international law. Domestic courts and agencies also play an important role in applying international rules.[150]

Concerns about independence also apply, therefore, to domestic courts. As many international treaties lack the corresponding international enforcement system, it is up to domestic courts to ensure the correct application of international law. This is not a great concern in general WTO law, because of its strong dispute settlement system, but is at least partially an issue in the application of some of the covered agreements, because the treaties delegate powers to administrative bodies of the WTO Members. As a result, domestic trade authorities, for instance, are competent to conduct investigations for assessment of the conferral of subsidies in foreign jurisdictions, and to impose countervailing measures on subsidized products.

Domestic administrative bodies, like domestic courts, might, however, tend to protect their home government by interpreting international law in a manner that is favorable to the government or other domestic players.[151] According to Benvenisti, "national courts tend to interpret

---

[146] For a broader discussion and application of these concepts to domestic trade authorities, see Caiado and Bär, "Die Rolle von nationalen Behörden im Subventionsregime des WTO-Rechts – wurde der Bock zum Gärtner gemacht?" p. 181.

[147] For a general study on international courts containing certain issues on independence, see Hersch Lauterpacht, The development of international law by the international court (Cambridge University Press 1982) 3.

[148] See, for instance, Thomas W Merrill, "Judicial Prerogative, The" (1992) 12 Pace L Rev p. 327.

[149] See Lauterpacht, The Development of International Law by the International Court p. 3.

[150] See Karen Knop, "Here and There: International Law in Domestic Courts" (1999) 32 NYUJ Int'l L & Pol p. 501.

[151] See Abbott and others, "The Concept of Legalization" p. 401.

international rules so as not to upset their government's interests, some-times actually seeking guidance from the executive for interpreting treaties."[152] This "home bias" is arguably even stronger in other domestic institutions that do not enjoy the autonomy that modern democracies commonly give their courts in order to shield adjudicators from external pressure, especially from the government.

International law has a relevant role to play, therefore, whenever domestic bodies are delegated powers to make determinations of breach: international law needs to consider the potential for home bias and regulate the domestic administration so as to minimize or neutralize it.[153] This could be achieved by various mechanisms. The first is to offer such domestic bodies a high degree of independence, protecting them from the pressure of domestic interest groups, including the gov-ernment. Without a certain degree of independence, domestic trade authorities, for example, could arguably favor domestic producers over foreign competitors by the imposition of WTO inconsistent counter-vailing duties. WTO rules that determine how such authorities are structured, and how they make decisions, are therefore of crucial importance.

2.3.2.2   Legal Review Aspects

When imposing control, states will inevitably face issues regarding reg-ulation of the opportunistic behavior of the other contracting party. This is simply an expression of the trade-off between the delegation of powers to the courts on the one hand, and the preservation of its own compe-tence for independent decision-making regarding appropriate response to a contingency on the other. Parties are reluctant to delegate too much control to courts because they fear that judicial decisions might wrongly constrain good faith measures. At the same time, if courts are not assigned enough competence, they will not have the power to punish an opportunistic measure imposed by the other contracting party.

One way for treaty parties to retain power is to limit the scope of review by the courts. Substantive and procedural legal constraints are an obvious way in which to exercise control over courts. Specification of commit-ments and establishment of decision-making procedures that define the delegated discretion with more or less precision might effectively guide

---

[152] Eyal Benvenisti, "Judicial Misgivings Regarding the Application of International Law: An Analysis of Attitudes of National Courts" (1993) 4 *Eur J Int'l L* p. 159, 161.
[153] See Abbott and others, "The Concept of Legalization" p. 401–13.

judicial decision-making toward the object and purpose of the agreement. A legal instrument often used by parties to limit review by the courts, referred to as "self-judging clauses" is discussed in more detail below.[154]

2.3.3 Flexibility through Default Rules

Default rules also function as a flexibility mechanism, by influencing parties in their decisions for or against compliance with treaty terms and in re-negotiation procedures.[155]

Default rules are "rules that define the parties' obligations in the absence of any explicit agreement to the contrary"[156] and serve to "resolve disputes that are not settled by the terms of the document itself."[157] If appropriately designed, and assuming that courts have full information, default rules could prevent opportunistic behavior[158] *ex post* by encouraging the parties to mimic the behavior they would have chosen *ex ante*, had they been in a position to write a complete contract.

The difficulty is to find an *ex ante* default rule that will create, *ex post*, the incentives necessary for both injurer and victim to act in good faith: one that is capable of distinguishing situations that are welfare-enhancing for both parties from those that are opportunistic.[159]

Inalienability, by contrast, is the prohibition of flexibility *ex post*.[160] It is the adequate protection rule of the complete contract[161] (which, the reader may recall, perfectly distinguishes forbidden from permitted behavior and requires no default rules) and of situations in which

---

[154] See Section 5.2.3.2.
[155] See Warren F Schwartz and Alan O Sykes, "The Economic Structure of Renegotiation and Dispute Resolution in the World Trade Organization" p. 2–4.
[156] Craswell, "Contract Law: General Theories" p. 1–2.
[157] Ibid.
[158] Schropp, Trade Policy Flexibility and Enforcement in the WTO: A Law and Economic Analysis p. 101–04.
[159] Ibid.
[160] Pauwelyn, *Optimal Protection of International Law* p. 32–33, also recalls that inalienability is a common feature in domestic legal systems. Classical examples are prohibitions to trade human organs or people. In such systems, even if an individual, for any given reason, wishes to sell himself into slavery, the law does not allow him to trade his entitlement to freedom.
[161] In a complete contract, all future contingencies and the respective welfare increasing behavior have been predicted and described and there is absolute no need for renegotiations or for parties to exercise regret in a welfare increasing manner. Therefore, it is best if the contract is simply enforced in any situation.

ex post deviation creates significant externalities that are always inefficient.[162] In legal terms, inalienability is usually compared to the rule of *jus cogens*,[163] referring to fundamental principles of international law that bind all states and from which no derogation is ever permitted.

PIL scholars and international judges recognize the existence of both *jus cogens* norms, and norms with a collective obligation status, the first making entitlements "truly inalienable" and the latter "prohibiting inter se transfers, a feature of inalienability."[164] Inalienability rules are obviously rather restrictive.[165]

There are two types of default rules, as discussed by Schwartz and Sykes, through which flexibility can be achieved: (i) liability rules; and/or (ii) property rules, which will encourage renegotiation.[166]

---

[162] As Pauwelyn puts it, if "the transfer cannot increase welfare, it is best to ban it," Pauwelyn, *Optimal Protection of International Law* p. 52. Other grounds include situations in which (ii) is contract-annihilating—occurs when a "unique level of commitment is indispensable for the functioning of the contract" (such as the treaties on anti-ballistic missiles); (iii) is immoral–human rights and jus cogens; (iv) in which goods are incommensurable; and (v) in situations in which governments act paternalistically. Paternalism is a controversial topic in the law and economics literature, having applications that could foster rational decisions of individuals, but that could also inefficiently limit individual freedom. For a literature overview and a discussion on the effects of paternalistic measures on rational individuals, see Anne van Aaken, "Begrenzte Rationalität und Paternalismusgefahr. Das Prinzip des schonendsten Paternalismus" in Michael Anderheiden and others (eds), *Paternalismus und Recht : in memorian Angela Augustin (1968–2004)* (Paternalismus und Recht : in memorian Angela Augustin (1968–2004), Mohr Siebeck 2006). For a literature review on the possible rational uses of inalienability rules in contracts, see Schropp, *Trade Policy Flexibility and Enforcement in the WTO: A Law and Economic Analysis* p. 105–07.

[163] See Pauwelyn, *Optimal Protection of International Law* p. 32–33.

[164] Other examples might include human rights treaties based on arguments of morality, and also paternalistic rules that could help smaller and less developed countries to deny certain treaty terms based on previous inalienable terms of a previously signed treaty. Despite these examples, there seems to be a lack of consistency and clear rules for the use of inalienability rules. In public international law there are good arguments for making the case for protection by inalienability in several areas. For instance, nuclear tests might have disastrous externalities on third parties and it seems reasonable to assume that bans on open tests or in certain areas be protected by inalienability rules. However, this system lacks clear criteria to determine which international law norms have such status and "decisions on inalienability seem predominantly subjective." See ibid. 122–23, and 19.

[165] As discussed in Section 2.4. However, allowing parties to exercise regret though flexibility mechanisms can be welfare enhancing to them.

[166] See Warren F Schwartz and Alan O Sykes, "The Economic Structure of Renegotiation and Dispute Resolution in the World Trade Organization" p. 4–6.

Liability rules allow a treaty party to make a unilateral decision as to whether it will perform or breach. Contracts generally contemplate that in the event of non-performance, the other party will be compensated.[167] Damages are generally the preferred form of compensation, based on the expectation that they will put the victim in as good a position as "if the injurer had performed" the contract; in other words that the harmed party receives damages in an amount corresponding to the gains it expected to receive under the contract. This is particularly relevant in the presence of an unforeseen event that benefits the injurer to an extent greater than the value of the harm done to the victim.[168] A liability rule in this situation will ensure that the payment of damages is included in the equation, so that a breach will only occur in cases in which the net value of the benefit to the injurer, after subtracting the value of the harm to the victim, remains larger than the assigned damages.[169]

Under a property rule, however, if a party wishes to breach a certain term of the agreement—to exercise an unforeseen flexibility, in good faith, for example—it must renegotiate the terms of the contract with the other party. There are serious shortcomings to this situation, since once a "good faith" breach has occurred, and the wrongdoer is in a position to negotiate compensation, it is feasible for the victim to overestimate its losses, an opportunistic behavior commonly known as a "hold out."[170]

---

[167] There are different levels of compensation that usually complement a liability rule. The most common being: (i) zero; (ii) restitution—establishes the *status quo ante* the contract—are smaller than those of reliance (which on its turn are smaller than those of a victims expectations); (iii) reliance—establishes the *status quo ante* the breach, compensating the victim for direct harms suffered and leaving out any indirect opportunities, such as efficiency gains that would have occurred in normal contractual performance); and (iv) expectation damage, which puts the victim in as good a position as if the other party had performed. For a literature review on the impact of different remedies on the behavior of rational contracting parties, see Schropp, *Trade Policy Flexibility and Enforcement in the WTO: A Law and Economic Analysis* p. 108–15.

[168] Ibid. p. 112.

[169] The use of expectation damages implies the existence of a third party competent to asses and to calculate harm and to determine the appropriate compensation. In the current multilateral trading system, this is done by WTO panels, AB and arbitrators. As noted by Schropp, there are costs and uncertainties associated to having such as system because: (i) injurer must gather information on the value of inflicted damage; (ii) creation and maintenance of an arbitrator raises costs and has collaborative issues; (iii) appealing to an arbitrator has costs for both parties; (iv) victims' subjective value must be monetizable; (v) arbitrators might make serious mistakes. Ibid. 115–17.

[170] Other transaction costs apply: (i) injurer incurs in information gathering costs to determine the size of the victim's expectation damages (which will probably be the reference for the negotiation); (ii) victim has to assess the potential gain of non-performance (from

2.4 Conclusion

Subsequent chapters will cover the economics of subsidies, the evolution of the rules on subsidies and the rules of the SCM Agreement currently in force.

This work is divided into three parts. The first part deals with commitment, analyzing the rationale behind the SCM Agreement and the choices determining the design of commitments. Its intent is to question when—and when not—to regulate subsidies and to sanction state behavior. The following parts focus on the effect of uncertainty in the SCM Agreement and discuss the introduction of flexibility mechanisms into the agreement. An in-depth analysis is provided by a focus on contractual mechanisms used to tackle three sources of uncertainty. It proceeds with a doctrinal analysis of the drafting of flexibility clauses in the SCM Agreement, and whether the current flexibilities provide an adequate system for differentiation of opportunistic measures from good faith behavior. The work concludes with a view as to whether the regulation of industrial subsidies achieved by the world trading system is adequate to prevent opportunistic behavior, while permitting good faith measures in times of crises and addressing legitimate non-trade concerns.

which she wants to take a piece of); (iii) costs of bargaining might destroy the gains from non-performance; (iv) the larger the number of victims, the more difficult is renegotiation. Endogenous transaction costs are also a problem. Even if both parties are aware of the contingency, they might be subjected to: (i) crowding out, which in a PR system leaves the victim with the incentive to negotiate for all gains of non-compliance; (ii) hold-out, i.e. the procrastination of negotiations with the objective of impacting ex post distribution to its own favor; or (iii) over investment, i.e. under LR, victim sees expectation damages as a guaranteed rate of return, which might lead her to disregard certain risks and thus surpass the optimum amount of investments or contractual commitment. Also, even in the presence of a court that could, if perfectly informed, determine whether a breach occurred and estimate the values of harm and compensation, problems of observability, verifiability, and quantification might lead to legal errors by judges and will result in decisions that do not correspond to the type of solution that would have been preferred *ex ante* by the parties. See ibid.

3

The Economics of Subsidies

3.1 Introduction

This section analyzes the economic rationale for use and regulation of subsidies, concluding that there are strong arguments to suggest that international cooperation on the matter might be beneficial. Assuming that cooperation takes the form of an international treaty, the section examines uncertainties that negotiators might face during their attempts to regulate, and discusses the need to introduce into the treaty flexibility mechanisms that are capable of adequate differentiation of opportunistic from good faith behavior.

The first part draws on standard microeconomic literature to examine the effects of subsidies and the use of subsidies by governments. It explains that under the standard economic assumptions of (i) perfect markets and (ii) global welfare-maximizing governments, states have no incentive to resort to subsidies. It also demonstrates how the scenario changes once there is economic recognition of potential for market failure and government pursuit of political gains. These assumptions provide reasons for governments to use subsidization to alter the competitive advantage of domestic firms, in order to overcome market failures or boost the welfare of organized groups.

Having set out the elementary rationale for use of subsidies, the effects of subsidization will be analyzed in light of two main theories of trade: terms-of-trade and political economy.[1] These theories were originally

---

[1] This has been a common distinction in the economic literature. For a detailed overview of its application to international rules on subsidies, see, for instance, David DeRemer, *The Evolution of International Subsidy Rules* (Working Paper ECARES 2013) p. 1–7; and for international trade rules in general, see Schropp, *Trade Policy Flexibility and Enforcement in the WTO: A Law and Economic Analysis* p. 143. The legal literature has

employed to explain international cooperation for regulation of tariffs, but there is a growing body of literature pointing to the potential gains to be had from cooperation over subsidies: it suggests, in essence, that states would be better off if they could negotiate mutually agreeable disciplines to regulate use of those subsidies that have potentially harmful cross-border effects.

The section discusses some of the major challenges that negotiators are likely to face in the process of drafting an agreement for the regulation of subsidies. Based on insights from the application of contract theory to international law, it concludes that there are significant reasons for policymakers to fear the inadequate regulation of subsidies. The first is that the use of subsidies to circumvent tariff commitments can cause cross-border effects (under-regulation problems) that are perceived by trade partners as harmful. Other issues relate to the use of subsidies as the policy instrument best able to tackle several types of market failure (over-regulation) and the difficulty of devising, on the basis of abstract models, a realistic definition of subsidy (either under- or over-regulation).

Contract theory predicts that uncertainty, if significant enough, will create an imbalance in regulation and lead unintentionally to restrictions on policymaking by states. When such imbalance occurs in areas such as public services in which subsidies play a vital role, it increases the risk that a state will not commit to an agreement that regulates subsidies.[2] If, therefore, uncertainties are not satisfactorily dealt with, the conclusion of an agreement becomes less likely or could produce undesirable outcomes.

---

often focused on arguments for regulation based on (i) aggregate efficiency arguments; and on (ii) externalities, concluding that only a subset of arguments of the second category are both economically and legally sound. For more details, see Alan O Sykes, *The Limited Economic Case for Subsidies Regulation* (E15Initiative Think Piece, 2015) p. 3. As both lines of argument are interconnected, this thesis will first analyze the economic arguments for intervention and will then examine the rationale from regulation.

[2] Throughout this work, we address these problems as the definitional issue or problem of subsidies. The issue could be explained by the fact that, by its economic nature, subsidies are a versatile policy instrument that can take many different legal forms, reach several possible policy goals, and benefit numerous economic sectors or players. In fact, economic theory argues that subsidies are the best available instrument to deal with several market failures and should therefore not be too restricted. This leads to difficulties in differentiating not only "good" from "bad" subsidies, but also subsidies from other governmental intervention measures (such as regulation). As a result, these problems raise the level of legal uncertainties to which negotiators are subjected to and might, therefore, make policymakers more reluctant to legally restrict the use of subsidies because of a fear of overregulation.

As discussed in Chapter 2, uncertainties derive from the bounded rationality of negotiators and costs associated with contractual transactions. It may be assumed, on the basis of such uncertainty, that policymakers are unable—or unwilling—to identify and describe all potential situations in which governments would like to use or restrict use of subsidies (their own or those of other states), thus resulting in an incomplete contract.

Incompleteness is an important legal issue because it necessitates *ex post* completion of the contract, which is associated with problems of opportunistic behavior by the parties. Completion *ex post* may occur by negotiation among the parties or by judicial decision. In contract theory, negotiation under uncertainty will require that policymakers adopt flexibility clauses in order to strike a mutually beneficial agreement regarding the use or restriction of subsidies. To understand the structure and function of such agreements, it is crucial to understand the economic rationale behind the use of subsidies and the corresponding uncertainties that haunt policymakers when considering the imposition of restrictions on their use.

3.2 The Microeconomics of Subsidies

The application of subsidies is a policy instrument by which states are able to influence the decisions of market players, regarding production, pricing, and investment in order to foster economic activity. Although consistently referred to as "subsidies" in the policy literature, the term is subject to various definitions.[3]

Attempts at definition suggest that government measures may be characterized as subsidies if they feature: (i) fiscal expenditure; (ii) resources of public origin; and (iii) conferral of a benefit.[4] The economic and legal literature expresses concern however that such

---

[3] This can be easily spotted in the records on the use of subsidies and public spending of domestic institutions and governments. Certain international organizations, for instance, include in their subsidies databases public expenses related to social programs such as minimum income and reduced interests for social housing plans. This is not a prerogative of international trade law. In EU law, where subsidies are also regulated, Marco Slotboom affirms that "[n]either the EC Treaty nor the implementing rules of the EC Council contain a definition of aid" Marco Slotboom, 'A comparison of WTO and EC law: do different objects and purposes matter for treaty interpretation?', London: Cameron May 2006) 101.

[4] Marc Bacchetta and Michele Ruta (eds), *The WTO, Subsidies and Countervailing Measures*, vol 19 (Critical Perspectives on the Global Trading System and the WTO,

a definition does not grasp the concept in its totality. Consider, for example, whether a tax exemption may be considered a subsidy: the fact that it is not a fiscal expenditure because there is no direct transfer of funding suggests that it is not a subsidy, but it does provide a benefit to corporations, which implies the contrary.

Characterization of a subsidy by reference to the public origin of resources can also be controversial, as governments may not act directly as the subsidizing agent but instruct a private entity to confer a subsidy. Similarly, it might be impossible to draw a clear distinction between the costs and benefits to companies associated with a plethora of taxes, governmental programs, and regulations, leaving the observer without certainty as to whether a company has received a benefit or is actually carrying a burden.[5]

Attempts at definition of "subsidy" by identification of common features across the literature indicates a convergence around the idea that "subsidization involves the government and results in benefits for somebody."[6] In textbook microeconomics, a subsidy is usually defined as a "payment to buyers and sellers to supplement income or lower costs and which thus encourages consumption or provides an advantage to the recipient."[7] Typical examples of subsidies include tax breaks, direct transfer of funds, public guarantees, and the supply of public services to a market agent. In relation to general trade policies, subsidies are distinguished from taxes and quotas, and the effects of subsidization on welfare are investigated in various economic sectors.[8] With this general

Edward Elgar 2011) p. xvi. The issue of defining subsidies is also seen as a context-based definition, in which legal, political, and economic aspects might play a role. See, for instance, Rubini, *The Definition of Subsidy and State Aid: WTO and EC Law in Comparative Perspective* p. 17. For an empirical overview of different definitions made by domestic and international bodies, see WTO, *Exploring the Links between Subsidies, Trade and the WTO* p. 47–54. For a legal definition contextualized by economics, see Gustavo Luengo, *Regulation of Subsidies and State Aids in WTO and EC Law: Conflicts in International Trade Law* (Kluwer Law International 2006) p. 5–8.

[5] For instance, one might consider that there is a subsidy in situations in which companies are allowed to use public roads without having to pay toll fees. However, if the company is subjected to higher taxation rates than its international competitors located abroad, it might be that the benefit accrued from using the roads does not compensate for the extra tax, potentially leaving the company in a competitive disadvantage despite of its access to a toll-free road.

[6] WTO, *Exploring the Links between Subsidies, Trade and the WTO* p. 48.

[7] Gregory Mankiw, *Principles of Macroeconomics* (7th edn, Cengage Learning 2014) p. 888.

[8] A report from the WTO Secretariat concluded that the incidence of subsidies had a significant variation across sectors, playing a relevant role in agriculture, industry, and services. WTO, *Exploring the Links between Subsidies, Trade and the WTO* p. 120–78.

approach government policies have been classified and analyzed on the basis of the societal group targeted by the measure, the effects of the measure on the behavior of the beneficiary, and its overall impact on the economy, or on the welfare of various groups.[9]

These studies focus largely on the effects engendered by subsidies in the behavior of firms,[10] reflecting perhaps the empirical perception that subsidies are directed to producers. In microeconomics, the general assumption is that "firms choose how much to produce in order to maximize profits."[11] Profit-maximizing firms strive therefore to strike a correct balance between *total revenue* and *total costs* of production, in relation to which they can determine the optimal amount to be produced.[12]

To determine the maximal profits in a market, a firm analyzes its costs and potential revenues generated by various levels of output, and will produce the "amount of output that leads to the greatest positive difference between the firms' revenue and its costs."[13] More precisely, a firm

[9] All these measures can be viewed as subsidies because, assuming that policymakers made a correct assessment of the market, the measures alter costs and revenues in a manner that influences the decision of consumers and firms concerning consumption, production, market entry and exit, pricing, and investment. As a result, the subsidy leads to an expansion (or at least the maintenance of a desirable level) in output of the supported goods and services and, incidentally, might support employment, income, economic growth, and tax revenue levels. In short, subsidies cause changes in the free-competition status quo. Such competition distortions "arise because the subsidized firm is prompted to change its behavior" by adjusting the "level of output, change price, or alter levels of research and development (R&D), thus altering the process and outcome of rivalry with its competitors," Office of Fair Trading of the UK, *Public Subsidies* (UNCTAD's Seventh Session of the Intergovernmental Group of Experts on Competition Law and Policy, 2004) p. 15.

[10] Defining the rationale behind the behavior of firms is an important step for understanding the usage and the rules on subsidies, as it can be associated with the rationale guiding the behavior of states when deciding to confer subsidies and to regulate them.

[11] David Begg, Stanley Fischer, and Rudiger Dornbusch, *Economics* (10th edn, McGraw-Hill Higher Education 2011) p. 122. This assumption is not free of critics. For instance, whilst a sole owner might prefer to maximize his total job satisfaction, managers at big companies could set production levels to maximize their own remuneration. However, the assumption of profit maximization prevails in the business and economic literature. See, for instance, Paul R Krugman, Maurice Obstfeld, and Marc Melitz, *International Trade: Theory and Policy* (The Pearson Series in Economics, Pearson Education Limited 2014) p. 196; and Mankiw, *Principles of Macroeconomics* p. 63–65.

[12] In order to assess its total revenue, the firm multiplies the number of output units sold by the price of each unit. For total costs, it calculates the costs of each input times each used input, adding up all inputs, Cooter and Ulen, *Law and Economics* p. 26.

[13] Ibid.

will expand output as long as marginal revenue exceeds its marginal cost.[14]

The assumption behind this assertion is that as production expands marginal costs tend to rise, while marginal revenue tends to fall. After an optimal level of output, therefore, profits start to decrease and firms will have no incentive to further increase their production.[15] The supply theory describes production from the perspective of a profit-maximizing firm.[16] In a specific market, however, to determine price and output firms must also evaluate the demand of the market from the perspective of the consumer.[17]

---

[14] This means that "producing and selling an extra unit adds more to total revenue than to total cost, raising total profit. If marginal cost exceeds marginal revenue, the extra unit of output reduces total profit," *Economics*, p. 124. Ibid. (italics in the original). This is an application to the supply side of the generalization of the microeconomics' assumption that rational individuals, including firms, act to maximize their benefit. In microeconomics theory, the decision-maker will continue to make marginal adjustments "so long as the marginal benefit exceeds the marginal cost, and he will stop making changes when the marginal cost of the last change made equals (or is greater than) the marginal benefit," Ibid. p. 22. For a simple mathematical explanation, see Begg, Fischer and Dornbusch, *Economics* p. 132–34.

[15] Besides output, there are other decisions that might be influenced by the profitability in a certain market. Changes in costs and revenues alter the foreseen profitability of a firm in the subsidized market and might therefore stimulate firms to enter, or not exit, this market. When deciding whether to enter a new market, companies estimate the profitability by balancing initial (construction of a factory, development of product) and production costs (raw materials, staff, banding) with expected revenues. By reducing costs, subsidies could enable undecided firms to enter a market. Similarly, a subsidy that reduces losses could influence the decision of a company to exit a market in which it already operates. By altering costs, subsidies can also have impact on pricing and output decisions. In economic terms, this is more likely to happen if a subsidy affects variable costs, rather than fixed costs, as the company would be in a position to reduce prices and gain market share to the detriment of its competitors. In reality, however, it might be difficult to establish a line between subsidies that affect variable or fixed costs only, and even subsidies that reduced fixed costs might have impact on price and output decisions. For instance, subsidized finance for the acquisition of new machinery may lead to a fixed cost reduction to the purchasing firm, but it may reduce variable costs as well if the company acquires more efficient machinery than it would be able to in the absence of the subsidy. Investment decisions are also affected by subsidies. Subsidies might reduce the costs of investments, thus making them more likely to occur. Depending on the design of the subsidy, the measure might canalize funding for areas prioritized by the policymakers. If the investment leads to better products, subsidied firms will be placed in a competitive advantage in detriment of non-subsidized companies. In case a new product is created, the subsidized firm will have a "first mover" advantage, which might raise entry barriers to competitors. Office of Fair Trading of the UK, Public Subsidies (UNCTAD's Seventh Session of the Intergovernmental Group of Experts on Competition Law and Policy, 2004) p. 1–14

[16] Begg, Fischer and Dornbusch, *Economics* p. 131.

[17] Ibid. p. 130.

On the assumption that consumers behave rationally in accordance with their preferences, microeconomic theory demonstrates an inverse relationship between price of a product and the quantity demanded.[18] It concludes therefore that consumers, and not only firms, may be considered interest-maximizing actors who interact in the market through production and consumption.

Based on the general economic assumption that the maximizing behavior of individuals or groups tends to push interaction toward equilibrium,[19] the interaction of supply and demand will establish an equilibrium between total production and price. More specifically, the "equilibrium price and quantity occur at the point of intersection of the aggregate supply and demand curves."[20] Should markets function in equilibrium, the result would be optimal production and allocation of resources in a manner that maximizes the welfare of market participants.

States can directly influence firm decisions regarding output in two fundamental ways. The first is by reducing costs to producers. A subsidy might for instance reduce the price of raw materials. The subsidy causes the marginal cost curve to shift downward. As a result, the costs to the firm decrease, and it decides to produce more.[21]

Another way that governments might directly influence firm decisions regarding output is to cause a shift in demand, which can be achieved, for example, by a consumption subsidy. With demand increasing, the marginal revenue curve also shifts upward. As a result, the level of optimal production by the company increases.[22]

This discussion suggests that governments have at their disposal a variety of instruments with which they are able to intervene in the market by influencing the behavior of firms and consumers.[23]

It is important, therefore, to understand why a government might feel the need to take such action. Why would governments decide to intervene in the level of output by firms? To address this question, Section 3.3 discusses the immediate costs and benefits of subsidies and describes

---

[18] Assuming elasticity of demand.

[19] It is irrelevant whether the maximizing agents intend or not to result the equilibrium. Simply by acting in a maximizing manner, the interaction tends to equilibrium. See Cooter and Ulen, *Law and Economics* p. 12–14.

[20] Ibid. p. 29.

[21] Robert Cooter and Thomas Ulen, Law and Economics (International Edition, New York: Pearson Addison Wesley 2008) p. 29.

[22] David Begg, Stanley Fischer, and Rudiger Dornbusch, Economics (10th edn, McGraw-Hill Higher Education 2011) p. 131.

[23] Ibid. p. 132.

different frameworks for analysis of governmental behavior. Later, this analysis will provide insight into the reasons for conferral of subsidies, as well as their regulation, and is therefore an important step in the proper investigation of the SCM Agreement.

3.3 The Rationale for the Use of Subsidies by Governments

Governments claim to pursue a variety of objectives in their use of subsidies, including, as noted by the WTO Secretariat: industrial development, increase in innovation, income redistribution, the supply of utilities such as water and telecommunications, regional development and integration, environmental protection, national security, and cultural policies.[24]

Irrespective of their perceived intentions, subsidization is only one of many policy instruments open to governments. Whether, and how effectively, subsidies are able to tackle a particular matter is determined by several variables, such as the presence of international competitors and the existence of market imperfections. In order to determine the situations in which rational governments can be expected to prefer subsidization over other policy mechanisms, including non-intervention, it is necessary to establish a coherent analytical framework.

3.3.1 Rational Choice Theory in International Law

Rational choice theory is used by international law and economics as a means of explaining state behavior. The concept of rationality has, until recently, been seldom used in traditional legal analysis, but it has been employed consistently for many years in the social sciences, economics, and international relations theory.[25] The adoption of this approach now enables legal scholars to liaise with the social sciences and so better equip themselves to understand the processes of law creation and the effect of

---

[24] WTO, *Exploring the Links between Subsidies, Trade and the WTO* p. 66.
[25] There are different applications of the concept of rationality. They mainly differ on the issue of preferences of policymakers. The Realist School understands the state as the central unitary rational actor that seeks to maximize its power at the international level. Similarly, but with a focus on elements other than power, institutionalism also sees the state as a "black box," giving little emphasis to the influence of domestic political groups. The influence of domestic groups on state behavior is then better captured by political economy approaches, discussed in Section 3.3.4. See Koremenos, "Institutionalism and International Law" p. 59; and van Aaken, "Opportunities and the Limits of an Economic Analysis in International Law" p. 31–32.

norms on state behavior.[26] The assumption of the rational choice theory in relation to states is that, like individuals and firms, they behave rationally, by acting to maximize their individual preferences.[27]

Rationality implies the interpretation of behavior through the identification and ranking of the preferences of the agent.[28] States, unlike firms, are often understood as a collective agent that coordinates the interests of multiple societal groups.[29] Their object of maximization is therefore not as

[26] There are, however, critics to the limitations of the approach. Rational choice analysis of international law is also commonly criticized for (i) abstracting from many intra-state relations and for disregarding the role of non-state actors and individuals in international law's creation and enforcement; (ii) for not having adequate tools to deal with the preferences of states that cannot be monetized, such as national security and (iii) for a certain ambiguity in dealing with the preferences of decision-makers, who might be concerned with overall welfare, but who might also be interested in fostering the welfare of the leaders of their home state or even their own. See, for instance, Pauwelyn, *Optimal Protection of International Law* p. 28–29. While relevant, these critics seem to be over-emphasized. As we have seen in Section 2.4, rational choice theory allows the researcher to analyze the behavior not only of states or international organizations, as PIL usually does, but also of domestic groups such as NGOs both in law-making as in law enforcement. This is an interesting departure and innovation in comparison to other legal fields. Also, public choice analysis is a growing field of research in international law and offers tools to understand and deal with the role of domestic interest groups and the influence that they might exercise over policymakers. See, for instance, van Aaken, "Opportunities and the Limits of an Economic Analysis in International Law" p. 31. The critique of incommensurability, however, seems to be of more substance, and international law and economics can certainly profit from more research on this topic.

[27] Rational choice theory "predicts phenomena as consequences of individual choices, which are themselves explained in terms of reasons," Daniel M Hausman, "Philosophy of Economics" in Edward N Zalta (ed), *The Stanford Encyclopedia of Philosophy*, vol Winter 2013 (The Stanford Encyclopedia of Philosophy, Stanford University 2013). The concept is based on the notion of individual choice, or methodological individualism, and of rational parties. The concept of methodological individualism claims that "that social phenomena must be explained by showing how they result from individual actions, which in turn must be explained through reference to the intentional states that motivate the individual actors." It is thus the explanation of the general result (macro) by means of individual behavior (micro), "Methodological Individualism," *Stanford Encyclopedia of Philosophy*. Rationality, on its turn, is understood as a behavior conditioned on "an agent's preferences (rankings of objects of choice)" that are "complete and transitive," that is to say that "the agent does not prefer any feasible alternative to what he or she chooses," ibid.

[28] The use of this concept, however, reaches a roadblock when the importance of different preferences is not easily identifiable. A common assumption defines this shortcoming: that economic analysis cannot tell us which preferences to maximize. That is to say, it seems problematic to wander into deductive terrain regarding whether, for example, a particular state values environmental protection more than it values economic growth. So, how to explain a behavior in the absence of clear preferences?

[29] See Koremenos, "Institutionalism and International Law" p. 59–64.

straightforward as that of firms, which seek to maximize profits. The preferences of states could be modeled in a number of different ways, but here it will be assumed that states aim to maximize either general net welfare, domestic welfare, or the welfare of certain domestic groups.[30]

Despite this potential for different preferences, economists understand rational states to achieve their preferences in a manner similar to that of other rational actors: in other words, they act in a way that maximizes their preferences, irrespective of what those preferences might be.

A variety of methods may be used for modeling the behavior of states attempting to maximize preferences.[31] The most common of the economic models for analysis of the adequacy of the tools used by states to achieve maximization are *price theory* and *cost and benefit analysis*.[32] In price theory models, all other things being equal, individuals will prefer cheaper goods over more expensive products. They will also prefer more efficient means to achieve a goal over less efficient paths to that same goal. Applied to public policy, this theory suggests that states will take into account not only the accrual of possible gains, but also the potential losses that flow from their measures. States will, moreover, weigh up the prospective effects of different measures and choose the most efficient of them, that being the one with highest net benefits.[33]

This process of weighing or balancing is carried out through an analysis of costs and benefits. Also known as "welfare analysis," "cost and benefit analysis" is an important economic instrument for the assessment of gains and losses that affect different societal groups, such as producers, consumers, and politicians.[34] By weighing the costs and benefits that accrue to the various groups, it is possible to determine the overall gains or losses in welfare that are likely to result from a certain policy, and to compare such outcomes to those associated with other policy alternatives.[35] As a general rule, rational governments will choose

---

[30] See, for instance, Schropp, *Trade Policy Flexibility and Enforcement in the WTO: A Law and Economic Analysis* p. 135–42.

[31] See Trachtman, *The Economic Structure of International Law* p. 4–9.

[32] See ibid.

[33] When discussing subsidies, for instance, Debraj Ray states that "[t]he mere fact that an export subsidy is effective, in the sense that it increases the country's revenue from exports, does not necessarily mean that it is a good thing. An evaluation depends on the gains and losses to all sorts of groups who are affected by the policy," Debraj Ray, *Development Economics* (Princeton University Press 1998) p. 681.

[34] See Cooter and Ulen, *Law and Economics* p. 6.

[35] Welfare analyses might take different effects of a measure into consideration. Commonly, they consider static effects, but might also ponder changes that occur over time, i.e.

the most efficient policy alternative: the one that achieves the highest gains at the lowest possible cost.[36]

In standard microeconomics, as discussed in more detail below, the welfare calculation assumes that accounting methods attribute the same weight to all groups: in other words, that government places the same value on one unit of welfare attributed to producers as it does to one unit attributed to consumer welfare.[37] This assumption usually supports calculations of net, general, or aggregate welfare, but as will be discussed below in relation to political economy, it is an assumption that can be relaxed. In effect, governments will, in certain conditions, place more importance on the welfare of some groups over others, with important implications for the policy decision-making process.

3.3.2   Welfare Considerations

In this section, a welfare analysis[38] is employed to explain the rationale of states for using subsidies. It considers first the effect of subsidies in a scenario of perfect competition, and concludes that benevolent (global welfare-maximizing) governments have no incentive to resort to subsidies. It then shows that even benevolent governments might resort to subsidies if their preference is domestic, rather than global, net welfare maximization. In the context of domestic welfare maximization, moreover, governments will find incentive for subsidization as a means of tackling market failures. Further, if governments were to prefer a certain

dynamic effects. In order to properly address the economic arguments for the use of subsidies, Section 3.3.2 introduces a welfare analysis of subsidization measures looking both at static and dynamic elements. For a more detailed discussion on the static and dynamic welfare implications of protectionist policies, manly tariffs and quotas, see Ray, *Development Economics* p. 665–76. In this analysis, Debraj Ray points out that static considerations do not take into account three important time-related possibilities, i.e. learning by doing, spillovers, and increasing returns. The current work discusses elements from both approaches, as well as the implications to policies related to subsidization. However, as the goal of this work is not to develop a novel microeconomic theory of the use of subsidies, it will not classify measures under different concepts, mainly working with the general concept of "welfare." See ibid.

[36] For a definition of efficiency as applied in microeconomics, see Cooter and Ulen, *Law and Economics* p. 13–14.

[37] This assumption can be relaxed. As detailed in the political economy section, governmental decision-making can place more value on the welfare of organized groups within society to the detriment of net welfare calculations. See Section 3.3.4.

[38] Welfare considerations are commonly applied in the international rules regulating the use of subsidies and dumping. See, for instance, Gabrielle Zoe Marceau, *Anti-dumping and Anti-trust Issues in Free-trade Areas* (Clarendon Press 1994) p. 15–19.

societal group, such as exporters, over general net welfare, they would have reason to subsidize in order to alter the competitive advantage of domestic firms, and thus boost the welfare of the organized group, even at the expense of aggregate domestic welfare.

3.3.2.1 Welfare Effects of Subsidies under Perfect Markets

A welfare analysis of subsidies first requires identification of the costs and benefits of subsidization measures. In the previous section, we examined the changes in the behavior of firms and consumers following government introduction of a subsidy.

As discussed, subsidies are desirable to companies because they cause profits and production to rise, while potentially reducing the price paid by consumers, relative to the pre-subsidy scenario. From the public perspective, however, a subsidy is a cost: the government must make an expenditure of funds that could otherwise be applied to different purposes.[39]

Given that it represents a cost to the government, the obvious question is: why would a rational government want to introduce a subsidy?[40] In addition to the suggestion that governments are left with nothing but costs, modern microeconomic theory considers the free market equilibrium—in which marginal benefit equates marginal cost, without intervention through subsidies—to be "socially optimal," and to result in the most efficient production and allocation possible.[41]

If one were to assume, therefore, that governments act in the general interest to maximize global net welfare, there is little room for action to improve socially optimal markets. In this scenario, government intervention can, in fact, lead only to reductions in efficiency, and should therefore be discouraged.[42]

This conclusion extends to the use of subsidies. Microeconomic theory demonstrates that, under perfect market conditions, subsidies will inevitably create inefficiencies by placing a wedge between

---

[39] Moreover, a subsidy might have negative implications to the overall economy because it generates inefficiencies. See Section 3.3.2.1.

[40] In the free market equilibrium, the introduction of a subsidy lowers the market price. As a result, consumers gain surplus and, because the subsidy raises the revenue of producers, it also increases their surplus. The cost of the subsidy, left to the government, equals the amount of the subsidy per unit of output, multiplied by the after-subsidy total output. In conclusion, the subsidy causes a general welfare deadweight loss, because its cost is larger than its benefit. See WTO, Exploring the Links between Subsidies, Trade and the WTO (World Trade Report 2006) p. 55.

[41] Cooter and Ulen, Law and Economics p. 38.

[42] As noted by WTO, Exploring the Links between Subsidies, Trade and the WTO p. 56–58.

prices that are socially optimal and those that are defined by marginal costs.[43]

In general, therefore, subsidies send producers distorted signals and favor production by less efficient companies, thus posing a problem of misallocation of resources. Government use of subsidies will thus create economic inefficiencies that depart from the optimal equilibrium.

In the long term "the effects of the advantages conferred on the subsidized firm may mean it faces less competitive pressure in the future,"[44], resulting in a potential decrease in consumer welfare. Assuming that markets function perfectly, therefore, subsidies would only worsen net welfare, and if governments care mainly to benefit overall welfare, then "no case can be made for a subsidy."[45]

The application of this domestic market analysis to economies that are open to international trade yields similar results: optimum market equilibrium is achieved without governmental intervention, and policy recommendations are that free trade is most efficient.[46]

As the WTO is mainly concerned with the trade, or international, effects of subsidies, it is necessary to examine in more detail the scenarios in which different types of subsidies, i.e. consumption, production, and export subsidies, impact trade.[47]

---

[43] The same is true for tariffs. Acting in a perfect market, benevolent governments who care about global overall welfare will not resort to tariffs and international regulation of the matter might therefore not be necessary.

[44] UK, *Public Subsidies* p. 21.

[45] WTO, *Exploring the Links between Subsidies, Trade and the WTO* p. 55. This is also true in an opened economy scenario. In both cases, subsidization would result in inefficient allocation of resources because of the costs it inflicts on taxpayers, and non-market signaling of prices due to the wedges between the world price and the subsidized price paid to domestic producers. In addition, a portion of domestic output would be determined by the subsidy, and not by world prices, thus raising domestic production above the optimum level. Under perfect market assumptions, therefore, one issue that would require explanation is, in the first place, the reason why governments would make use of subsidies. Subsidies thus may lead to at least three distortions on competition that could be harmful to consumers and the economy as a whole. First, it can distort market signals and lead firms to employ resources in less valuable uses (allocative inefficiency). Second, it may contribute to less efficient firms to gain market share (productive inefficiency). In addition, subsidies can stimulate firms to alter their investment level and type, leading to sub-optimal decisions on innovation (dynamic efficiency). See UK, *Public Subsidies* p. 16.

[46] WTO, Exploring the Links between Subsidies, Trade and the WTO p. 55.

[47] As noted by Luengo, the object of trade rules, either at the regional or international level, are "government measures that affect the production of goods or their marketing conditions can have harmful effects on trade," Luengo, *Regulation of Subsidies and State Aids in*

A consumption subsidy, when introduced for any reason in an environment in which imports are not hindered by other trade policies such as tariffs or quotas,[48] will stimulate consumption through a reduction in consumer prices. As a consequence of the subsidy, global production will increase, and efficient firms, irrespective of their location, will also benefit, while the government is left with the costs of subsidization. Overall, despite the gains to consumer and producer surplus, the inefficiency caused by the subsidy will generate costs in addition to those borne by the Treasury.

Production subsidies engender similar inefficiencies with potentially adverse effects on imports. Production subsidy provokes an expansion of domestic output and a retraction of imports, causing an additional economic cost of the subsidy relative to the free market scenario.[49]

Export subsidies also lead to inefficiencies in the home country. An export subsidy provides an incentive for firms to divert their output from the domestic to the foreign market. Their withdrawal of outputs from the domestic market causes domestic prices to rise, so that if re-importation is prohibited or imports are prevented by tariffs or other means, then the domestic consumer who pays the higher prices will suffer a welfare loss. The government will also bear the costs of subsidization. The exporter, on the other hand, experiences welfare gains associated with increases in the level of its exports.[50]

The welfare or cost-benefit analysis conducted demonstrates that state measures engender production and consumption distortions and imply a cost to the government. As government intervention leads to market inefficiency, free trade is apparently the optimum policy.

This preliminary overview of welfare effects of subsidies suggests therefore that governments would be better off to abstain from subsidization and other interventionist measures. Such a conclusion is nevertheless at

---

WTO and EC Law: Conflicts in International Trade Law p. 20. In this regard, subsidies are not per se negative for trade, and should be regulated by trade agreements to the extent to which they affect international trade.

[48] This assumption is important for the examination of the functioning of subsidies, but in reality subsidies are often used in conjunction with other trade remedies, such as tariffs, and conditionality, such as domestic content requirements, which function as a quota. In Section 4.3.2.3.1 we will consider the effects of domestic subsidies when conditionality is imposed on its use, such as the obligation to make use of domestically produced input. The introduction of other trade restrictive mechanisms would yield similar results as import substitution policy, i.e. favoring domestic over foreign producers and thus reducing imports in the subsidizing country.

[49] WTO, Exploring the Links between Subsidies, Trade and the WTO p. 55.

[50] Ibid. p. 57.

odds with current practices observed in the global arena, where many governments make extensive use of subsidies as a policy instrument.[51]

3.3.2.2   Welfare Gains

This analysis, as presented so far, has pointed out that subsidization has both positive and negative effects on the welfare of various market agents and the subsidizing government. It has also shown, however, that assuming conditions of perfect competition, the effect of subsidies on general economic welfare is an unambiguous net negative outcome due to the production of inefficiencies and costs to the government.

Despite this clear inference, which would advocate against state use of subsidies, the empirical economic literature highlights the fact that subsidies are a commonly used policy tool. One explanation for this departure from the usual pro-free trade economic position is that governments perceive certain gains from subsidization that are not often captured by standard domestic welfare analyses.

The literature of trade policy offers three elements for further consideration. First, subsidies have an effect on terms-of-trade, which could be perceived as a gain to the domestic economy. Secondly, producer surplus might be under-valued by standard models of market failure, in which measures of consumer welfare do not accurately reflect the social gains.[52] Thirdly, governments may choose to place more emphasis on the welfare of specific domestic groups than on general net welfare.

These further assumptions support the conclusion that the use of subsidies can be a rational policy response of governments seeking to maximize either net welfare or the welfare of organized groups within society. They deserve, therefore, a more detailed analysis, which is undertaken immediately below.

3.3.2.2.1   Terms-of-Trade

The first argument in favor of government intervention in free trade derives directly from the cost-benefit analysis. In welfare terms, it is possible for a large country to influence domestic as well as world prices, and thus generate a terms-of-trade gain that outweighs the losses usually associated with an interventionist policy. As manipulation of terms-of-trade can generate a net gain to domestic welfare in the interventionist state, it would be rational for a government to attempt it if the domestic gains, which would normally be negative due to inefficiencies

---

[51] Ibid. p. 56.
[52] Krugman, Obstfeld, and Melitz, *International Trade: Theory and Policy* p. 247.

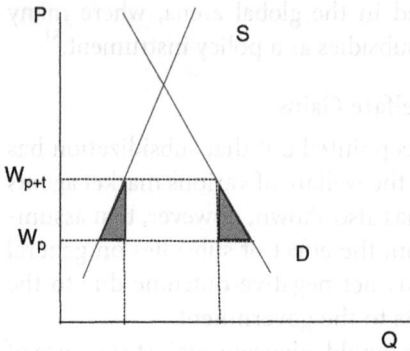

Figure 3: Cost benefit analysis of a tariff in an open economy.
Source: Adapted from Krugman[57]

created by the interventionist policy,[53] are expected to dominate global aggregate effects.

The application of tariffs is usually considered the best trade policy available to states for the manipulation of terms-of-trade. The economic literature suggests that if a state is free to set tariffs, there is no reason for it to use other domestic policies for the purpose of manipulating terms-of-trade.[54] Tariffs are thus a country's "first-best" instrument for effecting this kind of change, but while optimal for unilateral purposes, their use has negative implications globally.

Consider, first, the effect of a tariff on imports in the absence of terms-of-trade gains. Domestic producers and the government experience gains due to correspondingly higher prices on "like" domestic products and increased tariff revenue. Consumers, however, will suffer a loss that is greater than the combined gains of importers and government.[55] Moreover, the tariff restricts world trade and generates net inefficiencies to production and consumption as shown in Figure 3.[56]

Figure 3 depicts the welfare effects of an import tariff on production and consumption. The triangle in the left of the figure stands for loss due to production distortion caused by the over-production of the good. The triangle to the right represents the loss due to domestic consumption

[53] See DeRemer, *The Evolution of International Subsidy Rules* p. 2–14.
[54] See ibid.
[55] See Krugman, Obstfeld and Melitz, *International Trade: Theory and Policy* p. 247.
[56] Domestic inefficiencies also occur through the use of quotas, export subsidies, and other policies that affect trade. See ibid. p. 252–57.
[57] See ibid. p. 269.

distortion caused by under-consumption. In the absence of the tariff, net welfare is depicted by the area of the triangle above the baseline Wp-D, which is clearly preferable to the result following imposition of the tariff indicated by the area of the smaller triangle above the baseline determined by the price (Wtp+t).

Once terms-of-trade effects come into play, the domestic net welfare results become more complex. In the case of a small country, which cannot significantly influence world prices, the effect in terms-of-trade drops out and "the costs of a tariff unambiguously exceed its benefits."[58]. Use of tariffs by a large country, however, produces a net gain in terms-of-trade, depicted in the terms-of-trade area in Figure 4, "which results from the decline in the foreign export price caused by a tariff."[59]

Figure 4 depicts the welfare effects of an import tariff on domestic production and consumption. The triangles stand for distortion losses and the square labeled "ToT" for terms-of-trade gains. If a tariff is set at a low enough level, the gains in terms-of-trade will be higher than the losses, and it becomes rational for a government to make use of it.

The tariff, as mentioned, is considered the ultimate policy instrument for this sort of unilateral manipulation, despite the fact that it results in losses to trading partners. Given however that this effect, usually referred

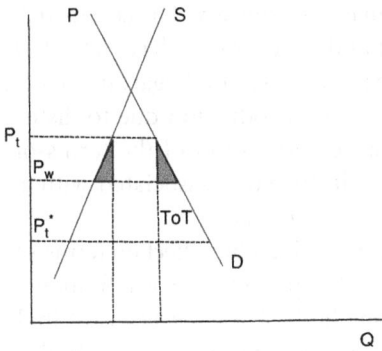

Figure 4: Cost benefit analysis of a tariff in an open economy including terms-of-trade gains.
Source: Adapted from Krugman[60]

---

[58] Ibid. p. 249.
[59] Ibid.
[60] See ibid. p. 269.

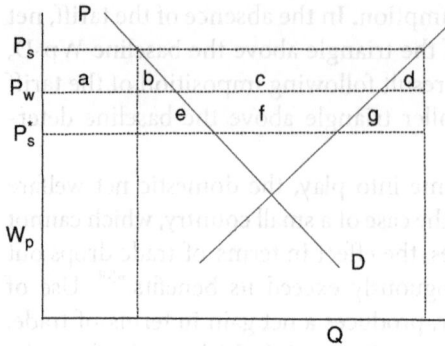

Figure 5: Cost benefit analysis of export subsidy including ToT.
Source: Adapted from Krugman[62]

to as "beggar thy neighbor," is subject to regulation *inter alia* by the GATT,[61] and that tariff levels are subject to ongoing reduction through a multilateral process of binding and lowering, large nations might turn from tariffs to subsidies as the second best option for improvement of their welfare in terms-of-trade.

A subsidy that is contingent upon exports, however, will, despite a positive impact on exporters, generate costs that exceed its benefits. The net effect of an export subsidy on terms-of-trade will therefore be negative.

Figure 5 demonstrates the effects of an export subsidy. The cost-benefit analysis suggests that consumers (a+b) and government (b+c+d+e+f+g) are hurt, while producers gain from the policy (a+b+c). Regarding losses, b and d represent losses to consumption and production due to distortions, and e, f, and g losses arising from deterioration of the terms-of-trade of the exporting country. As a result, the costs associated with an export subsidy "unambiguously" exceed its benefits.

As discussed in Section 3.3.2.2.2, the way in which this effect on terms-of-trade differs from that of tariffs is of crucial importance for justification of rules regulating the use of subsidies. On the basis of the terms-of-trade arguments, there is clearly a rationale for restricting domestic subsidies, because they, like tariffs, might be used as a "beggar thy neighbor" policy, but there is little reason for regulating export subsidies. In fact, export

---

[61] Schropp, *Trade Policy Flexibility and Enforcement in the WTO: A Law and Economic Analysis* p. 225.
[62] See Krugman, Obstfeld, and Melitz, *International Trade: Theory and Policy* p. 250.

subsidies should be welcomed by foreign trade partners, who will experience resulting gains in terms-of-trade *vis-a-vis* the subsidizing state.

3.3.2.2.2   Market Failure   Market failure is also used to provide economic justification for subsidization. As previously discussed, subsidies and other interventionist policies cause net losses in welfare when used in perfect markets. The classic assumption of the perfect market is often relaxed, however, in order to provide a theoretical explanation for government measures, such as the use of subsidies,[63] that are not otherwise easily elucidated.

Market failure is defined as "a situation in which scarce resources are not allocated to their most efficient use."[64] The result of a market failure is that the market "does not provide a good or service even though the economic benefits outweigh the economic costs."[65] In response, "public policy should be directed at improving the efficient functioning of the market by correcting the market failures, as long as the benefits of intervention outweigh the costs."[66] One relevant economic hypothesis is that state intervention might "improve the functioning of markets"

---

[63] While perfect competition theory is an important benchmark for economic and legal studies, it has been noted in the literature that " . . . the conditions necessary for perfect competition are extremely unlikely to be observed in practice." After all, it "requires that on any particular market there is an infinite number of buyers and sellers, all producing identical (or 'homogeneous') products; consumers have perfect information about market conditions; resources can flow freely from one area of economic activity to another: there are no 'barriers to entry' which might prevent the emergence of new competition, and there are no 'barriers to exit' which might hinder firms wishing to leave the industry." In light of these elements, "a market structure satisfying all these conditions is unlikely, if not impossible," Richard Whish and David Bailey, *Competition Law* (Oxford University Press 2015) p. 7–8. Similarly, Thirlwall states that "The conditions required for markets to perform their allocative and creative functions in an optimal manner are very stringent, and are unlikely to be satisfied in any economy, let alone developing countries. The true benefit of output may not be reflected in price because of externalities; price may not reflect marginal cost because of market imperfections; and many developmental goods and services may not be produced at all because markets are incomplete of missing entirely, and therefore cannot perform their creative function. In other words, there are likely to be market failures. In addition, there is the problem that there is nothing in the market mechanism that guarantees an equitable distribution of income in society, or that will direct adequate resources away from present consumption to build up the means of production for a higher level of consumption in the future," Anthony Philip Thirlwall, *Economics of Development: Theory and Evidence* (Palgrave Macmillan 2011) p. 307.

[64] Mankiw, *Principles of Macroeconomics* p. 886.

[65] Hans W. Friederiszick, Lars-Hendrik Röller, and Vincent Verouden, "European State Aid Control: An Economic Framework" in Paolo Buccirossi (ed), *Handbook of Antitrust Economics* (Handbook of Antitrust Economics, The MIT Press 2008) p. 633.

[66] Ibid.

in situations in which competition is "unlikely to produce efficient outcomes in terms of prices, outputs and use of resources."[67]

Subsidization might thus be construed as the rational action of benevolent governments seeking to "improve the functioning of markets."[68]
Bhagwati and Ramaswami[69] for instance, as well as Johnson,[70] argue that
a production subsidy is the most efficient tool of government intervention in the presence of domestic distortions,[71] those market conditions in
which there is a difference "between the actual price and the socially
optimal price."[72] As noted by Bacchetta and Ruta, "this argument implies
that, at least in the presence of domestic distortions, an international
trade treaty should leave scope for flexibility to governments in their
choice of production subsidies."[73]

There are various sources of market failure. The failure known as an
externality is "the uncompensated impact of one person's action on the
well-being of a bystander (third party)."[74] Externalities occur when the
action of a market player imposes positive or negative consequences,
such as innovation spillover or pollution,[75] on other agents. A common

---

[67] Ibid. p. 632.

[68] Ibid.

[69] A seminal paper in the issue of subsidies concludes, for example, that an optimum subsidy
"is necessarily superior to any tariff when the distortion is domestic," Jagdish Bhagwati
and Vangal K Ramaswami, "Domestic Distortions, Tariffs and the Theory of Optimum
Subsidy" (1963) *The Journal of Political Economy* p. 44–50, 50.

[70] For Johnson, "the correction of domestic distortions requires a tax or a subsidy on either
domestic consumption or domestic production or domestic factor use, not on international trade." By focusing on consumption, production, or factor use, the intervention
could "offset the existing distortions without introducing new distortions," thus leading
to a "situation of Pareto optimality," Harry G Johnson, *Optimal Trade Intervention in the
Presence of Domestic Distortions* (Rand McNally 1963) p. 10.

[71] Market failures are distortions caused by the absence of certain elements of perfect
competition in which several producers and consumers act in a market of homogeneous
goods.

[72] WTO, *Exploring the Links between Subsidies, Trade and the WTO* p. 58.

[73] However, as subsidies can be used to explore the terms-of-trade externality tackled by
a trade agreement, a subsidies agreement should "strike a balance between the benefits of
government flexibility in setting subsidies to offset domestic distortions and the costs of
using subsidies for uncooperative behavior in the international arena," Bacchetta M and
Ruta M (eds), *The WTO, Subsidies and Countervailing Measures*, vol 19 (Critical
Perspectives on the Global Trading System and the WTO, Edward Elgar 2011).

[74] Mankiw, *Principles of Macroeconomics* p. 885.

[75] Externalities are an important economic feature used to justify governmental intervention in the marketplace. It derives from the notion that, in certain economic sectors,
investments may not be undertaken on a socially optimal level by private firms. This is
because the social benefits of production can exceed those that private investors are able
to enjoy individually or due to the fact that producers do not take into account external

perception is that the role of governments is to "curb negative external-ities through regulation or taxation" and to "promote positive external-ities through subsidies."[76] Subsidies can, moreover, foster activities capable of competing with industries that characteristically generate negative externalities, as illustrated by the promotion of renewable energy over traditional polluting energy sources.[77]

Subsidies can also play an important role in creating markets for *public goods*, which may be construed as an extreme externality. Given that a public good is, in economic terms, "neither excludable nor rival,"[78] it is troublesome to prevent it from being used or to charge for its use. There is therefore an incentive for actors to "free ride": to receive the benefit of the good but avoid paying for it.[79]

Public goods have no price attached to them, so "if one person were to provide a public good, such as a national defense system, other people would be better off, and yet they could not be charged for this benefit."[80] In the presence of a free rider problem, private producers might fail to produce and supply the good, resulting in market inefficiency because they are not in a position to appropriate the private benefits of production. This could, in turn, lead to underproduction or no production of a socially desirable good. Typical examples of public goods include national defense,[81] basic research,[82] and social goals such as the fight against

---

costs associated with its product. As a result, production and/or consumption levels are set below or above the optimum, leading to positive and negative externalities such as R&D spillover and pollution respectively. Market failures then are used justify state intervention as a means to induce the socially optimal level of production by private firms.

[76] Thirlwall, *Economics of Development: Theory and Evidence* p. 309.

[77] Gregory Mankiw, Principles of Macroeconomics (7th edn, Cengage Learning 2014) p. 203–04.

[78] Mankiw, *Principles of Macroeconomics* p. 887.

[79] Ibid. p. 224.

[80] Ibid. p. 223.

[81] In case of foreign aggression, it is not possible to exclude people from using the "defense" good, and additionally the use of it by a person does not reduce the benefits conferred to others. Under such a scenario, the private market, under normal conditions, will not provide the good and governmental intervention is necessary. Ibid. p. 224.

[82] The creation of knowledge can also be understood within a public good context. As knowledge, once it is produced, might be broadly available free of charges; "profit-seeking firms tend to free ride on the knowledge created by others and, as a result, devote too few resources to creating new knowledge." A system of protection for intellectual property might soften the problem, but not eliminate it. In general, technological knowl-edge can be subjected to patents and made excludable, but general knowledge is not excludable. Ibid. p. 224–25.

Table 3: *The classification of goods according to excludability and rivalry.*

		Rival?	
		Yes	No
Excludable?	Yes	Private goods • Clothing	Natural monopolies • Cable TV
	No	Common resources • Environment	Public goods • National defense

Source: Mankiw[85]

poverty.[83] Subsidization may be an effective response to public goods problems as a means of fostering production of such goods and achieving a more efficient market outcome.

The nature of public goods would normally render their production unsustainable in a competitive economic market. In theory a good may be classified according to its excludability or the extent to which its owner is able to exclude or prevent others from accessing and using it, and its rivalry referring to the extent to which consumption or use of the good by one person diminishes the ability of another to use it. Most private goods, such as clothing, are both excludable and rival. Public goods, however, are neither excludable nor rival. This implies that the use of a public good cannot be prevented, and that its use by one person does not diminish the ability of others to make use of it.[84]

---

[83] The magnitude of certain social problems, such as elimination of poverty, makes it difficult for a single private party to eliminate the issue. Moreover, the private market for charity is also subjected to the free riding problem, as those who do not donate might still enjoy the benefit less inequality generated by those who do contribute to charity. Ibid. p. 225–26.

[84] Other types of goods, following this classification, are common resources, which are rival but not excludable and natural monopolies, i.e. goods that are excludable nut not rival. Fish in the ocean are a clear example of common resources. As the catching of a fish excludes prevents other from catching it, this is an example of rival good. However, it is non excludable, as due to the size of the ocean it is virtually impossible to prevent fishing boats to catch fish. Natural monopolies, on its turn, are excludable but non rival, such as the fire service. It is easy to prevent the fire service from attending an emergency and thus letting a house burn down, however, as most of the time there is no emergency, protecting an extra house should not have a great impact of the protection available to the others. Ibid. 223–23.

[85] Ibid., p. 222–23.

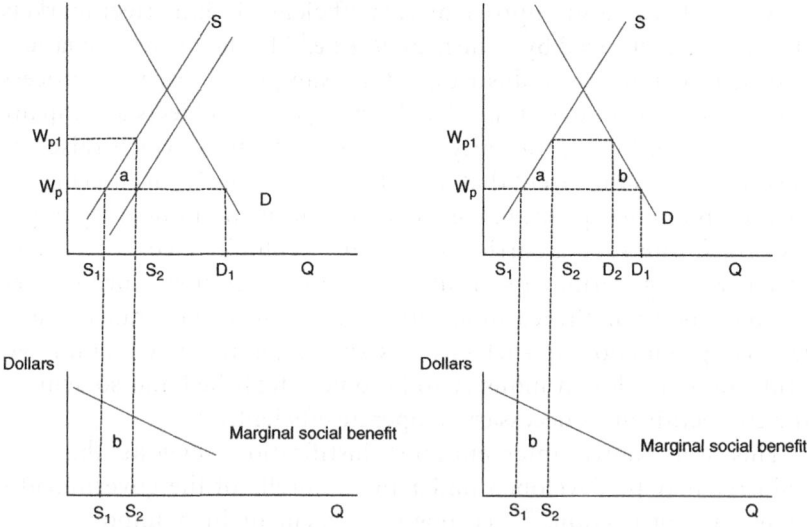

Figure 6:   Analysis of subsidies and tariffs used to correct market failures.
Source: Adapted from Krugman[87]

Where there is a discrepancy between the private and the social benefits
of production, such that the supply of a good is at stake, a domestic subsidy
is viewed as the best mechanism by which to address it. The subsidy has the
effect of raising the producers' surplus, which then has a positive impact on
the quantity produced. This allows production to increase to the socially
optimal level of output, and while the subsidy causes production distortions, it is less distortive than a tariff, which would lead also to consumption losses.[86]

Both subsidies and tariffs are used as a means of increasing the revenue
of producers, see Figure 6. While tariffs produce both consumer and
producer inefficiencies, indicated by triangles a and b in the top right of
Figure 6, subsidies result only in production inefficiencies, as shown by
area in the top left of the graph. Considering that lower costs are incurred
by subsidies to achieve the same policy objective, policymakers ought to
prefer them over tariffs when tackling such externalities.

[86] See Cooter and Ulen, *Law and Economics*; and also Mankiw, *Principles of Macroeconomics*
p. 222–23.
[87] See Krugman, Obstfeld, and Melitz, *International Trade: Theory and Policy* p. 250.

A subsidy can also improve market efficiency in imperfect markets that are characterized by *industries of scale.*[88] In the nuclear, aviation, and semi-conductor industries,[89] for example, a learning process causes costs to fall over time. The learning curve subjects a company to a period of loss in the early stages of production, which raises its costs overall, to the extent that it might be prevented from entering the market in the first place. Large fixed costs at the point of entry might also constitute such a barrier. Potentially prohibitive costs create an incentive for governments to subsidize until the company or industry reaches a point on the learning curve at which it can generate efficient levels of production. In such circumstances, it is arguable that limited protection enables an industry to become established and so achieve the competitiveness necessary to operate efficiently.

This well-known interventionist justification suggests that "an industry may be developed under the umbrella of the government's temporary protection."[90] Through a system of high import tariffs and subsidization of the domestic industry, a government can establish a "rent redistribution mechanism, from domestic consumers to local producers, that may help the local industry to overcome the initial cost disadvantage and thus survive in the long run."[91]

The problem of substantial fixed costs is not the only important issue to be addressed by such a policy framework. The perception of increasingly significant returns in some industries is also an issue. A delay in generation of returns does not necessarily mean that domestic producers are inefficient, but that average costs of production are so high that profitable activity is precluded until large scales of production are achieved. As efficiency might also require a period of learning, protection could facilitate development of the capacity of domestic firms to compete with foreign companies. Further, as certain sectors have positive external spillover effects, state support for industrial development might help overcome failures of coordination between industry sectors.[92]

---

[88] See WTO, *Exploring the Links between subsidies, Trade and the WTO* p. 59.
[89] See ibid. p. 60.
[90] Kenneth A Reinert, Ramkishen S Rajan, and Amy Joycelyn Glass (eds), *The Princeton Encyclopedia of the World Economy*, vol 2 (Princeton University Press 2009) p. 622.
[91] Ibid.
[92] Ray, *Development Economics* p. 669–76.

This "infant industry argument" for state intervention is "based on the existence of some type of market failure and dynamic positive externalities"[93] and is the "main rationale underlying most advocacy of industrial policy."[94] As in other externality cases, the best available policy instrument with which to address it may be the provision of subsidies to domestic producers.

Despite its appeal as a justification for trade policy, the infant industry argument does not give benevolent governments a rationale for provision of unlimited assistance to firms. Rational governments will, in fact, ensure that any infant industry-based protectionism is contingent on the existence of externalities, and the demonstration of long-term cost-saving viability, and will make a credible commitment to restrict such protection to temporary measures.[95]

Once protection is in place, however, there is a serious concern that firms will have inadequate incentive to become efficient. There is evidence that, rather than optimize their production, companies will on the contrary invest their resources and efforts into prolonging the protective benefits,[96] if possible on an indefinite basis.

This rent-seeking behavior of industry is exaggerated by the fact that there may be little incentive in future for governments to lift the protection, as this is usually a costly political endeavor. Moreover, economists question the ability of governments to adequately identify market failures and correctly assess the cost-benefit impacts of the policy.[97]

The preceding analysis of government intervention by subsidization has concentrated largely on production subsidies, reflecting the prevalence, in the economic literature, of the use of domestic measures for correction of

---

[93] Bernard M Hoekman and Michel M Kostecki, *The Political Economy of the World Trading System* (Oxford University Press 2009) p. 553.

[94] Ibid.

[95] Ibid. See also ibid. p. 463–65.

[96] Two commonly cited examples are Latin America and certain Asian countries. Both have actively promoted import substitution policies during the second half of the twentieth century. However, whereas the Asian experience is usually positively evaluated, much due to its early introduction of an outward element which fostered exports and competition for foreign markets, the South American case is perceived as a failure because of its inward focus. See, for instance, Ray, *Development Economics* p. 674–76.

[97] This can prove to be a complex task in which governments need to "accurately predict the learning dynamics of each particular industry to be protected as well as the cost that such protection generates to domestic consumers and firms," Reinert, Rajan, and Glass (eds), *The Princeton Encyclopedia of the World Economy* p. 623.

market failures.[98] Export subsidies are not usually associated with treatment of market failure, though one strand of literature perceives a correlation between them in the presence of information asymmetries.[99]

As asymmetry of information between supply and consumer demand can result in market failure. An efficient domestic firm, unknown in foreign markets, if confronted with such asymmetry in relation to its domestic consumers, might benefit from an export subsidy that enables it to build a reputation with foreign consumers.[100] Once again, financial assistance by way of subsidy contingent on export could result in a better outcome for the company than that expected under free market principles.

3.3.3   Redistributive and Noneconomic Objectives

There are at least two other important justifications for the use of subsidies related to the roles they play in fostering redistribution, and in supporting non-economic policy goals.

Government intervention in the market is often carried out for redistributive purposes: to promote social and regional cohesion by, for instance, favoring families or regions that suffer economic disadvantage. Subsidization in support of redistributive objectives is rationalized on the basis that, although such policies might not directly contribute to improving overall economic efficiency, they respond to the express concerns and preferences of citizens.

Subsidies may also enable governments to achieve non-economic objectives. Commonly cited objectives include self-sufficient production of food and energy, and protection of public interests, such as national defense.[101]

---

[98] A seminal paper in the issue of subsidies concludes, for instance, that an optimum subsidy "is necessarily superior to any tariff when the distortion is domestic," Bhagwati and Ramaswami, "Domestic Distortions, Tariffs and the Theory of Optimum Subsidy" p. 50.

[99] The classical example being as follows: firms seeking loans usually have a better understanding of their activities than the financing agent does, especially if the firm has recently been founded and does not yet have a credit record with the bank. In this case, the bank might be in a difficult position to access the credit risk and end up rejecting profitable ventures. In this case, a subsidy might help to overcome the effects of asymmetric information. See Kyle Bagwell and Robert W Staiger, "The Role of Export Subsidies When Product Quality Is Unknown" (1989) 27 *Journal of International Economics* p. 69-89.

[100] WTO, *Exploring the Links between Subsidies, Trade and the WTO* p. 199.

[101] For a detailed description of economic and non-economic justifications used by governments for subsidizing, see ibid. This is also a concern in European law, as in

Table 4: *The rationale for the use of subsidies.*

	Rationale for the use of subsidies						
	Efficiency based					Equity based	Non-economic
Externalities	Public goods	Information asymmetries	Imperfect competition	Market power	Learning process	Return of scale	Redistribution	Societal values

Source: Elaborated by the author

3.3.4   Political Economy Argument

The explanations for subsidy use provided so far have been based on an assumption that governments care for the maximization of domestic welfare, or diverse non-economic goals, that would not be achieved under usual market conditions. Another assumption, however, might be that it is the welfare of certain organized societal groups, such as producers or exporters, that is the primary concern of governments. Such considerations of political economy might motivate governments to use subsidies opportunistically for protectionist purposes to boost the competitive advantage of domestic firms.[102]

The potential for state protectionism is an assumption that is critical to political economic analysis. The rationale for state action in political-economy approaches to international law is found in the set of domestic forces at play.[103] The "political function" combines

---

Leigh Hancher, Tom Ottervanger, and Piet Jan Slot (eds), *EU State Aids* (Sweet & Maxwell 2012).

[102] The basic assumption of the model is that politicians are concerned about the impact of their actions on groups of potential voters and campaign contributors. This concern derives from his rational attempt to maximize his interest to be re-elected. The concept of re-election is broad enough to cover many preferences, from personal financial goals to possible benevolent preferences such as to stay in power in order to advance a program of income distribution. Important in this definition is that whatever the determinant element of preference negotiator, policymakers prefer to stay longer in office and for that they need the support of the electorate in general, in the form of votes, and the support of special interest groups (SIGs), in the form of political support and funding. See, for instance, Schropp, *Trade Policy Flexibility and Enforcement in the WTO: A Law and Economic Analysis* p. 134–43; and van Aaken, "Opportunities and the Limits of an Economic Analysis in International Law" p. 27–28.

[103] There are two main variations of the model. In the first, politicians will use their actions (including subsidies) as an instrument to foster the welfare of a majority of voters. In the second, they will be more concerned with the welfare of SIGs in order to attract funding, for instance, from an association of industries, and votes for organized groups, such as labor unions. Under the medium voter model, voters will consider the costs, for instance a raise in taxes, associated to a subsidy program. Those voters that benefit from the subsidy might support the program, but those not eligible to receive the benefit tend to be contrary to the subsidy. From the policy-market perspective, he or she might "maintain political support if they pursue policies that the majority of voters care about." Under such a scenario, subsidies tend to reach a greater number of beneficiaries, and "highly target or specific subsidy programs are unlikely to be implemented." The scenario changes if we consider that policymakers care not only for votes, but also for political support and funding from SIGs. This second approach, in which we focus here, is detailed in WTO, *Exploring the Links between Subsidies, Trade and the WTO* p. 64, and also Schropp, *Trade Policy Flexibility and Enforcement in the WTO: A Law and Economic Analysis* p. 134–43.

concerns for the welfare of both the general population and special interest groups (SIGs), the result of which is to guarantee political and financial contributions to policymakers. In short, the political function is a weighted average of general welfare, which will normally generate votes, and SIG welfare, which ensures political support.[104]

Every subsidization policy has an impact on both general welfare and the wellbeing of SIGs which, in relation to trade, include exporters, importers in competing domestic sectors, foreign exporters, labor unions, and environmental or civil liberty groups.[105] Decisive for this analytical framework, however, is the notion that the organization of SIGs renders them more effective than the general public at lobbying as a means of promoting their interests[106] and maximizing the welfare of their participants. Public policy might, therefore, favor the particular interest of an organized group over more diffuse interests, even if it causes a decrease in general domestic or global welfare. Where this involves subsidization, it suggests that "subsidies that are provided to a specific industry are not intended to correct a market failure, but to improve the economic standing of the special interest group, who will then reward"[107] the policymaker. An evaluation of political economic considerations thus suggests that there is a close link between subsidization and protectionist measures.[108]

---

[104] For a more detailed analysis of these issues, see Schropp, *Trade Policy Flexibility and Enforcement in the WTO: A Law and Economic Analysis* p. 134–43. This political decision rationale is close to what Baldwin described as "Politically realistic objective function"; see Richard Baldwin, "Politically Realistic Objective Functions and Trade Policy PROFs and Tariffs" (1987) 24 *Economics Letters* p. 287–90, 289.

[105] Schropp, *Trade Policy Flexibility and Enforcement in the WTO: A Law and Economic Analysis* p. 138.

[106] Political economy motivation is often seen with distrust. For instance, Johnson defines it as "the political power of various economic groups in the community, as measure by their capacity to extort transfers of income from their fellow-citizens," Johnson, *Optimal Trade Intervention in the Presence of Domestic Distortions* p. 8.

[107] WTO, *Exploring the Links between Subsidies, Trade and the WTO* p. 63.

[108] Under political economy assumptions, the behavior of governments is still explained by welfare maximization, but the way in which governments perceive the welfare of different domestic groups vary. Under this political economy theory, governmental actions tend to favor politically organized constituencies, such as exporters and importers, to the detriment of less organized groups, such as consumers. This serves to explain, for instance, why policymakers might make use of subsidies that have a negative impact on overall welfare, or why they might favor the domestic industry interests by imposing countervailing duties on subsidized exports.

Table 5: *What do domestic players want?*

Domestic players							
Pro protection		Pro export			General Electorate		
Subsidies	Trade protection	Export subsidies (Additional access)	Open markets (Cheaper sourcing)	Cheaper Products	Efficient allocation	Employment	Higher wages

Source: adapted from Caiado[109]

[109] José Caiado, "From Coordination to Collaboration: Explaining International Disputes over Tariff Classification" (2012) 3 *Economic Analysis of Law Review* p. 95–108.

This correlation between subsidies and protectionism is especially evident in relation to ongoing tariff regulation. As tariff levels have been bound and progressively reduced since the advent of the GATT, their utility as a tool of protectionist trade policy has been diminished, thus encouraging politically motivated governments to turn to subsidies and other non-tariff measures, such as technical barriers and rules of origin, as means of implementing protectionist policies. Political economy thus offers not only a rationale for use of the production subsidy, which mimics the protectionist effects of a tariff, but also for the export subsidy, which was initially excluded from the terms-of-trade discussion.[110] The literature suggests, in fact, that exporters constitute one of the most organized groups in society: one that is influential enough that governments will channel resources for the benefit of exporters, to the detriment of domestic net welfare overall.[111]

3.3.5   Rationale for International Cooperation and Subsidy Control

The analysis has so far considered subsidies largely as one general policy instrument, but a great part of the literature, both economic and legal, addresses them according to a distinction between two types: subsidies that are contingent upon export performance (export subsidies) and

---

[110] In such case, whereas production subsidies would still find benevolent justifications, export subsidies would have the clear intent of placing domestic export groups in a competitive advantage vis-à-vis their foreign competitors. This advantage could lead domestic exporters not only to circumvent tariff commitments in a foreign country, but also to take over third markets from other foreign export groups. Moreover, should the export subsidy result in a decrease in world prices, foreign producers would also lose profitability.

[111] For instance, in US – Softwood Lumber, the alleged subsidy stimulated exports, meaning that for the importing country the net effect of the subsidy is because it reduces the prices of import and improves the terms-of-trade. Nevertheless, the effects of the subsidy might be unevenly distributed between different market players in the importing country, i.e. consumers of the subsidized product benefit from lower prices, but domestic producers might face a loss. For the government, the aggregate effect depends on how the government weighs their impact on the welfare of the different domestic groups and, depending on its preferences, the government may perceive the costs to the industry as dominating other possible gains. Similarly, for the subsidizing state, the subsidy worsens its terms-of-trade and creates a net loss, but exporters are likely to gain, and in the preferences of the government, gains to exporters might dominate the cost to taxpayers. As a result, it is possible that a subsidy "may simultaneously benefit the exporting country government, and harm the importing country government," Horn and Mavroidis in Bacchetta and Ruta (eds), The WTO, Subsidies and Countervailing Measures p. 809–10.

those that are conferred regardless of the destination of the output[112] (production subsidies). The relevance of the distinction is that each type implies a different outcome in terms of efficiency and resource allocation.

As previously discussed, if one assumes perfect and closed markets, "production subsidies to firms have the effect of expanding output, reducing the price paid by consumers and creating an overall welfare loss."[113] If the market is open to international trade, however, a grant of subsidy to a firm competing with imports will lead to an "expansion in domestic output at the expense of imports."[114] After the subsidy, prices will remain the same, but domestic production will increase, leading to either an expansion of exports or contraction of imports.

The effect of a production subsidy in the domestic environment is to diminish the efficiency of both production and consumption, because the same goods could be imported for less than it costs to produce them at home. Outside the domestic market the subsidy has spillover effects, and the reduction of domestic imports corresponds to a loss of market share and profits by foreign exporters. Import contraction is, in effect, a cost to foreign firms located in other states. In terms of domestic efficiency, however, the losses that it represents could be outweighed by production subsidies that generate gains in terms-of-trade. There is thus a rationale for the governmental application of production subsidies, but because they would make foreign countries worse off, there is a concomitant rationale for their regulation and control.

The effect of an export subsidy is to displace firm output from the internal to the international market. Assuming there is no re-importation, an export subsidy will affect not only the volume of production, but also its price. In response therefore to the contraction of available product in the internal market and increased external supply domestic prices will tend to rise and, if the exporting state is large enough to influence international prices, global prices will fall.

In terms of welfare, however, the country conferring the export subsidy faces a net loss. This is a notable departure from the production subsidy, which generates a net gain to the conferring government through an improvement in terms-of-trade. Despite expansion of domestic output, which benefits domestic producers, the welfare loss faced by domestic

---

[112] Production subsidies could also impact exports if conferred to firms participating in international trade. WTO, *Exploring the Links between Subsidies, Trade and the WTO* p. 55.

[113] Ibid., p. 56.

[114] Ibid.

consumers, who are unable to access product in the cheaper global market, predominates. The additional losses in terms-of-trade reinforce that the outcome of the export subsidy in an unambiguous welfare loss to the economy of the conferring government.

The overall impact of export subsidies on trade partners is, however, positive. In the importing country, the consumer benefit arising from lower prices outweighs losses suffered by producers who are unable to cope with reduction in revenues caused by the new prices.[115] The exception to this claim is a situation involving market failure in the country importing the subsidized product. Aggregate losses might occasionally occur if the social cost is less than the private cost, in which case the standard model would underestimate the loss of producer surplus caused by the foreign subsidy. In such cases, "if the social loss is large enough, it can outweigh the benefit to consumers."[116] Aggregate losses might also occur if the country is a third market competitor rather than an importer of the subsidized export, in which case consumer gains in the competing country are outweighed by losses to producers.[117]

The political economy literature suggests, moreover, that production and export subsidies might each be used to foster domestic groups, at the expense of foreign producers, despite that the net welfare of such politically motivated subsidization might be losses to the home country.

Table 6: *The rationale for regulation of subsidies.*

Rationale for regulation			
Terms-of-trade		Political economy	
Production subsidies	Export subsidies (competing market)	Export subsidies	Production subsidies

Source: Elaborated by the author

[115] Ibid. p. 58.
[116] Gene M Grossman and Petros C Mavroidis, "US–Lead and Bismuth II: United States–Imposition of Countervailing Duties on Certain Hot-Rolled Lead and Bismuth Carbon Steel Products Originating in the United Kingdom: Here Today, Gone Tomorrow? Privatization and the Injury Caused by Non-Recurring Subsidies" (2003) 2 *World Trade Review* p. 170–200.
[117] Ibid.

3.4 Conclusion

The foregoing analysis demonstrates the existence of numerous rationales for the use and regulation of subsidies. Importantly, in relation to trade, it points to two main bases for international regulation of subsidies. First, the connectivity of nations through international trade facilitates the potential of subsidies to create cross-border spillover[118] effects in foreign markets. Secondly, the fact that governments are susceptible to influence by domestic protectionist groups increases the likelihood that subsidization will favor domestic companies over foreign competitors. Together these suggest that states may benefit from cooperation in the international regulation of the use of subsidies.[119]

Economic theory provides a series of explanations regarding the use of subsidies and related externalities. Three aspects deserve attention for their relevance to international regulation. First, subsidies can cause externalities to trade partners, even when used by benevolent governments to tackle recognized market failures. Such effects include alteration of trade volumes, trade diversion, reduction in the market share of competitors, and shifting of profit in favor of domestic producers. In short, subsidies can impose negative externalities on companies and governments abroad.[120]

Secondly, governments may consciously employ subsidies to manipulate terms-of-trade[121] to their benefit, and alter trade volumes and welfare to the detriment of foreign competitors. The potential to "beggar thy neighbor" through use of production subsidies enables governments to foster their own domestic welfare to the detriment of trade partners.

---

[118] Other possible rationales are the commitment and global efficiency rationales. According to the first, international agreements could be used as an instrument for governments to shift to the WTO the political costs of unpopular measures. The second argues that through an international agreement states wish predominantly to foster global welfare levels even if that would affect their domestic welfare in the short term. See, for the first, Daniel Brou and Michele Ruta, "A Commitment Theory of Subsidy Agreements" (2013) 13 *The BE Journal of Economic Analysis & Policy* p. 239–70; and also Friederiszick, Röller, and Verouden, "European State Aid Control: An Economic Framework" p. 640–41. For a discussion about the efficiency argument for regulation, see Sykes, *The Limited Economic Case for Subsidies Regulation* p. 2–5.

[119] This is also the case for cooperation on regulating subsidies: "When individual decisions lead to a sub-optimal collective outcome, ostensibly there is a need for coordination," Hancher, Ottervanger and Slot (eds), *EU State Aids* p. 36.

[120] Friederiszick, Röller, and Verouden, "European State Aid Control: An Economic Framework" p. 22.

[121] For an overview of this explanation, see DeRemer, *The Evolution of International Subsidy Rules* p. 8–9.

This potential for "strategic" use of trade policy has guided much of the economic literature on trade agreements.[122] Unilateral action by the importing state, without consideration of the loss of the foreign exporter, will result in imposition of a negative externality that reduces the profits of the exporter and might worsen the terms-of-trade of the foreign state. The foreign country in such a situation would be reluctant to unilaterally reduce its trade barriers "for fear that it might deteriorate its terms-of-trade and possibly make it worse off."[123] Should states have unilateral discretion to choose an appropriate level of domestic protectionism, they would therefore be stuck in an inefficient non-cooperative equilibrium.

The problem of strategic subsidization is even clearer in relation to agreements for regulation of tariff use, since subsidies can be used in an opportunistic manner to circumvent the agreed balance of concessions. This facility to divert from the expected contractual outcome of the trade agreement provides states with incentive to use subsidies to gain a market share that is higher than that previously agreed, or to prevent its domestic industries from losing market share.

Thirdly, it has long been recognized that neither the terms-of-trade nor strategic use literature fully explain the rules on subsidies as developed within the modern multilateral trading system. In particular, trade rules have long regulated *export* subsidies, despite the fact that they benefit foreign importing trade partners. While the importing country experiences a net welfare gain, export subsidies might actually worsen the terms-of-trade of the subsidizing country and result in a loss to its overall welfare. The importing state should in theory send a "thank you" note, therefore, to the foreign subsidizing government whenever an export subsidy is granted.[124] Further, by boosting trade volumes, an export subsidy

---

[122] Such as optimum tariffs on imported products as in Harry G Johnson, "Optimum Tariffs and Retaliation" (1953) 21 *The Review of Economic Studies* p. 142–53.

[123] Douglas A Irwin, Petros C Mavroidis, and Alan O Sykes, *The Genesis of the GATT* (The American Law Institute Reporters' Studies on WTO Law, Cambridge University Press 2008) p. 178.

[124] For an overview of the economics of subsidies, especially as relevant for the multilateral trading system and the WTO rules on industrial subsidies, see Dominic Coppens, *WTO Disciplines on Subsidies and Countervailing Measures: Balancing Policy Space and Legal Constraints* (Cambridge International Trade and Economic Law, Cambridge University Press 2014) p. 18; and DeRemer, *The Evolution of International Subsidy Rules* p. 6–10. As DeRemer points out, "[e]xport subsidies improve the terms-of-trade for importing countries and increase trade, so there is no reason to constrain them in conventional trade theory. When the only cross-border effect of export subsidies is the terms-of-trade improvement of the importing country, then the export subsidies are like a gift from

may also be able to resolve inefficiencies resulting from high tariffs. Even though the subsidy itself might also give rise to inefficiencies, these would be borne by the exporting country, leaving the importer with an increase in national welfare and no reason to complain.

The logical conclusion of this train of thought, which is apparently the non-regulation of export subsidies (or at least indifference by importing countries), will be different if we assume that states place a sufficient degree of importance on the welfare of specific domestic groups.[125] As previously discussed, it is apparent that governments will take measures to protect the welfare of such groups, even if such actions decrease the domestic welfare as a whole. Policymakers might feel compelled therefore to act against export subsidies that reduce the profits of domestic producers and exporters,[126] even if such action precludes domestic consumers from the benefits of subsidized imports.

Moreover, in relation to the GATT or other existing trade agreement that restricts tariffs, domestic and export subsidies might be used by states parties to it to alter the market access commitments originally negotiated.[127] This might contradict irrespective of the assumption that governments act in order to maximize their

abroad, and there is no reason for all countries to restrict their use." Ibid. p. 2 (footnote omitted).

[125] The assumption that policymakers behave in a manner so as to achieve higher general welfare can also be relaxed. Political economy scholars argue that the behavior of governments and policymakers is not primarily determined by overall welfare levels, but by the welfare of certain organized groups who can successfully lobby for their interests. To this regard, governments might subsidize activities that are beneficial to the groups those receiving the subsidy, but that may cause a decrease in general economic welfare, either globally or domestically.

[126] When analyzing domestic subsidies with export promotion incentives, DeRemer considers that restrictions on domestic subsidies that also benefit exporting companies that might end up being exported are a welfare-improving measure for policymakers if import tariffs have already been reduced, such as in the GATT. The reason being that, despite the GATT framework, countries still do not account for several possible effects of their higher subsidies on foreign jurisdictions. When focusing on the profit-change effect of subsidies, DeRemer concludes that the net effect for the importing country might be negative if the policy-market highly values profit of the subsidized economic sector, thus justifying multilateral coordination to restrict the use of domestic subsidies that have such effects. DeRemer, *The Evolution of International Subsidy Rules* p. 2–6.

[127] According to the idea of policy substitution, once tariffs are reduced and bounded by a trade agreement, such as the GATT, governments have a clearer incentive to use subsidies as a substitute for the tariffs. Subsidies then need to be regulated, as they can be used to circumvent the market access commitments present in the trade agreement. For a detailed analysis on the substitutability between tariffs and subsidies and the preference

interests. Benevolent governments, in their preparation of policy, are more concerned with the corrective effects of their own measures than with market distortions produced abroad. Subsidization of domestic innovation, for instance, might inadvertently act as a disincentive to foreign firms to compete in that sector, reducing in the long term their share of the domestic market in favor of subsidized local firms.[128] There is little incentive, however, for governments to take into account the propensity of their subsidy measures to distort the previously negotiated "balance of concessions."

As a policy recommendation, therefore, two conclusions may be emphasized. On the one hand, assuming that markets are indeed permeated with imperfections, subsidies can function as a best available policy instrument with which to foster efficiencies and improve aggregate welfare. The implication of this is that any regulation dealing with subsidies should allow for a certain degree of policy discretion. On the other hand, subsidies can be used as a strategic policy instrument to the detriment of trade partners. Production subsidies may be used to manipulate terms-of-trade. Export subsidies can adversely affect the profits of foreign competitors in third markets. Production and export subsidies may be employed as protectionist tools to circumvent market access commitments negotiated under the GATT. The potential damage associated with

of governments for the later once tariffs have been regulated by trade agreements, see Henrik Horn, Giovanni Maggi, and Robert W Staiger, "Trade Agreements as Endogenously Incomplete Contracts" (2010) 100 *The American Economic Review* p. 394–419. Economists have therefore long praised GATT's limitation on domestic policies that could circumvent the negotiated market access commitments. In legal terms, GATT restricted the use by its contracting parties of any measure that would nullify or impair the benefits that another contracting party should expect from the market access commitments. This restriction applied to measures that expressed a failure of a contracting party to fulfill its obligations under the GATT, but, more interestingly, it also gave contracting parties a legal claim against measures that did not conflict with the rules of the GATT. Considering that the GATT did not prohibit domestic subsidies, these so called "non-violation claims" could potentially challenge subsidies that, although not prohibited, had the effect of nullifying or impairing the benefits accruing from the GATT.

128 Although the underlying assumptions of the terms-of-trade and the political economy theories might diverge, the externalities caused by the use of subsidies, whether looked from one or the other perspective, have the similar effect of externalizing (to a foreign country) the costs of the protectionist measure either by changes in the terms-of-trade, or by imposing profit loses to relevant industries of the trade partner.

strategic subsidization suggests that governments may benefit from international cooperation that aims to restrict the use of those subsidies that generate adverse outcomes. The complex task of striking a balance between good and bad subsidies is discussed in detail in the following sections.

4

The SCM as an Incomplete Contract

4.1 Introduction

Despite sharp critique of the feasibility and relevance of regulation of industrial subsidies, recent legal and economic studies suggest that there exists a coherent rationale behind any agreement that aims to discipline the topic. A subsidies agreement can be understood as a mechanism for maximization of the preferences of states: establishing rules to prevent opportunistic use of subsidies for circumvention of tariffs and potentially distributing profits among industries.[1] By entering into a contract with such effects, states determine to restrict subsidies in an attempt to maximize their domestic welfare and the welfare of at least some of their constituents.

In addition to these disruptive effects, subsidies can act as an instrument for implementation of public policies in "good faith." Subsidies are, for example, considered the best available policy instrument with which to tackle domestic market failures, such as under-investment in innovation. They can also be an important tool with which to address crisis situations, and are closely related to non-economic values, both governmental, such as defense, and societal, such as the promotion of culture.

---

[1] The WTO agreements are trade related agreements, i.e. they regulate trade issues among WTO Members. The main function of a trade agreement is to neutralize externalities caused by unilaterally set trade policies. By granting mutual concessions of market access, states regulate and reduce the effects of such externalities. As subsidies can be used to circumvent the agreed "balance of concessions," there are incentives for states to use them opportunistically so as to gain a higher market share than previously agreed. Moreover, subsidies can cause further externalities by being used as a mechanism to opportunistically shift profit from foreign to domestic industries. An agreement regulating subsidies should also take this cross-border effect into account.

Drafters of the SCM Agreement have arguably tried to constrain the use of subsidies for opportunistic purposes, while at the same time permitting their use in "good faith."[2] The key issue for the design of the Agreement is thus the differentiation of opportunistic and "legitimate" uses of a subsidy.

In any contract, such a distinction is ideally achieved by an accurate description of permitted and prohibited behavior. A treaty on subsidies is, however, subject to severe uncertainties that make this difficult to achieve. If uncertainties are not remedied sufficiently and in a timely manner, they prevent parties from extracting the foreseeable contractual gains. They render every subsidies agreement "incomplete," a fact that parties must take into consideration at the outset of the treaty-making process.

In the negotiation of a subsidies agreement, uncertainty arises in the form of technical issues that stem from the complexity of the regulated subject, and the difficulty with which this is translated into legal terms. The nature of uncertainty, in a more profound sense, is that the intrinsic limitations of the parties prevent them from foreseeing all possible contingencies in a volatile economic and political environment. Given these nuanced perspectives on uncertainty, contract theory commonly distinguishes between "unforeseeability" (uncertainty regarding the future), "asymmetrical information" (uncertainty related to the actions of the other players), and "textual ambiguity" (uncertainty as to the meaning and scope of contractual provisions).

Such uncertainties render contracts incomplete, leaving room for opportunistic behavior by the parties. In theory, there are three contractual legal tools with which the incompleteness of a treaty may be overcome: treaty language, delegation of judicial powers, and remedies. This categorization provides a basis for the analysis in this chapter regarding the capacity of the rules of the SCM Agreement to cope with uncertainty and incompleteness.

---

[2] Though by means of frameworks other than "incomplete contract theory," several legal scholars have identified a similar rationale for the SCM Agreement and discuss how to best tailor international rules so as to tackle opportunistic uses of subsidies and/or to avoid externalities resulting from their use. See, for instance, Simon Lester, "The Problem of Subsidies as a Means of Protectionism: Lessons from the WTO EC—AIRCRAFT Case" (2011) 12 *Melbourne Journal of International Law* p. 2–28; Green and Trebilcock, "The Enduring Problem of World Trade Organization Export Subsidies Rules"; Coppens, *WTO Disciplines on Subsidies and Countervailing Measures: Balancing Policy Space and Legal Constraints*; and Rubini, "Ain't Wastin' Time No More: Subsidies for Renewable Energy, The SCM Agreement, Policy Space, and Law Reform."

Chapter 2 has already established how the analytical framework of contract theory applies to international treaties. Chapter 3 introduced the economic rationale for the use of subsidies by states, with a special focus on their effects on international trade. Chapter 4 now addresses the application of the contractual framework to the substantive field of regulation. It first identifies the preferences of WTO Members, evaluating the incentives on them to pursue a multilateral trade agreement for regulation of industrial subsidies, and the corresponding obligations that derive therefrom. Secondly, it classifies types of uncertainty and related incompleteness as they pertain to a subsidies agreement, and discusses the need for flexibility mechanisms.[3] The analysis provided here will introduce the obligations and flexibility rules currently in force under the SCM Agreement, laying the groundwork for discussion of the rationale for the non-performance rules.

4.2   Rationale for International Cooperation and Control of Subsidies

In international law and economics, a treaty or international agreement is a formal legal instrument that creates obligations with binding effect on governments. Its use by states is intended to overcome problems of international cooperation by facilitating transactions in jurisdiction, as a means of addressing excessive unilateralism.[4] Underlying the decision of the parties to adopt the specific legal form of a treaty or contract as a means of regulation, there is the *intent* of parties to solve a specific cooperation problem.

It is important to understand this contractual intent, and the corresponding problem underlying the treaty, because it influences the choices of the parties with respect to the design of the treaty. In particular, the overall rationale for a specific treaty will determine the clauses that are used to define and exchange entitlements and establish contractual remedies. In other words, the rationale determines the design of the treaty.

---

[3] For a broader discussion about the role of preferences and uncertainties in contractual theory, see Section 2.1.1, and specially Cooter and Ulen, *Law and Economics* p. 43–48 and, in an application to international trade law, see Schropp, *Trade Policy Flexibility and Enforcement in the WTO: A Law and Economic Analysis* p. 77.

[4] States are the subject of international law *par excellence*, but other subjects also have competence to enter into treaties, such as international organizations, certain territories, etc. See Trachtman, *The Economic Structure of International Law* p. 119.

Chapter 3 concluded that there are numerous rationales for regulation of the use of subsidies. The most important of these is that, due to international trade networks, there is potential for subsidies to generate cross-border spillovers.[5] Further, because governments are susceptible to lobbying by protectionist groups, subsidies might be used to promote domestic firms over foreign competitors. Subsidies nevertheless remain an important mechanism for the promotion of public policies.

Chapter 3 further concluded that the subsidy is, on the one hand, the best available policy instrument with which to foster efficiencies and improve aggregate welfare, while on the other it is a strategic policy tool that can be used to detrimental effect on international trade. Production subsidies may be used to manipulate terms-of-trade to adversely affect trade partners. Export subsidies can undermine the profits of foreign third market competitors. Production and export subsidies may be used to circumvent market access commitments under the GATT. The potential for harmful effects suggests that governments might benefit from international cooperation aimed at limiting the use of such subsidies.

This opposition between good and bad subsidies poses a challenge for negotiators, who must strive to draft a contract that captures the contractual intent regarding solution of the cooperation problem and translates these complexities into appropriate legal language.

As discussed, subsidies constitute a complex policy tool that can take many different forms. The initial classification of subsidies distinguishes between export subsidies and domestic subsidies, and is then expanded into "prohibited" subsidies and "actionable" subsidies, as demonstrated in Section 4.3.2.3.[6]

---

[5] Other possible rationales are commitment and global efficiency. According to the first, international agreements could be used as an instrument for governments to shift to the WTO the political costs of unpopular measures. The second argues that through an international agreement states wish predominantly to foster global welfare levels even if that would affect their domestic welfare in the short term. See, for the first, Brou and Ruta, "A Commitment Theory of Subsidy Agreements"; and also Friederiszick, Röller, and Verouden, "European State Aid Control: An Economic Framework" p. 640–41. For a discussion about the efficiency argument for regulation, see Sykes, *The Limited Economic Case for Subsidies Regulation* p. 2–5.

[6] See DeRemer, *The Evolution of International Subsidy Rules*; also John Jackson, *The Perplexities of Subsidies in International Trade*, Chapter 11 (The World Trading System, MIT Press 1997) p. 285–93; and Irwin, Mavroidis, and Sykes, *The Genesis of the GATT* p. 156–58.

Table 7: *The case for flexibility x rationale for regulation.*

	Terms-of-trade	Market access		Political economy	Case for flexibility
		Domestic	3rd market		
Export subsidies	–	–	X	X	Weak
Domestic subsidies	X	X	–	X	Strong

Source: Elaborated by the author

The prior discussion reveals how this classification corresponds to the harmful effects of subsidies that require international regulation. Such regulation will address terms-of-trade management, issues of political economy and closure of market access, and the economic case for flexibility. In a nutshell, domestic subsidies are usually associated with terms-of-trade, political economy and domestic market closure, while export subsidies are more closely related to loss of market share in third markets and motives in relation to political economy. There is, at the same time, an economic case for flexibility mechanisms that pertains most strongly to domestic subsidies. There is a weaker case for granting flexibilities in relation to export subsidies, as they can be used only exceptionally as a means of overcoming market failures.[7]

In order to overcome these problems in the drafting of a treaty, policymakers will arguably have to constrain the uses of subsidies that produce negative externalities, while at the same time permitting legitimate uses of them.[8]

While the perfect balance could be achieved by an *ex ante* complete contract between the parties, legal theory suggests that policymakers are confronted by a number of uncertainties that prevent them from writing such complete contracts.

---

[7] See Chapter 3, Section 3.5, for references; see especially Green and Trebilcock, "The Enduring Problem of World Trade Organization Export Subsidies Rules"; and WTO, *Exploring the Links between Subsidies, Trade and the WTO* p. 116.

[8] For references on negative externalities of subsidies, see DeRemer, *The Evolution of International Subsidy Rules* p. 2–13. For an overview of the role of externalities, see Chapter 2, Section 2.1.3, and specially Trachtman, *The Economic Structure of International Law* p. 119–49.

Table 8: *Contractual intent of a subsidies agreement.*

Contractual intent		
Protect market access commitments	Undistorted competition for third markets	Policy space for legitimate uses

Source: Elaborated by the author

The following section tests this hypothesis in the substantive area of subsidies, and discusses its implications for a subsidies agreement. It concludes that because the definition of subsidy is ambiguous, potentially encompassing several policy instruments, subsidies regulation is subject to a high level of uncertainty. This suggests that flexibility mechanisms will have a significant role in any attempt to address the matter through international regulation.[9]

4.3   Regulating Subsidies through Incomplete Contracts

A critical aspect of contract law is the underlying rationale or original motivation that leads states to cooperate in regulation. This not only guides the definition of rights and obligations by the parties, but also influences the level of flexibility that is ultimately built into the treaty.

An agreement regulating subsidy use, especially in relation to international trade, is thought to mutually benefit the parties by constraining opportunistic use of subsidies.[10] The economic literature identifies two main opportunistic uses. The first is the circumvention of commitments

---

[9] Similar issues have already been explored in other areas of trade and investment law but no comprehensive study has been done for the rules on subsidies. In order to determine what the optimal flexibility mechanisms are, we should first clearly identify the uncertainties to which policymakers are subjected when drafting rules that restrict subsidies. For the issue of incomplete contracts and international trade, see Schropp, *Trade Policy Flexibility and Enforcement in the WTO: A Law and Economic Analysis* p. 6. Also, investment treaties have been analyzed through a similar method by van Aaken, "Smart Flexibility Clauses in International Investment Treaties and Sustainable Development" p. 843.

[10] Economists have long defended that certain domestic subsidies might be used by governments to manipulate trade volumes to the benefit of their own terms-of-trade. This shows a rather straightforward case for restricting the use of domestic subsidies. Export subsidies, on the other hand, worsen the terms of trade of the subsidizing country, and their restriction finds little justification under the traditional economic approach to trade agreements. However, once the perfect market assumption is relaxed, export subsidies might also negatively affect trade partners and need to be regulated. For an overview of

to tariff reduction, in response to which the parties to a tariff regulating agreement, such as the GATT, might wish to regulate subsidies as well ("policy substitution" or "market access problem"). The second such use is profit-shifting in favor of the subsidized industry ("profit shifting problem"), which impacts the competitiveness of foreign firms. Even if a subsidy improves terms-of-trade or the net welfare of an importing state,[11] it could have a negative impact on the welfare of a domestic group or groups, such as domestic producers. Should a government (for strategic policy or political reasons) value the welfare of such a group, however, a negative reaction by policymakers toward subsidization might be triggered. As unilateral responses to subsidies, such as increased tariffs or cross subsidization are usually wasteful, states may be caught in an inefficient uncooperative relation, often seen as a prisoner's dilemma game, which could be improved by agreement.[12]

An agreement to address these problems would be expected to include commitments that limit the sovereignty of states to prevent them from employing subsidies in ways that cause the damaging effects. Predictably, however, the negotiation of such an agreement is a complex task, due to fundamental uncertainties that affect the regulation of subsidies.

4.3.1 Historical Overview of Negotiations

The claim that an economically informed legal framework is useful for explaining the current rules on subsidies finds support not only in the *lege lata*, but also in the historical development of these norms. The complexity of the current regulation is the result of decades of negotiations among states: government concern with negative externalities and spillover effects of foreign policies has been at the heart of the multilateral trading system since its inception after the Second World War.[13]

The common narrative about this period suggests that international economic cooperation was the way to overcome the damaging "beggar thy neighbor" trade and monetary policies that had been implemented

---

the economic theory of the regulation on subsidies, see DeRemer, *The Evolution of International Subsidy Rules* p. 8–9.

[11] For instance, by raising the welfare of consumers of the subsidized imported good.

[12] For issues of cooperation and the use of treaties as an instrument to overcome them, see Trachtman, *The Economic Structure of International Law* p. 127–30.

[13] Historical studies argue that states were concerned with trade wars and "beggar thy neighbor" policies. See for instance Irwin, Mavroidis, and Sykes, *The Genesis of the GATT* p. 176–97.

unilaterally between the World Wars, resulting in negative externalities on the welfare of states and policymakers.[14] The collective response of states was to design a series of international economic treaties and organizations that would provide a mandate for regulation of a considerable spectrum of international economic relations.[15]

Among the treaties devised during this period was the Suggested Charter for an International Trade Organization of the United Nations ("Suggested Charter"),[16] which had a clear trade focus. The aim of the

[14] Countries used to dedicate their efforts to boycotting each other's economies in order to promote their own, generating a cycle of vain economic disputes led by the principle of reciprocity. Continuous and irresponsible subsidization was one of the main policies that created profound distortions on international trade. As described by Krugman, this is known as a "prisoner's dilemma," a situation in which "each government, making the best decision for itself, will choose to protect," Krugman, Obstfeld, and Melitz, *International Trade: Theory and Policy* p. 286. See also Coppens, *WTO Disciplines on Subsidies and Countervailing Measures: Balancing Policy Space and Legal Constraints* p. 30; and Thomas W Zeiler, "The Expanding Mandate of the GATT: The First Seven Rounds" in Amrita Narlikar, Martin Daunton, and Robert M Stern (eds), *The Oxford Handbook on The World Trade Organization* (The Oxford Handbook on The World Trade Organization, Oxford University Press 2012) p. 102. One possible manner to cooperate was through the creation of several international institutions responsible for mediating and regulating economic relationships. As recalled by Luengo, *Regulation of Subsidies and State Aids in WTO and EC law: Conflicts in International Trade Law* p. 36–37, "[t]he purpose of the H[avana] C[harter] was to create an International Trade Organization [...] which, together with other multilateral institutions such as the World Bank and the International Monetary Fund, would contribute to stabilizing the economic, political and social situation following World War II." The World Bank "was set up to facilitate post-war recovery and to otherwise assist economic development," Coppens, *WTO Disciplines on Subsidies and Countervailing Measures: Balancing Policy Space and Legal Constraints* p. 31; and the IMF "was created to provide a stable monetary regime based on the US dollar as the reserve currency" as in Ivan D Trofimov, "The Failure of the International Trade Organization (ITO): A Policy Entrepreneurship Perspective" (2012) 5 *J Pol & L* p. 56. For a description focusing on the world monetary system, see Krugman, Obstfeld, and Melitz, *International Trade: Theory and Policy* p. 550–51.

[15] Negotiations that led to the GATT could be historically divided into (i) bilateral negotiations between the US and the UK, which set basic understandings between two of the leading economic players of the post-war period; and (ii) multilateral negotiations which managed to strike a deal on the texts of the GATT and the Havana Charter. See Irwin, Mavroidis, and Sykes, *The Genesis of the GATT* p. 5–22.

[16] For a detailed description of the history of the negotiations between the US and the UK, see ibid. p. 12–76. As recalled by Luengo, *Regulation of Subsidies and State Aids in WTO and EC Law: Conflicts in International Trade Law* p. 37, "[n]ear the end of 1945, the US Department of state invited a number of countries to start negotiations for the purpose of establishing a multilateral trade agreement. At the same time, the United Nations began its task of coordinating incentives for international cooperation. During the first session of the United Nations Economic and Social Commission in February of 1946, the US suggested the establishment of the 'United Nations Conference on Trade

Suggested Charter "was to create an International Trade Organization [. . .] which, together with other multilateral institutions such as the World Bank and the International Monetary Fund, would contribute to stabilizing the economic, political and social situation following World War II."[17]

The Suggested Charter proposed rules for establishment of the core structure of the ITO and its *modus operandi*.[18] Negotiations also included rules on subsidies. The Suggested Charter initially stipulated (i) the need for notification by the subsidizing country in the event of application of subsidies to domestic or other products, with intent to increase exports or decrease imports; and (ii) the prohibition and abolition of export subsidies within three years.[19]

The final version of the Suggested Charter (the "Havana Charter") "was divided into various Chapters, which detailed the provisions on trade policy, economic development and reconstruction, employment, restrictive competition practices, dispute settlement and the creation of an institutional framework suitable for the ITO to carry out its functions."[20] Having been elaborated in successive rounds of negotiations in London, New York, Geneva, and Havana, it was signed in 1948.[21] Meanwhile, the General Agreement on Tariffs and Trade (GATT) was signed in 1947 during the Geneva Round of the United Nations Conference on Trade and Employment, provisionally coming into force in 1948.[22]

and Employment' to draft the foundational charter for the ITO as well as negotiate tariff reductions on a worldwide scale."

[17] Coppens, *WTO Disciplines on Subsidies and Countervailing Measures: Balancing Policy Space and Legal Constraints* p. 31.

[18] Suggested Charter for an International Trade of the United Nations – Chapter VII; as noted by Luengo, *Regulation of Subsidies and State Aids in WTO and EC Law: Conflicts in International Trade Law* p. 39.

[19] Suggested Charter for an International Trade of the United Nations – Chapter IV, section E. Further negotiations were necessary to finally strike a final agreement. These resulted in the rules included in the GATT and in the Havana Charter.

[20] Suggested Charter for an International Trade of the United Nations – Chapter VII; as noted by Luengo, *Regulation of Subsidies and State Aids in WTO and EC Law: Conflicts in International Trade Law* p. 39.

[21] The Charter was constituted by a series of propositions on international trade, but concerning the scope of this work, what deserves attention is the creation of an agreement on tariffs (GATT) and of a multilateral organism for international trade (ITO) in accordance with Bretton Woods.

[22] The development of the Havana Charter negotiations, including its rules on subsidies, has recently been subjected to more detailed studies. For a comprehensive description of the evolution of negotiations and treaty drafts on several trade issues, see Irwin, Mavroidis,

Despite all the effort that went into negotiating the Havana Charter, the US Congress did not ratify the text, and the ITO never came into existence. After public announcement of congressional opposition to the ratification, the US president, in 1950, closed the door on US approval of the ITO, leaving the GATT as the central legal piece in the multilateral trading system.

With the failure of the Havana Charter,[23] the GATT was to assume more responsibility for subsidies than was originally intended. Initially, the GATT regulated only domestic subsidies, but during a review session of 1954–55 the GATT rules were amended to include rules on export subsidies.[24]

The modern contours of the rules on subsidies were shaped in the 1970s, in the "Agreement on Interpretation and Application of Articles VI, XVI and XXIII of the General Agreement on Tariffs and Trade," commonly known as the Subsidies Code.[25] The Tokyo Round of Multilateral Trade Negotiations was marked by a declared concern with non-tariff barriers, including subsidies. In its paragraph 3(b), the Ministerial Declaration of the Tokyo Round called negotiators to:

and Sykes, *The Genesis of the GATT*. For a detailed description with a focus on the rules on subsidies, see Luengo, *Regulation of Subsidies and State Aids in WTO and EC Law: Conflicts in International Trade Law* p. 35–96. It is our understanding that a correct appreciation of the rules of the ITO and its preparatory work are important, because "[a]lthough the ITO never saw the light, the provisions on subsidies contained in the HC were progressively, almost entirely incorporated into the GATT" (ibid., p. 37) and might therefore have explanatory power over the current rules, as well as legal force for their interpretation.

[23] As recalled by Luengo, *Regulation of Subsidies and State Aids in WTO and EC Law: Conflicts in International Trade Law* p. 38, "[f]or the negotiation of the ITO, the US government had the mandate to conclude the resulting agreements on tariff reductions without the need for Congress's approval. However, the approval of the Congress was necessary for agreements incorporating the US into an international organization" [footnotes omitted].

[24] At the Review Session, an important milestone was created on subsidies with the addition of a section B to Article XVI of the GATT, entitled "Additional Provisions on Export Subsidies." For an overview of the GATT subsidies regime, see Michael J Trebilcock, *Advanced Introduction to International Trade Law* (Edward Elgar Publishing 2015) p. 77–79.

[25] These negotiations were marked by a conflict of different proposals: The American and the British. The USA was claiming for "more stringent rules on subsidies for non-primary products, and the EU and other countries, aiming at disciplining the extensive use of CVDs by the US during the 1970s," Coppens, *WTO Disciplines on Subsidies and Countervailing Measures: Balancing Policy Space and Legal Constraints* p. 35.

reduce or eliminate non-tariff measures or, where this [would] not [be] appropriate, to reduce or eliminate their trade restricting or distorting effects, and to bring such measures under more effective international discipline.[26]

Finally, at the Uruguay Round, the current subsidies rules were drafted, in the form of the Agreement on Subsidies and Countervailing Measures (SCM Agreement).[27] In addition to regulating the use of industrial subsidies, this Agreement imposed disciplines on the use of countervailing measures, thus consolidating certain trends that had been expressed throughout the negotiating process.[28]

In keeping with the economic literature, negotiators initially chose to address export and domestic subsidies and several of their effects. The basic classification, distinguishing export from domestic, remained consistent throughout the negotiating history, but as negotiations advanced, the two categories were refined and expanded to further distinguish prohibited from actionable subsidies.

Means of enforcement of the rules on subsidies was contemplated by a larger regulation on trade measures, which subjected subsidies to the general WTO rules of dispute settlement promulgated by the system. More specific rules were also developed to address unilateral reactions to foreign subsidies ("countervailing measures").

The relevance of this negotiating history is that it contextualizes the origin and development of the regulation of subsidies within the general multilateral trading system. Its particular significance will be revealed in the rest of this chapter in the examination of the progressive development of subsidies regulation: the attempt to strike a balance between rules for prevention of subsidies that cause trade externalities, and means of facilitation of subsidization as an economic and social policy instrument. The achievement of this balance, as already pointed out, constitutes the main challenge for any agreement regulating subsidies.

4.3.2   Setting the Entitlements: Restrictions on Subsidies

Earlier, Chapter 3 identified the core entitlements around which a subsidies agreement should be structured: the restriction of subsidies that create negative externalities, and facilitation of good faith subsidies

---

[26] GATT, Ministerial Meeting, Tokyo, 12–14 September 1973.
[27] WTO, "Multilateral Negotiation Rounds" 2016 <www.wto.org> accessed 08.18.2016.
[28] See Luengo, *Regulation of Subsidies and State Aids in WTO and EC Law: Conflicts in International Trade Law* p. 84–86.

through comprehensive flexibility rules. Negotiators attempted to achieve such regulation by defining the specific commitments, or rights and obligations, of each of the contracting parties. An analysis of the adequacy of the current rules on subsidies requires, therefore, that these commitments be further investigated.

4.3.2.1 Development of the Rules

Negotiators, as already mentioned, drew a primary distinction between domestic subsidies and export subsidies. During negotiation of the Havana Charter[29] it was determined that the GATT text would include rules on trade-affecting domestic subsidies,[30] including a requirement of notification by the subsidizing party and the right of affected Contracting Parties to trigger consultations upon request.

Export subsidies were, with certain exceptions, prohibited, and were to be phased out within a certain period of time after the creation of the ITO.[31] In 1947, during the New York Round, however, it was decided that the part of the GATT on export subsidies would be reallocated from the draft GATT to the draft ITO Letter, where it remained outside of the GATT text.[32]

---

[29] Other substantive and institutional issues were also at the center of the discussions in London. As recalled by Luengo, *Regulation of Subsidies and State Aids in WTO and EC Law: Conflicts in International Trade Law* p. 38, "[i]n the midst of the first meeting of this Conference, held in London (1946), the US proposal for the ITO was discussed, the procedures for the multilateral negotiations for tariff reductions were agreed upon, and it was concluded that the General Agreement on Tariffs and Trade (GATT) would be necessary to safeguard such tariff concessions."

[30] For a detailed description of the development of GATT/WTO rules, see Irwin, Mavroidis, and Sykes, *The Genesis of the GATT*. For a historical study of the rules on subsidies within the GATT/WTO system, see Luengo, *Regulation of Subsidies and State Aids in WTO and EC Law: Conflicts in International Trade Law* p. 35–96.

[31] Irwin, Mavroidis, and Sykes, *The Genesis of the GATT* p. 156–57.

[32] The meeting in New York also discussed the contents of the GATT, and as "it was expected that the GATT were to be a specific agreement on trade within the framework of the ITO" it was "not deemed necessary to include other provisions of social policy or development in the GATT that were going to be present in the founding Charter of the ITO." A similar argument was used to remove export subsidies regulations from the GATT and to replace them to another agreement within the ITO framework. See Luengo, *Regulation of Subsidies and State Aids in WTO and EC Law: Conflicts in International Trade Law* p. 38. According to a recent study about the New York Conference, "[a] majority of countries felt that the discipline on export subsidies should be part of the ITO Charter, but not the GATT. Consequently, the provision on export subsidies was included in Article 30 of the New York Draft ITO Charter, but not in Article XIV of the New York Draft GATT," Irwin, Mavroidis, and Sykes, *The Genesis of the GATT* p. 157–58.

The draft ITO Letter, signed in 1947–48 during the Havana Round, foresaw: (1) a duty to notify all subsidies that maintained or increased exports, or that reduced or prevented an increase in imports;[33] (2) a prohibition of certain export subsidies, especially those resulting in export prices lower than the domestic price of the product;[34] and (3) special trade rules to, (a) permit international agreements to regulate commodity prices;[35] and (b) prohibit export subsidization of a commodity sector if it would result in a "non-equitable share" of the market.[36]

Havana Charter Article 25, which dealt with subsidies generally, obliged ITO Members to notify subsidies, including any form of income or price support the effect of which was to maintain or increase exports from, or decrease imports into, its territory. Members were also intended to discuss the reduction of any subsidy that caused or threatened to cause serious prejudice to the interests of other ITO Members. Article 26 prohibited export subsidies that undercut the domestic market by causing export prices to drop below those charged in the domestic market. Conditions included a two-year margin for the application of these restrictions,[37] and an exception permitted states to counter-subsidize in order to offset the effects of subsidies by other Members. Articles 27 and 28 dealt with subsidies to primary products.[38]

With the failure of the ITO, the regulatory framework constituted by the GATT came into force.[39] A description of entitlements in relation to

---

[33] Havana Charter Article 25.
[34] Ibid. 26.
[35] Ibid. 27.
[36] Ibid. 28.
[37] Export subsidies, with the exception of primary products (which received special treatment), should be abolished within a term of two years beginning from the date the Charter enters in force. See Havana Charter Article 26.
[38] For a detailed overview on these articles as well as the conditions foreseen in Article 26, see Luengo, *Regulation of Subsidies and State Aids in WTO and EC Law: Conflicts in International Trade Law* p. 39–40.
[39] As stated in a previous work, "with the failure of the Havana Charter, never ratified by the United states, the GATT Agreement arose as the main international trade agreement in force. GATT's Article XVI had a detailed obligation requiring states not only to notify their subsidies, but also their 'estimated effect [. . .] on the quantity of the affected product [. . .] imported into or exported from its territory' and 'the circumstances making the subsidization necessary.' Later amendments reinforced the differentiation between industrial and agricultural subsidies while the rules on export subsidies were also strengthened. Once more, there was no explicit provision about the legitimate use of subsides, suggesting that all others were presumably consistent with their international obligations and therefore the text of the agreement only obliged states to avoid certain export subsidies. If Article XVI had been taken seriously, there would have certainly existed a need to

regulated subsidies was found in GATT Article XVI, which obliged Contracting Parties to disclose information about subsidizing measures, both domestic and export.[40] The GATT avoided any definition of a subsidy.

In the absence of a clear definition, scholars sought to extract from Article XVI some notion of the concept of subsidy that "was implicit in that provision."[41] Notably, Article XVI refers to the Contracting Party as the "entity granting the subsidy," hinting that a subsidy is given by governments or public bodies, a feature that would later be reflected in the SCM Agreement. Secondly, it conceives subsidy broadly, to include "all forms of income or price support" capable of boosting exports or hindering imports, causing material injury to third parties.

There are at least two problems with this informal definition gleaned from Article XVI. First, its overbroad conception of "subsidy" has the potential to capture a wide range of governmental measures that might influence the volume of imports and exports. Secondly, it fails to incorporate by reference the common effects of subsidization, such as its propensity to increase domestic production, or the negative externalities associated with a rise or shift in profits.[42] A description with such breadth of scope and lack of awareness of effects poses a threat to legal certainty: the GATT makes no provision for clarification as to which measures fall under the regulation, or for determining causality between a measure and economic effect.

The import of this lack of detail is that it permits extension of the reach of the rules beyond a desirable level, to target legitimate subsidies and other policy measures with similar effects. Doubts about the scope of the subsidies rules arose because the implications of Article XVI were broader than initially foreseen, and legal certainty had been undermined, increasing the risk of legal adversity. Export subsidies, moreover, remained unregulated by the agreement.

---

clarify the extension of its obligations concerning notification and restriction of subsidies. However, as many articles of the GATT, this provision had little effectiveness," José Caiado and Thomas Berghaus, *R&D Subsidies: A Law & Economics Analysis of Regional and International Rules* (2012) p. 4–5.

[40] See Luengo, *Regulation of Subsidies and State Aids in WTO and EC Law: Conflicts in International Trade Law* p. 43.

[41] Ibid. p. 46.

[42] There were also critics about the disconnection of the notion of "serious prejudice" in Article XVI, and Article VI, which regulated CVDs and used a different terminology, such as "material injury." The GATT was silent about the relation between these two possibly similar terms. See ibid.

Rules on export subsidies were eventually introduced during the Review Session of 1954–55.[43] The new text, Section B of Article XVI, resembled that of the earlier ITO draft, which had recognized that "the granting by a Contracting Party of a subsidy on the export of any product may have harmful effect for other contracting parties."

In Article XVI, Section B, clause 4, two restrictions on the export of non-primary products[44] were imposed. The first prohibited the grant of new export subsidies. The second introduced a "cap and reduce" clause on existing export subsidies.[45]

---

[43] Following the establishment of the GATT as the legitimate legal framework for the conduction of world trade, negotiations on tariff reductions and non-tariff measures were implemented through negotiation rounds. Some of the features of the current "negotiation round" model, such as (positive) consensus-based decisions and the "single undertaking" approach have been heavily criticized as being responsible for the deadlock of negotiations in the Doha Round, as described in Peter van den Bossche and Werner Zdouc, *The Law and Policy of the World Trade Organization: Text, Cases, and Materials* (3rd edn, Cambridge University Press 2013) p. 90. Despite the critics to the modern variation of such "negotiation round" model, rounds provided negotiators with the "opportunity for package deals" and "political momentum" to strike a deal on the reduction of several tariff lines and, at a later stage, on the regulation of non-tariff barriers, and seem to have been an important factor to expand trading rules both geographically and in legal substance, including rules on subsidies. Both these elements potentially play an important role in allowing parties to reach an agreement. Package deals elevate the range of interests under negotiation, offering an opportunity for parties to exchange concessions in different tariff lines and other areas of trade barriers, potentially facilitating an agreement that could strike a balance in concessions. For instance, during the Uruguay Round, the US is said to have insisted on having other parties to make commitments on intellectual property issues, whereas Europeans clearly valued rules on geographic indications and developing countries would like to see fewer restrictions on trade in agriculture. While certainly making negotiations more complex, this broader range of topics also allowed parties with different interests to get something from the negotiations. Political momentum is also an important issue, as governments have to make concessions and thus impose losses on certain domestic players who might oppose the agreements. Having a firm commitment by governments to finalize negotiations on a certain deadline could be an incentive for policymakers to more firmly advertise the domestic advantages of the agreement to its constituents and progressively build support for the domestic approval of the trade treaties. For a short description of the role of these instruments, see ibid. p. 87. Also, see Guzman, *How International Law Works: A Rational Choice Theory* p. 161–81.

[44] There were also new rules on primary products. According to Luengo, *Regulation of Subsidies and State Aids in WTO and EC Law: Conflicts in International Trade Law* p. 49, the "reforms introduced in the GATT in 1955 on export subsidies for primary products were weaker than the obligations for such products in the H[avana] C[harter]."

[45] See ibid. p. 48, who refers to this clause as a "standstill clause in order to freeze and reduce the export subsidies." An interpretative note to this clause actually stated that the intention of parties was to reach an agreement before the end of 1957 to abolish all

Despite the substantive regulatory expansion brought about by the GATT Review Session, a clear definition of subsidies was still absent from Article XVI, and the strongly worded obligations agreed by the parties were not systematically enforced. Apart from the new export subsidies provisions added by way of Section B, treaty interpreters were left with the general elements of Section A and associated uncertainty.[46]

To conclude, the amended GATT rules on subsidies retained (in Article XVI Section A) the historic obligation to notify subsidies, and created (in Section B) new rules on export subsidies. Recognizing the potentially harmful effects of export subsidies, these rules attempted to both cap (at January 1, 1955 levels) and to prohibit (from 1958) any export subsidy that results in the sale of exported goods at a lower than domestic price.

The amendments did not have a fully satisfactory outcome, as the obligation to notify subsidies stumbled into two problems. First, the lack of a clear definition of subsidy left Contracting Parties some room for maneuver regarding what and how to notify. Secondly, although the problem of form was partially solved through the efforts of Working Groups to design detailed notification templates,[47] Contracting Parties were still reluctant to handle information that could trigger foreign action against them. The right of an allegedly affected Contracting Party to request consultations proved to be a weak remedy, obliging subsidizing parties to merely "discuss the possibility" of limiting their subsidization. The absence of a definition of subsidy was also problematic. Although the Article XVI identification of a few conceptual features facilitated interpretation and application of the subsidies rules, this lacuna was a significant source of uncertainty in the system.[48]

---

remaining export subsidies. See Interpretative Note to Article XVI:4 of the GATT. Such an agreement, however, was never reached. See ibid. p. 49.

[46] See Sections 4.1 and 4.2.

[47] The templates seem to have been very comprehensive and required states to report the reason and legal basis for subsidization, the beneficiary of the subsidy, the total expenses, and per unit amount of subsidy, and the estimated effects of the subsidy on quantities imported and exported. Luengo, *Regulation of Subsidies and State Aids in WTO and EC Law: Conflicts in International Trade Law* p. 53.

[48] There were attempts to create lists of specific measures that would be considered as export subsidies. the OEEC (Organization for European Economic Cooperation, which preceded the OECD) drafted a document with an extensive list determining prohibited "aids to export." In 1960, when the OECD was created, there was an unsuccessful attempt to transfer this list to the GATT headed by France, since only 16 countries adhered to this policy. For more details, see Coppens, *WTO Disciplines on Subsidies and Countervailing Measures: Balancing Policy Space and Legal Constraints* p. 34. Also at the GATT,

Some of these issues were dealt with by further negotiation, resulting for example in the introduction of new rules of entitlement and enforcement through the Tokyo Round Subsidies Code of 1973–79. The general entitlement rule in Article 8 of that Code recognized that although subsidies provide governments with an important policy instrument with which to achieve social and economic objectives, they can also have adverse effects on other parties.[49]

In addition to augmenting the GATT rules with a more detailed description of regulated effects, the Code required Contracting Parties to "seek to avoid" the use of subsidies with potentially adverse effects, especially those that caused injury to domestic industry, prejudice to another Contracting Party, or nullification or damage to the benefits of another GATT signatory.[50] The Code also created the "possibility for any party to request information from another Contracting Party about the nature and amount of the subsidy"[51] granted by the party.

The Code, moreover, maintained the GATT prohibition on use of export subsidies in relation to industrial goods. In the face of an ambiguous concept of subsidy, the Code expanded the "Illustrative List of Export Subsidies," adding a number of examples of permitted domestic subsidies. In the context of the longstanding and controversial debate over the definition of "subsidy," this list demonstrates a certain mutuality of understanding among the Contracting Parties regarding those practices that should be considered export and domestic subsidies.[52]

---

a "Working group in 1960 prepared a non-exhaustive list of specific practices that were considered export subsidies," Luengo, *Regulation of Subsidies and State Aids in WTO and EC Law: Conflicts in International Trade Law* p. 62.

[49] Luengo, *Regulation of Subsidies and State Aids in WTO and EC Law: Conflicts in International Trade Law* p. 68–71.

[50] For more details, please see ibid. p. 68.

[51] As noted by Rubini, the specificity test is linked to the idea that "specific subsidies would especially interfere with the allocation of resources domestically – and hence internationally – thus shifting artificially comparative advantages between countries," Rubini, *The Definition of Subsidy and State Aid: WTO and EC Law in Comparative Perspective* p. 360. It is also noted, not without critics to this perception, that general measures not captured by these tests are "increasingly linked to, for example, social investments in health, education, law and order, basic research, and physical infrastructure," ibid. p. 361. Low, for instance, defends the use of the specificity test as a "rule of thumb" to restrict the scope of the SCM Agreement to more distorting subsidies.

[52] It should be mentioned that the Code had special rules for developing countries, granting them S&D (special and differential) treatment relating subsidization, opposing to the MFN principle. On the one hand, they had recognition that domestic measures, including those targeting export promotion, for production support were legitimate, but on the other were still subjected to CVDs. According to the text of the Code: "this

While the descriptive language of the Subsidies Code may be capable of tackling uncertainty associated with regulation of domestic and export subsidies, the domestic subsidies commitments in the Code, which merely require states to attempt avoidance of their use, are perceived as weak. Further, the application of the prohibition on export subsidies, as minimally defined in the Code, was inhibited by restriction to its signatories and the lack of a strong enforcement mechanism.[53]

As discussed in Chapter 3 the effects of terms-of-trade manipulation provide one explanation for the necessity of international restriction of subsidies use. The rationale is that because production subsidies can improve the terms-of-trade of the subsidizing state, there is incentive for rational governments to use them. Despite domestic gains, however, the use of subsidies to manage terms-of-trade levels can also worsen the terms-of-trade of a trade partner, and is perceived as a cost to other states.

The correction of the terms-of-trade externalities problem requires international rules, and because international regulation explains the advance of the multilateral trading system, especially the rules on tariffs, it might also be expected to extend to the rules on subsidies with tariff-like "beggar thy neighbour" effects on trade partners. At first glance, however, this is not the case. While the draft Havana Charter imposed both notification requirements and restrictions on production subsidies, the GATT adopted a more lenient approach, requiring mere notification of domestic subsidies.

Although notification might reduce uncertainty around subsidizing country behavior by helping to ensure that subsidies are not used for terms-of-trade management, this GATT mechanism for notification does not seem to have been much used by the Contracting Parties. For this reason, most of the legal scholarship shares a critical view of the GATT

Agreement shall not prevent developing country signatories from adopting measures and policies to assist their industries, including those in the export sector. In particular, the commitment of Article 9 shall not apply to developing country signatories, subject to the provisions of paragraphs 5 through 8 below," Subsidies Code, Article 14.2. Even though such protection was stipulated, developing countries were still supposed to dedicate some effort to reduce subsidies, otherwise they would be exposed to CVDs as much as developed countries. This decision was pushed by the USA as a retaliation to the new discipline on CVDs and to the S&D treatment given to developing countries. See Coppens, *WTO Disciplines on Subsidies and Countervailing Measures: Balancing Policy Space and Legal Constraints* p. 37–38.

[53] Note that the Code was a "plurilateral" agreement, i.e. it has a limited number of participants and was not automatically applicable to all GATT Contracting Parties.

rules on domestic subsidies. This legal criticism is also founded largely on the absence of clear rules for restriction of production subsidies. Without a definition of "subsidy," there are considerable gaps in the GATT rules that could undermine the general objective of regulating unilateral subsidy policies that have harmful trade effects.

This conclusion supports the case proposed by legal scholars for more detailed regulation,[54] which would also serve to address other substantive gaps in the original GATT. Evolution of the rules, through the Tokyo Round agreements and the current SCM Agreement, seems to have addressed these concerns.

With respect to export policies, the Havana Charter, contrary to the terms-of-trade literature, imposed a prohibition on export subsidies. This prohibition should however, in keeping with the political economy scholarship described in Chapter 3, help eliminate externalities such as profit-shifting in competition for third markets and tariff circumvention policies.

With the fiasco of the Havana Charter and the failure of the final text of the GATT to restrict them, export subsidies remained unregulated and thus a potential source of externalities. The problem was partially addressed by the Review Session of 1954–55, which recognized the potential for export subsidies to generate harmful effects and attempted to cap, as well as prohibit, subsidies to foster exports. This trend was preserved in both the Tokyo Round agreements and the SCM Agreement. The SCM Agreement also restricts subsidies related to import substitution policies. The provision is a source of controversy because, as economists agree, on the one hand such subsidies have a direct effect on trade flows and might be used for reasons of political economy, while on the other they constitute an important public policy instrument capable of fostering economic activity, especially in developing countries. This dichotomy will be addressed in more detail after a general introduction to the SCM Agreement.

---

[54] There is a discussion in the literature about the necessity of more stringent rules on domestic subsidies. Economists tend to favor a system based on less rules and non-violation claims, whereas lawyers usually argued for more obligations and a more consistent enforcement mechanism. See more details in Section 4.3.2.5.2.2, on non-violation claims.

4.3.2.2   Overview of the SCM Agreement

The SCM Agreement defines a subsidy as a "financial contribution by a government" that confers a "benefit" and is "specific."[55] These constitutive elements of subsidy have been described in the SCM Agreement with varying degrees of precision, and application of the definition has required interpretative efforts by the WTO adjudicating authorities.[56]

The issues associated with definition of subsidies are highly complex, requiring a detailed analysis that is outside the scope of this work. More than one PhD dissertation has focused exclusively on this question, and a vast number of dispute settlement decisions discuss the application of the concept to concrete facts.[57]

Some elements of subsidy must nevertheless be addressed here, due to the central role that its definition plays in the SCM Agreement, in that it determines the scope of application of the rules. In general terms, the matter of definition of subsidy constitutes a significant source of uncertainty. On the one hand, if the concept is interpreted too broadly, policymakers may find their hands tied in several areas of public policy, simply because they could not anticipate the reach of the rules.[58] On the other, it provides a powerful source of flexibility through interpretation and application of the concept in concrete situations.

The likelihood that this will happen is increased by the fact that terms of limited precision were employed by negotiators in the definition of subsidy, in order to delegate power to third parties to facilitate adequate application of the concept *ex post*. Interplay between financial contribution, government benefit and specificity, may be used, within the

---

[55] See Article 1-2 of the SCM Agreement.

[56] For instance, the concept of financial contribution contains a list of governmental practices that fall under Article 1 of the SCM Agreement. The notion of benefit, however, does not contain such a list. See Article 1.1(a)–1.1(b) of the SCM Agreement. This differentiation is relevant because, according to contract theory, the use of more or less precise language could signify the delegation of more powers to adjudicating third parties. In this sense, the WTO interpreters would have more interpretative margin when analyzing the concept of benefit. This will be further discussed in Chapter 5.

[57] See Rubini, *The Definition of Subsidy and State Aid: WTO and EC Law in Comparative Perspective* p. 17–18.

[58] For a description of the role of the definition of subsidy on the interpretation of the object and purpose of the SCM Agreement, see Jan Wouters and Dominic Coppens, "An Overview of the Agreement on Subsidies and Countervailing Measures Including a Discussion on the Agreement on Agriculture" in K Bagwell, G Bermann, and P Mavroidis (eds), *Law and Economics of Contingent Protection in International Trade* (Law and Economics of Contingent Protection in International Trade, Cambridge University Press 2010) p. 13–28.

boundaries of interpretation, to promote efficient *ex post* adjustment. This will be further analyzed in Chapter 5.

For now, it is relevant to note that even in situations in which a measure meets the definition of subsidy, and therefore falls within the scope of the SCM Agreement, it is not automatically prohibited. As pointed out by the Appellate Body, "the granting of a subsidy is not, in and of itself, prohibited under the SCM Agreement. Nor does granting a 'subsidy', without more, constitute an inconsistency with that Agreement."[59] This statement is derived from the classification of subsidies set out in the SCM Agreement, discussed in detail in the next section.

4.3.2.3 Basic Entitlements

The SCM Agreement is the result of negotiation of provisions in relation to GATT subsidies and countervailing duties (CVD). Like the GATT, it applies to subsidies related to the trade of manufacturers.[60] Subsidization of the agriculture and services sectors were left to specialized agreements.[61] The object and purpose of the SCM Agreement is defined as the imposition of "multilateral disciplines on subsidies which distort international trade."[62]

In the absence of preambular provisions, the substantive rules of the SCM Agreement have an important role in determining its object and purpose.[63] Articles 1 and 2 define the concept of subsidy and narrow its scope to subsidies that are deemed to be "specific," or granted to a specified industry, industrial sector, or region.[64] These provisions impose no obligations, but serve as a "threshold for the application of the disciplines prescribed by Parts II [prohibited subsidies], III [actionable subsidies], IV [non-actionable subsidies] and V [countervailing measure] of the SCM Agreement."[65]

---

[59] Canada Aircraft 21.5 para. 47.

[60] Wouters and Coppens, "An Overview of the Agreement on Subsidies and Countervailing Measures Including a Discussion on the Agreement on Agriculture" p. 11–13.

[61] WTO Agreement on Agriculture and General Agreement on Trade and Services, respectively.

[62] Panel Report, Brazil – Export Financing Programme for Aircraft (Brazil – Aircraft), WT/DS46/R, adopted 20 August 1999, as modified by Appellate Body Report WT/DS46/AB/R, DSR 1999:III, p. 1221, para. 7.26.

[63] Wouters and Coppens, "An Overview of the Agreement on Subsidies and Countervailing Measures Including a Discussion on the Agreement on Agriculture" p. 11–13.

[64] Ibid.

[65] Ibid. p. 33.

The substantive rules of the SCM Agreement also classify subsidies by reference to three categories: prohibited, actionable, and non-actionable. [66] Frequently referred to as the traffic light system, the categories are dubbed red light, yellow light, and green light, respectively.[67]

The economic effect of subsidies on international trade is fundamental to the understanding and interpretation of the SCM Agreement, an assertion that is supported by both legal doctrine and the competent authorities that interpret the Agreement. Crucial to the analysis, however, is a correct determination of the extent of coverage of the legal rules, and a proper evaluation of the relationship between this legal perspective and the economic rationale. For these, it is necessary to examine, in more detail, the rights and obligations set out in the SCM Agreement in relation to the use of subsidies and countervailing measures.

4.3.2.3.1 Prohibited Subsidies The category of prohibited subsidies comprises subsidies that are *contingent*[68] upon export performance and upon the use of domestic over imported goods.[69] The definition of export

[66] See WTO, *Exploring the Links between Subsidies, Trade and the WTO*; also Trebilcock, *Advanced Introduction to International Trade Law* p. 79; and Luengo, *Regulation of Subsidies and State Aids in WTO and EC Law: Conflicts in International Trade Law* p. 97–102.

[67] As described by Wouters and Coppens: "On the one end, two types of subsidies are principally prohibited in and of themselves (red light) because of their direct trade-distortive effect, namely export subsidies and local content subsidies (Part II SCM Agreement). On the other end, three types of subsidies, in other words, for research activities, disadvantaged regions, or for the adaption to environmental requirements, were deemed nonactionable (green light) and thus in principle were allowed under the SCM Agreement (Part IV SCM Agreement). All other subsidies are actionable subsidies (rest category, yellow light), meaning that they can be challenged or countervailed if they cause adverse effects (Part II SCM Agreement)," Wouters and Coppens, "An Overview of the Agreement on Subsidies and Countervailing Measures Including a Discussion on the Agreement on Agriculture" p. 33–34.

[68] The agreement explicitly makes use of the term "contingent," which has been interpreted to mean "conditional." As noted by Wouters and Coppens, "this conditionality can be in law but also in fact, which prevents governments from circumventing the provision by linking subsidies to export [or import substitution] performance without prescribing it explicitly in their laws," Wouters and Coppens, "An Overview of the Agreement on Subsidies and Countervailing Measures Including a Discussion on the Agreement on Agriculture" p. 35. See also Panel Report, Brazil – Taxation, para. 7.385, and para. 7.1147.

[69] Article 3, SCM Agreement. For an overview, see WTO, *Exploring the Links between Subsidies, Trade and the WTO* p. 199–200; and Wouters and Coppens, "An Overview of the Agreement on Subsidies and Countervailing Measures Including a Discussion on the Agreement on Agriculture" p. 34–49. See also Green and Trebilcock, "The Enduring Problem of World Trade Organization Export Subsidies Rules" p. 127–30; and Jackson, *The Perplexities of Subsidies in International Trade* p. 293–300.

and import substitution subsidies is rather broad, and encompasses several public measures that are tied *de jure* or *de facto* to a requirement to export or to make use of domestic input.

Although not explicitly mentioned in the SCM Agreement, legal doctrine and caselaw consider such subsidies to be prohibited *per se*.[70] This means that, in the context of a dispute over the conformity of a measure, it is irrelevant whether or not the measure has actually produced harmful effects. It is sufficient for a complainant to prove that the measure is a prohibited subsidy, upon which the measure will be deemed inconsistent with the SCM Agreement.

Prohibition *per se* may be contrasted with the effect-based rule, which prohibits "a behavior if it produces certain undesirable effect."[71] A *per se* prohibition is thus more restrictive, and less flexible, than effect-based norms.[72] It has the advantage that it is more easily applied and does not require a "high level of expertise and knowledge from those who would administer it,"[73] resulting in a lower probability of error in the measurement of effects and a higher level of legal certainty.[74] The *per se* prohibition is an appropriate tool, therefore, for the prevention of measures that are always harmful or opportunistic, when it can be presumed that the measures will cause adverse effects.

[70] See Trebilcock, *Advanced Introduction to International Trade Law* p. 87.
[71] This distinction is much applied in competition law. See William E Kovacic and Carl Shapiro, "Antitrust policy: A Century of Economic and Legal Thinking" (2000) 14 *The Journal of Economic Perspectives* p. 43–60. For a discussion on the use of effect-based rules as a flexibility instrument in the GATT/WTO system, see Marc Benitah, *The Law of Subsidies under the GATT/WTO System* (Kluwer Law International 2001) p. 11–35. Benitah, however, takes a slightly different view, arguing that there are elements of the rules on prohibited subsidies that require an effect-based analysis. Although this might be correct for a few elements, it is not adequate to the general understanding of the provision which clearly omits any reference to the need to demonstrate that negative effects have been produced by the measure. In this regard, it could be said that the effect is inferred, and that the measure is *per se* prohibited.
[72] As noted by Marceau, "a rule of reason offers more flexibility and should allow for the introduction of more sophisticated defenses for particular business decisions. On the other hand, a rule of reason requires a fairly high level of expertise and knowledge from those who would administer it." Marceau, *Anti-Dumping and Anti-Trust Issues in Free-Trade Areas* p. 298.
[73] Ibid. p. 298–99.
[74] On the other hand, when assessing the consistency of a measure, effect-based norms take into consideration more details and offer a more case-tailored result. Legal certainty is however an important element because it is "more precise for guidance to business enterprises and entrepreneurs in the world," Jackson, *The Perplexities of Subsidies in International Trade* p. 301.

Subsidies that are deemed "prohibited" generally involve concessions that are offered subject to adoption of certain performance requirements, notably export and import substitution requirements.

Performance requirements are legal obligations that may entail "minimum export ratios, import ceiling, local content-specification, and the like,"[75] including production within a particular geographic locale, achievement of certain employment levels over a period of time, and implementation of additional rules regarding transparency in the employment of public funds. Such conditions may reflect general principles for protection of the public interest, but are frequently used to enhance the accomplishment of policy objectives.[76] Conditions particularly relevant to international trade include local use requirements that prefer domestic over imported input, and export performance.[77]

Prohibited subsidies fall into two sub-categories: "export" subsidies and "import substitution" subsidies. The first comprises subsidies that are subject to export requirements,[78] including both *de facto* and *de jure* export subsidies.

---

[75] Dani Rodrik, "The Economics of Export-Performance Requirements" (1987) 102 *The Quarterly Journal of Economics* p. 633–50, 633.

[76] Performance requirements are often costly to firms; after all, they impose a condition which the profit-maximizing firm would not, in the absence of the regulation, normally choose to follow. However, should the performance requirement be associated to a benefit, such as a subsidy, and assuming that the benefits of the subsidy are set at higher level, firms might be willing to accept the conditionality.

[77] Subsidies contingent on localization requirements usually stipulate a determined geographic region within the territory of the state granting the subsidy where the subsidized firm must develop its production activities. By stimulating firms to settle in a pre-determined region, governments intend to foster regional development of less advanced areas within the territory.

Localization requirements also include the obligation to use domestically produced input in the production of the final good. Import substitution mechanisms boost domestic production levels to the expense of foreign products and directly affect international trade. Similarly, subsidies contingent on the export of produced goods may directly affect foreign trade if the subsidized goods compete internationally. Moreover, if the subsidizing state is large enough, export subsidies may reduce global prices and suppress profitability of competitors thus causing an extra welfare loss to foreign producers.

[78] In fact, many subsidy programs combine both LCRs and export performance requirements. As noted by Thirlwall, Latin American trade policy was incapable of fostering export, despite export subsidies, due to the high costs associated with LCRs. In his words, "In Latin America, policies became more outward-looking but still favoured production for the domestic market. Although subsidies were given to exports, exporters were still required to use domestic inputs produced under protection, and the subsidies were generally insufficient to provide an incentive to export that was comparable to the protection of domestic markets, and thus there was a continued bias in favour of import substitution," Thirlwall, *Economics of Development: Theory and Evidence* p. 539.

"Export requirements" might be directed at the number of production units dedicated for export, the proportion of production attributable to imports, the extent of foreign ownership in domestic production, and the value of repatriated dividends.[79] The problem is that subsidies that are conditional upon exportation of the subsidized goods prevent firms from selling their product in the domestic market, and may foster the effects[80] previously discussed: displacement of exports from other countries and a negative impact on world prices.[81]

As exports grow, foreign producers will encounter increased competition in third markets that can reduce sales and prices, and ultimately shrink profits. Foreign domestic producers will similarly face an increase in competition as a result of the presence of subsidized exports[82] in the foreign country.

The economic literature consequently mistrusts these measures, as export requirements are often imposed in pursuit of the promotion of political economy rather than justifiable policy objectives.[83] It recognizes certain exceptions, however, such as the use of export subsidies to overcome information asymmetries, as previously discussed.

Import substitution subsidies constitute the second sub-category of prohibited subsidies. Also referred to as having "local content requirements" (LCRs), these subsidies are commonly used to impose a localization requirement.[84] It is estimated that in 2010 LCRs affected

[79] Rodrik, "The Economics of Export-Performance Requirements" p. 637.
[80] As a general definition, "export promotion generally comprises the encouragement of various types of manufactured products that range from light manufactures, such as footwear and textiles, all the way to more sophisticated items, such as automobiles or memory modules for computers," Ray, *Development Economics* p. 677.
[81] See Section 3.5.
[82] Performance requirements, whether in terms of localization or export performance levels, pose an additional source of potential negative spillovers of subsidies. Performance requirements may come with a clear trade restrictive component (in the case of LCRs) and a direct impact on trade flows and prices (export performance) and are commonly viewed as a burdensome restriction to international trade. In many aspects, the effects are even more onerous than those of the subsidies itself. Local content requirements function partially as quotas and do not necessarily have a correlation with the correction of market failures, but the same does not apply to most export performance subsidies.
[83] As discussed in Chapter 3, subsidies might be used to correct for market failures. However, most of this theory is based on domestic subsidies. Bhagwati and Ramaswami, "Domestic Distortions, Tariffs and the Theory of Optimum Subsidy" p. 50.
[84] Sherry Stephenson, *Addressing Local Content Requirements in a Sustainable Energy Trade Agreement* (2013) p. 13.

nearly five percent of global trade in goods and services, amounting to $928 billion worldwide.[85]

The criteria for local content vary from measure to measure. LCRs commonly refer to local content as a predetermined proportion of the components used in the assembly of a final product. While LCRs usually determine local content by stipulating a percentage of tangible inputs, such as 45% of assembled car parts, more sophisticated measures might also refer to intangible goods, such as domestic R&D. Common to all LCR measures, however, is the criterion that production of the subsidized good involves the use of locally produced goods or services.

The effect of LCRs is to prevent producers from purchasing the most efficient (or least expensive) components on the world market, which causes production costs to go up and firms to suffer loss.[86] Forced local production will by definition raise the costs incurred by a firm, thus reducing its profit.[87] The subsidy might, however, despite such loss, generate sufficient benefit to provide profit-maximizing companies with an economic rationale for production or purchase of the less efficient local inputs that will enable it to meet the threshold content requirement.[88]

The consequences for foreign trade are equally direct. The reader will recall that a grant of subsidy to a domestic producer gives the subsidized product a competitive advantage vis-à-vis its foreign competitors, thereby increasing domestic production and reducing imports. A local content requirement will in effect subsidize the component industry as well as the final good, thus extending the effects of subsidization through-out the supply chain of the good and multiplying the protectionist effect

---

[85] Ibid.

[86] In fact, such requirements might be seen as a tax on producers, as in Thirlwall, according to whom the problem with import substitution policies and protection in general is that "they breed inefficiency, and more importantly act as a tax on exports by keeping costs . . . high." Thirlwall, *Economics of Development: Theory and Evidence* p. 539.

[87] There is evidence that this is particularly true for capital goods. According to a recent study, the use of localization barriers to trade "often raise the cost of critical capital goods inputs" particularly for general purpose technologies (GPTs) such as information and communications technology, and this stunts innovation and productivity growth across all sectors of an economy, thereby compromising broader economic growth," Robert Atkinson, Stephen Ezell, and Michelle Wein, *Localization Barriers to Trade: Threat to the Global Innovation Economy* (Information Technology and Innovation Foundation 2013) p. 42.

[88] In other words, "if it made economic sense to localize production in the destination country, they would have already done so," Stephenson, *Addressing Local Content Requirements in a Sustainable Energy Trade Agreement* p. 37–38.

of the subsidy.[89] As domestic production of equipment, for example, grows, it will displace efficient imports, with the result that local producers benefit, while foreign firms suffer a loss due to the fall in importation levels.

From an economic viewpoint, it is understandable, therefore, that drafters of the SCM Agreement paid special regulatory attention to export and import substitution subsidies. As each type of prohibited subsidy seems to have inevitable distorting effects on trade, and export subsidies only weakly correlate to the correction of domestic market failures, the discussion has centered mainly on whether restrictions have been set at an appropriate level. A complete ban, for example, is a rather strong instrument that leaves no margin for individual appreciation and should therefore be used only in exceptional circumstances. Economic arguments suggest that export and import substitution subsidies might sometimes constitute a rational good faith policy for use by states. Export subsidies can be used to overcome information asymmetries, and local content subsidies to tackle well-known market failures, such as the underproduction of innovation.

The *per se* prohibition established by the SCM Agreement, however, strictly regulates prohibited subsidies, leaving little room for state discretion in the devising of measures. Some use of flexibility mechanisms might nevertheless enable states to tailor the provision to situations in which these subsidies are used in good faith.

Potential for flexibility lies in the nuances of the regulation adopted by the SCM Agreement, including an important distinction between export and import substitution subsidies. In relation to subsidies contingent on export performance,[90] the SCM Agreement

---

[89] Local content policies might have trade effects similar to quotas, as described by Krugman, Obstfeld, and Melitz, *International Trade: Theory and Policy* p. 257–59.

[90] The list reads: "Illustrative List of Export Subsidies: (a) The provision by governments of direct subsidies to a firm or an industry contingent upon export performance; (b) Currency retention schemes or any similar practices which involve a bonus on exports; (c) Internal transport and freight charges on export shipments, provided or mandated by governments, on terms more favorable than for domestic shipments; (d) The provision by governments or their agencies either directly or indirectly through government-mandated schemes, of imported or domestic products or services for use in the production of exported goods, on terms or conditions more favorable than for provision of like or directly competitive products or services for use in the production of goods for domestic consumption, if (in the case of products) such terms or conditions are more favorable than those commercially available on world markets to their exporters; (e) The full or partial exemption remission, or deferral specifically related to exports, of direct taxes or social welfare charges paid or payable by industrial or commercial enterprises; (f)

incorporates by annexation an illustrative list that, on the one hand, asserts a clear prohibition of certain subsidizing measures, and on the other permits a certain level of flexibility. In relation to import substitution or subsidies contingent on the use of domestic over imported goods, no exceptions to the prohibition are articulated and, as already addressed, other means of flexibility would have to be devised to deal with such measures.

The illustrative list of export subsidies in Annex I of the SCM Agreement contains several examples of measures to be considered export subsidies.[91] The diverse selection of measures ranges from direct support to the provision of services to the use of currency schemes. Common to them is the notion that the measure makes provision in some way for benefits contingent upon export.[92]

While limiting the scope for further interpretative refinement of the regulatory language by WTO adjudicators, the list also opens a door to a certain degree of flexibility. Government provision of export loans and guarantees is for instance not a prohibited subsidy and is therefore consistent with WTO regulation as long as interest rates are compatible with OECD rules.[93]

The allowance of special deductions directly related to exports or export performance, over and above those granted in respect to production for domestic consumption, in the calculation of the base on which direct taxes are charged" [footnote omitted]. See Annex I, "Illustrative List of Export Subsidies" of the SCM Agreement.

[91] Proposals concerning the expansion of this list have been a contiguous topic in the Doha Round negotiations. See Debra Steger, "The WTO Doha Round Negotiations on Subsidies and Countervailing Measures: Issues for Negotiators" (Symposium on Economic Restructuring in Korea In Light of the Doha Development Round Negotiations on Rules) p. 3–5; and Wouters and Coppens, "An Overview of the Agreement on Subsidies and Countervailing Measures Including a Discussion on the Agreement on Agriculture" p. 34–35. Similarly, Trebilcock suggests that, with relation to actionable subsidies, an improvement to the SCM Agreement would be "to permit a range of non-trade-related justifications for such subsidies (analogous to those set out in Article 31 of the Tokyo Round Subsidies Code, Article 8 of the SCM Agreement on non-actionable subsidies, and Article XX of the GATT), provided that these are the least trade-restrictive means available for achieving such non-trade-related policy goals (analogous to the necessity test under Article XX), and provided that they meet conditions like those in the chapeau to Article XX, in particular that they are not a disguised restriction on or distortion of trade," Trebilcock, *Advanced Introduction to International Trade Law* p. 88.

[92] See Green and Trebilcock, "The Enduring Problem of World Trade Organization Export Subsidies Rules" p. 133–39.

[93] See Section 4.3.2.3.1; see also Wouters and Coppens, "An Overview of the Agreement on Subsidies and Countervailing Measures Including a Discussion on the Agreement on Agriculture" p. 43–45.

This was precisely the issue in *Brazil Aircraft*,[94] in which Brazil argued that: i) subsidized loans and guarantees were used merely to level the playing field against financing that was subject to lower interest rates;[95] and ii) similarly, that the SCM Agreement list of prohibited subsidies constituted a potentially "affirmative defense" of the use of incentives to export.[96] The decision suggests agreement by WTO drafters that even subsidies that ultimately foster exports might have a legitimate economic role in the development of trade in certain markets, and that a policy balance needs to be struck between commitment and flexibility.[97]

The prohibition of import substitution subsidies, on the other hand, is subject to no such exception, and subsidies contingent on local content are therefore in principle more strictly regulated than those contingent on export performance.[98] The SCM Agreement deems all import substitution subsidies to be inconsistent with WTO law, leaving the courts virtually no room of appreciation with which to decide whether a measure falls under Article 3(b) of the SCM Agreement.[99]

In the absence of a detailed illustrative list, adjudicators could in principle interpret "financial contribution" in the context of import substitution subsidies so as to introduce a certain level of flexibility,[100] but WTO law has so far given the concept a broad interpretation capable of encompassing a myriad of governmental measures.

---

[94] Panel Report, Brazil – Export Financing Programme for Aircraft, WT/DS46/R, adopted 20 August 1999, as modified by Appellate Body Report WT/DS46/AB/R (Brazil – Aircraft), DSR 1999:III, p. 1221.

[95] For an overview of the case, see Oliver Stehmann, "Export Subsidies in the Regional Aircraft Sector—The Impact of Two WTO Panel Rulings against Canada and Brazil" (1999) 33 *Journal of World Trade* p. 97–120.

[96] See Footnote 59 of the SCM Agreement. For its interpretation, see Wouters and Coppens, "An Overview of the Agreement on Subsidies and Countervailing Measures Including a Discussion on the Agreement on Agriculture" p. 40–42.

[97] For a discussion of positive effects regarding flexibilities in export subsidies, see Green and Trebilcock, "The Enduring Problem of World Trade Organization Export Subsidies Rules" p. 125.

[98] This affirmation takes into consideration the inexistence of express provisions regarding the justification of import substitution subsidies. As it will be discussed, however, other flexibility mechanisms, such as those introduced by legal interpretation, may apply. See Section 5.2.

[99] As noted by the doctrine, "the SCM Agreement does not provide any ground for justification for local content subsidies," Wouters and Coppens, "An Overview of the Agreement on Subsidies and Countervailing Measures Including a Discussion on the Agreement on Agriculture" p. 48–49.

[100] See the discussion on Coppens, *WTO Disciplines on Subsidies and Countervailing Measures: Balancing Policy Space and Legal Constraints* p. 115.

The adoption of a broad interpretation of "financial contribution" is directly related to the language of Article 1, which refers to both positive and negative government actions, including for example both actual and potential "transfer of funds" as well as the act of foregoing "government revenue." WTO Panels and the Appellate Body have therefore interpreted the concept accordingly as encompassing innumerable activities by a state.[101]

An alternative judicial approach would be to adopt a flexible interpretation of other constituent concepts of subsidy. If a measure is not made by the government or does not confer a benefit, it is outside of the scope of the SCM Agreement and therefore not a subsidy in the first place, rendering irrelevant the question as to whether it promotes exports or import substitution.[102] This was an issue in *Canada-Renewable Energy*,[103] in which the Appellate Body, deciding in favor of a strict interpretation of the term "subsidy," found the Canadian measure to be acceptable by reason that it fell outside of the scope of the SCM Agreement, thus permitting its elements of import substitution. These issues will be addressed in more detail in Chapter 5. For now, it is important to understand the second and third categories in the tripartite SCM Agreement classification of subsidies, notably actionable and non-actionable subsidies.

4.3.2.3.2 Actionable Subsidies In the second category of regulated subsidies, referred to as "actionable," are those domestic subsidies that are not contingent on import substitution.[104] Wouters and Coppens describe this group as defined by "default," meaning that a specific subsidy "if not prohibited ... constitutes an actionable subsidy."[105] Actionable, or "yellow light" subsidies are, like prohibited subsidies, subject to the dispute settlement system and to countervailing

---

[101] Wouters and Coppens, "An Overview of the Agreement on Subsidies and Countervailing Measures Including a Discussion on the Agreement on Agriculture" p. 16.

[102] As noted by Rubini, "the classification of a government measure of financial support [...] as subsidy may produce significant consequences in terms of constraint of governmental prerogatives," Rubini, *The Definition of Subsidy and State Aid: WTO and EC Law in Comparative Perspective* p. 376.

[103] Panel Report, Canada – Renewable Energy.

[104] As noted by Wouters and Coppens, local content subsidies "are the only type of domestic subsidy that is prohibited," Wouters and Coppens, "An Overview of the Agreement on Subsidies and Countervailing Measures Including a Discussion on the Agreement on Agriculture" p. 48.

[105] Ibid. p. 49.

measures.[106] To successfully challenge an actionable (as opposed to a prohibited) subsidy, however, it is not enough to prove that the subsidy exists; it is also necessary to demonstrate that it is the cause of certain effects that have an adverse impact on the interests of other WTO Members.[107]

If a subsidy is neither prohibited nor causes any adverse effect (or the effect has been removed), the subsidy falls outside the scope of the SCM Agreement. The "effect-based" rules defining actionable subsidies are by definition less strict than *per se* prohibitions on export subsidies and import substitution subsidies.[108] The "adverse effects test," a crucial element of the SCM Agreement, acts as a sort of "mediation principle" by which WTO Members[109] negotiate conflicted interests between their own use of such subsidies and avoidance of harm due to foreign use of them.

An understanding of the effects test requires evaluation of the definitions of the various adverse effects to which a subsidy might give rise, and an analysis of the notion of causation between subsidy and effect. The relevant effects are: (a) injury to the domestic industry of another Member; (b) nullification or impairment of benefits; and (c) serious prejudice to the interests of another Member.

---

[106] For an overview of the legal elements for this category, see ibid. p. 49–52. For an analysis connecting legal and economic aspects of this regulation, see Robert Howse, "Do the World Trade Organization Disciplines on Domestic Subsidies Make Sense? The Case for Legalizing Some Subsidies" in Kyle W Bagwell, George A Bermann, and Petros C Mavroidis (eds), *Law and Economics of Contingent Protection in International Trade* (Law and Economics of Contingent Protection in International Trade, Cambridge University Press 2009) p. 85.

[107] There effects are: (a) "injury to the domestic industry of another Member"; (b) "nullification or impairment of benefits accruing directly or indirectly to other Members under GATT 1994 in particular the benefits of concessions bound under Article II of GATT 1994"; and (c) "serious prejudice to the interests of another Member," Article 5 SCM Agreement. For a descriptive overview of the main elements and sub-elements of adverse effects, see Luengo, *Regulation of Subsidies and State Aids in WTO and EC Law: Conflicts in International Trade Law* p. 166–77.

[108] See Section 4.3.2.3.1; and also Benitah, *The Law of Subsidies under the GATT/WTO System* p. 11–35.

[109] Jackson, *The Perplexities of Subsidies in International Trade* p. 294. As noted by Jackson, "if the subsidized goods are not harming or causing injury in the importing country, then why bother about any response? On the other hand, if the subsidized imports create sufficient distress in the importing country to rise to some threshold level of 'material injury', or 'serious prejudice', perhaps at that point a response such as a countervailing duty is justified," ibid.

The concept of "injury" includes material injury, or threat thereof, to a domestic industry, and the retardation of domestic industrial establishment. An injury determination requires evidence related to the "effect of the subsidized imports on prices in the domestic market for like products" and "the consequent impact of these imports on the domestic producer."[110] Evaluation of the impact of the subsidy should consider economic factors such as decline in output, sales, market share, profit, productivity, utilization, prices, and investments.[111]

Another adverse effect under SCM Agreement Article 5(b) is "nullification and impairment," which is language typically used in the GATT to describe the harm that measures might cause to benefits accrued by WTO Members through negotiation of tariff reductions.[112] Given that subsidies can be used as an alternative to tariffs for protectionist purposes, the SCM Agreement regulates the use of those that have such effect.

Finally, subsidies also have an adverse effect if they cause "serious prejudice" to the interests of another WTO Member. Serious prejudice is found where the subsidies "displace or impede" imports or exports of a like product to the market of a WTO Member (either the subsidizing member or a third market),[113] "significant price undercutting or price suppression, price depression or lost sales,"[114] or an "increase in the world market share of the subsidizing Member."[115]

The adverse effects test, by incorporating several economic elements, offers a fairly comprehensive coverage of the potentially harmful uses of subsidies. It encompasses not only effects of subsidies on domestic industry, as exemplified by tests controlling for failing imports, exports, prices, and investments, but also, through the nullification and impairment test, effects associated with tariff-related uses of subsidies. Notable, however, is the absence of any computation of the potentially positive

---

[110] Bossche and Zdouc, *The Law and Policy of the World Trade Organization: Text, Cases, and Materials* p. 580. Note that the determination of injury also requires proof of other elements, such as like products and domestic industry. For an overview, see Coppens, *WTO Disciplines on Subsidies and Countervailing Measures: Balancing Policy Space and Legal Constraints* p. 144–46.

[111] See Article 15.4 SCM Agreement. Note that the list contained in Article 15.4 is not exhaustive, and other relevant economic factors might be taken into consideration in the analysis. See also Bossche and Zdouc, *The Law and Policy of the World Trade Organization: Text, Cases, and Materials* p. 580.

[112] See ibid. 582–83 and fn 350.

[113] Article 6.3(a) and 6.3(b) SCM Agreement.

[114] Article 6.3(c) SCM Agreement.

[115] Article 6.3(d) SCM Agreement.

effects of subsidies, especially on consumers, an issue that was touched on in the analysis developed in Chapter 3.

Chapter 3 discussed how an economic cost benefit analysis will typically take into consideration the impact of a measure on the welfare of several groups, including producers and consumers, in relation to which subsidies cause significant effects. A domestic subsidy, for instance, can raise consumer welfare by increasing production and decreasing prices, while an export subsidy similarly benefits foreign consumers by lowering the export price of subsidized goods.

International trade law, however, is often silent on the protection or consideration of consumer welfare, despite the importance of its inclusion in any comprehensive analysis of welfare. By disregarding the effect of a measure on consumers, a cost benefit analysis will tend to overestimate the impact of the measure on other economic agents, such as governments and producers.

This "bias favoring national producers," which neglects to account for the fact that subsidies (though possibly inefficient overall) are commonly of benefit to consumers, can result in an incomplete assessment of the overall welfare impact, overemphasizing the adverse effects of subsidies that are normally associated with a competing industry.[116]

4.3.2.3.3 Non-Actionable Subsidies

The SCM Agreement presents a further third category of subsidies that are "legal" or "non-actionable." Initially, this "green light" group encompassed several subsidies, such as innovation subsidies, that reflected economically justifiable policies.

---

[116] As noted by a panel, "we see no basis in the SCM Agreement for the notion that an increase in 'consumer welfare' constitutes a defense to a claim of adverse effects caused by subsidies. Nothing in the text of the Agreement, or in its object and purpose, supports the proposition that the panel can or should take into account possible 'positive' effects on competition of subsidies in evaluating claims of serious prejudice. It may often be the case that subsidies in fact contribute positively to consumer welfare – for instance, in US – Upland Cotton, the panel found price suppression caused by subsidies, and concluded that the United States' use of subsidies caused adverse effects to Brazil's interests. However, that price suppression presumably also resulted in prices for textiles and clothing that were lower than they otherwise would have been, which is a 'positive', while it also reduced revenues to cotton farmers, which is a negative. There is no mention of this in either the panel's or the Appellate Body's decision, and absolutely no basis to think that panels should somehow engage in a consideration that might 'balance' these competing effects," Panel Report, European Communities and Certain Member States – Measures Affecting Trade in Large Civil Aircraft, WT/DS316/R, adopted 1 June 2011, as modified by Appellate Body Report, WT/DS316/AB/R (EC and certain member States – Large Civil Aircraft), DSR 2011:II, p. 685, para 7.1991.

Today, however, it is limited to those subsidies identified in Article 8.1, namely non-specific subsidies that are excluded from contestability by SCM Agreement Article 1.2. Others set out in Article 8.2, such as regional, environmental, and R&D subsidies, have, by force of SCM Agreement Article 31, been actionable since January 1, 2000. This means that if an R&D subsidy, for instance, results in demonstrably negative effects on the industry and benefits or interests of another Member, it can now be unilaterally countervailed and challenged at the dispute settlement system of the WTO.[117] As non-actionable subsidies function as an explicit flexibility, it will be analyzed in more detail below.[118]

4.3.2.4 Entitlement Protection

In the SCM Agreement, WTO Members adopt further rules for protection of their subsidies commitments.[119] In relation to prohibited subsidies, a successful challenge by a WTO Member requires simple proof of existence, without the necessity of demonstrating that the subsidy has caused any specific harm. In legal jargon, there is a presumption that such subsidies cause harmful effects. The only way for Members to bring such a measure into compliance with WTO law is to "withdraw the subsidy without delay."[120]

Until the violating policies are brought into compliance and the dispute is settled, remedies available to Members for prohibited subsidies take the form of property rules. In contrast to a liability rule, a property rule requires that "someone who wishes to remove the entitlement from

---

[117] See WTO, *Exploring the Links between Subsidies, Trade and the WTO* p. 199–200; and Howse, "Do the World Trade Organization Disciplines on Domestic Subsidies Make Sense? The Case for Legalizing Some Subsidies" p. 96–101.

[118] The legal treatment given to actionable subsidies differs substantially both in terms of commitments as well as in flexibilities. Besides the effect-test, which as discussed in this item is a less restrictive rule than a *per se* prohibition, non-prohibited subsidies are also tested for their specificity, i.e. for their discriminatory use among different economic sectors. For a detailed description of the specificity rule, see Coppens, *WTO Disciplines on Subsidies and Countervailing Measures: Balancing Policy Space and Legal Constraints* p. 100–15; and also Luengo, *Regulation of Subsidies and State Aids in WTO and EC Law: Conflicts in International Trade Law* p. 129–41. See also Benitah, *The Law of Subsidies under the GATT/WTO System* p. 88–90, for an economic contextualization of the legal concept of specificity.

[119] This section draws on the unpublished paper Jelena Baeumler, José Caiado, and David DeRemer, "How Do the WTO Articles on Actionable Subsidies Function as Liability Rules?" (2014).

[120] Article 4.7. SCM Agreement.

Table 9: *The multilateral regulation of subsidies over time.*

	Havana Charter	GATT (pre-review)	Review	Tokyo	SCM
Export	Prohibited (2 years' period) except primary products	Not approached	Prohibited except for primary products	Prohibited for industrial products	Prohibited
Domestic	Subjected to notification and restriction	Mere procedural disciplines on trade affecting subsidies	Same as GATT	General guidelines	Actionable
Explicitly legal					Non-actionable

Source: Elaborated by the author

its holder must buy it from him in a voluntary transaction."[121] Pauwelyn suggests that property protection stands out in international law as the "default form of protection unless special circumstances arise."[122]

Liability protection is distinct from property protection. Among the WTO agreements that address domestic policies, the SCM Agreement, in its rules on actionable subsidies, is one of the few to establish a liability protection system. Whereas most remedial systems require that compliance be achieved solely by alteration of the illegal policy, the SCM Agreement contemplates a further remedy for actionable subsidies in that Members might "take appropriate steps to remove the adverse effects" of the subsidy.[123]

The rules on actionable subsidies, which are not prohibitive and make removal of adverse effects an available remedy, ensure that "WTO Members can engage in certain conduct that is condemned (yet, not unlawful) if only they 'pay for it.'"[124] Recent trade law and economics literature follows the classification of Pauwelyn,[125] and also of Maggi and Staiger, who consider actionable subsidies to be a "clear" example of liability rules.[126] WTO Members that are noncompliant in their use of such subsidies have the option of removing the adverse effect, while retaining the subsidy itself.[127]

---

[121] Ibid.

[122] See Pauwelyn, *Optimal Protection of International Law* p. 5; and Giovanni Maggi and Robert W Staiger, "Trade Disputes and Settlement" (2013) Department of Economics—Yale University p. 3–4.

[123] Article 7.8 of the Agreement on Subsidies and Countervailing Measures.

[124] See Pauwelyn, *Optimal Protection of International Law* p. 5; and Maggi and Staiger, "Trade Disputes and Settlement" p. 3–4.

[125] Pauwelyn focuses on extending the Calabresi and Melamed analysis to the international law setting. See Pauwelyn, *Optimal Protection of International Law* p. 6. He applies his general proposed framework to explaining why actionable subsidies are subject to liability rules. Ibid. p. 107. He calls the actionable subsidy rules a "democratic safety valve" by which a population "who changes its mind and democratically opposes a treaty obligation [...] can be given effect, yet without harming others as liability protection implies full compensation of all victims," ibid. p. 59. He also mentions transaction costs of bargaining and the problem of incomplete contracts, but he does so in the context of the GATS rather than the actionable subsidy rules.

[126] Giovanni Maggi and Robert W Staiger, "Optimal Design of Trade Agreements in the Presence of Renegotiation" (2015) 7 *American Economic Journal: Microeconomics* p. 109–43.

[127] Subsidies that were formerly non-actionable, such as those identified in SCM Agreement Article 7.8, are also subject to liability rules and remedies.

Table 10: *Enforcement mechanisms.*

Enforcement		
Unilateral	Multilateral	
CVMs	Violation claims	Non-violation claims

Source: Elaborated by the author

4.3.2.5   Delegation of Powers in the SCM Agreement

In international economic law, enforcement mechanisms can take a variety of different forms. In WTO law, the standard dispute settlement system is elaborated in the Dispute Settlement Understanding. Other WTO covered agreements, however, as set out in a list provided at DSU Appendix 2, provide for special or additional rules and procedures on dispute settlement.[128]

Included in the list is the SCM Agreement which provides, in addition to multilateral dispute settlement, a unilateral method by which Members might countervail subsidies.

These two methods—the multilateral remedy provided by the DSU, and the unilateral remedy offered by the SCM Agreement—can be used by Member states to tackle prohibited and actionable subsidies. Together they constitute the WTO enforcement system for protection of subsidies entitlements.[129]

4.3.2.5.1 Unilateral Unilateral measures against subsidies are referred to as "countervailing measures" (CVMs) or "countervailing duties" (CVDs). They are essentially "a special duty levied for the purpose of offsetting ... any subsidy bestowed, directly, or indirectly, upon the manufacture, production or export of any merchandise."[130] Under GATT/WTO rules, CVDs are usually classified as a unilateral measure similar to antidumping and safeguards. Among the weapons (such as antidumping, safeguards, and anti-subsidies measures) in the arsenal of

---

[128] These act as *lex specialis* to the DSU, as provided in Article 1, para. 2 of the DSU.

[129] Although reputation might be considered an important element of enforcement mechanisms in international law, this work will focus on the systems prescribed by the GATT/WTO system. For details on reputation as an enforcement instrument, see Guzman, *How International Law Works: A Rational Choice Theory* p. 71–118.

[130] Art IV GATT and footnote 36 to the SCM Agreement. See also Bossche and Zdouc, *The Law and Policy of the World Trade Organization: Text, Cases, and Materials* p. 585.

trade remedies, those targeting subsidies have been explored to a lesser degree, at least in absolute numbers, than the ones aimed at offsetting dumping margins. This might explain why there is a relatively higher academic interest in dumping practices and antidumping measures than in subsidies and countervailing measures. Recent data analysis, however, reveals an increasing number of anti-subsidies cases, leading scholars to observe a "potential shift toward governments relying [more] on the countervailing duty (anti-subsidy) policy."[131] There are two main reasons for this, namely: i) the change in behavior by important states that only recently accepted use of anti-subsidies measures against China; and ii) the international response to the series of bailout programs that succeeded the 2008–2009 global economic crisis. The topic of countervailing duty policy thus deserves further consideration, both for the lack of attention that it has received in the past and for its increasing importance to governments as a trade remedy tool.[132]

CVDs originate in domestic law.[133] The steps generally required to impose a CVD are as follows. A legal person (industry, union, or trade association) petitions the competent local authority with a statement that it is competing against "illegally" subsidized products, and a request that duties of a certain amount be applied to them. The local government undertakes an inquiry to investigate whether an actionable subsidy is, or was, in place, and whether the domestic industry has been injured by it. If both questions are answered in the affirmative, duties will be administered.

The economic rationale of CVD measures is debatable because, in practice, subsidies in the exporting country shift the supply curve to the right, as if the importing country were receiving a direct transfer of funds from taxpayers of the subsidizing state, which potentially raises its welfare. Sykes, adopting this welfare approach in his examination of the legal system of CVD in the United States, concluded that "none of the plausible efficiency justifications for countervailing duties can persuasively explain or justify the existing countervailing duty laws of the United

---

[131] Chad P. Bown, "Taking Stock of Antidumping, Safeguards and Countervailing Duties, 1990–2009" (2011) 34 *The World Economy* p. 1955–98, 1963–64.

[132] Ibid.

[133] The United States' anti-foreign subsidy legislation remounts to the end of the nineteenth century. See Sykes, *The Limited Economic Case for Subsidies Regulation* p. 7; and Alan O Sykes, "Countervailing Duty Law: An Economic Perspective" (1989) 89 *Columbia Law Review* p. 199–263.

States," and therefore, "abolition of the countervailing duty laws might best serve the national economic interests."[134]

Efficiency arguments aside, Goetz et al propose a protectionist rationale, asserting that the underlying motivation for CVDs is the protection of national firms from competition by subsidized companies.[135] They identify two divergent conceptions of this rationale. The first is that CVDs act as a deterrent: they dissuade companies from accepting subsidies, and governments from conferring them. The second is the "neutralization" conception in which states accepts subsidization, but attempt to protect domestic firms by neutralizing its effects on competition.[136] The authors advocate for the latter. Assuming that the use of subsidies can, even in the exercise of legitimate domestic policies, cause negative effects abroad, they suggest that the role of the CVD law is to neutralize these effects, rather than to influence decision-making as to whether a subsidy is accepted or granted in the first place.[137]

Baylis found further justification for use of CVDs in the economic literature. The strategic trade theory, for instance, implies that it may be rational for the importing government, given certain oligopolistic conditions, to use some form of countervailing tariff, which would offset the

---

[134] Sykes, "Countervailing Duty Law: An Economic Perspective" p. 263. A similar argument is made by Trebilcock and Howse for whom the traditional argument is that subsidies lead to an inefficient allocation of global resources by distorting comparative advantages. However, it is also possible to argue that many subsidies enhance efficiency by correcting market failures/externalities. Assessing such efficiency effects is intimidating and indeterminate. But even if subsidies do distort trade, to determine whether CVDs law can improve allocation is a total different matter, being clear that current US law, for instance, does not take this into consideration when determining or imposing such duties. Also puzzling is that CVDs in most cases reduce domestic welfare in the importing country (where it is defined as maximization of producer, consumer, and government surplus), because of heavy consumers' losses. Michael J Trebilcock and Robert Howse, The Regulation of International Trade (Psychology Press 2005) p. 283. This suggests that rather than condemning, countries should support foreign subsidization. A second argument relates to the use of subsidies as a form of support to predatory pricing, but there seems to be little theoretical or empirical basis for such allegations, at least in the international trade sphere. Also here, current law does not support the allegation that CVD are paying much attention to this claim.

[135] Charles J Goetz, Lloyd Granet, and Warren F Schwartz, "The Meaning of 'Subsidy' and 'Injury' in the Countervailing Duty Law" (1986) 6 International Review of Law and Economics p. 17–32.

[136] Ibid. p. 18–19.

[137] Ibid. p. 30–32.

effects of the subsidy in the domestic market but may or may not dissuade the exporting state from conferring it.[138]

Political pressure, another factor to which CVD use is attributed, is well addressed by political economy. Recognizing that politicians might favor pressure groups at the expense of domestic social welfare, the political economy of trade policy offers explanations both as to why states might confer subsidies, and why they are likely to impose CVD as a trade barrier. In this analysis, indicators of political power, size, and population, apart from the economic conditions associated with strategic trade theory, may point to the groups that can successfully lobby for subsidies and tariffs.[139]

Lastly, CVDs may be employed as a means of warning foreign governments against future behavior, creating a little-explored disincentive for subsidization.

Thus, there are a mix of rationales for the use of CVDs. While the majority of the explanations for CVD use presented in the literature rest on political economy, concerns about future behavior, as noted by Baylis, cannot be disregarded. Although welfare scholars agree that multilateral enforcement and other cooperative solutions are superior to unilateral measures, CVDs may still be understood as a second best alternative (albeit a limited one, due to the difficulty of addressing spillover effects in the domestic market of subsidized exports to third markets[140]) in which unilateral action is permissible in only very specific cases, such as high export subsidies.[141]

That the use of CVDs seems rooted primarily in political economy or protectionist motives is a concern aggravated by the fact that CVD investigation and the imposition of duties are undertaken by national

---

[138] Kathy Baylis, "Countervailing Duties" in William A Kerr and James D Gaisford (eds), *Handbook of International Trade Policy* (Handbook of International Trade Policy, Edward Elgar Publishing Limited 2007) p. 176–79.

[139] Ibid.

[140] Without a clear mechanism to neutralize such externalities, there were concerns with cross-subsidization, i.e. the use of subsidies by a state to fight subsidization by another state, which increased even more the distortions produced by subsidies and that the regulation was supposed to reduce and control. Coppens, *WTO Disciplines on Subsidies and Countervailing Measures: Balancing Policy Space and Legal Constraints* p. 32.

[141] See Trebilcock and Howse, *The Regulation of International Trade* p. 291, for whom, ideally, the multilateral system should, instead of allowing for CVDs, facilitate negotiation on the topic with the WTO taking a more transparency role by notification and surveillance mechanisms, "monitoring subsidy policies and calculating subsidies in tariff equivalents, or effective rates of protection, providing a kind of common bargaining currency," ibid.

authorities. As discussed in Chapter 2, administrative bodies might harbor certain "home biases," and "tend to interpret international rules so as not to upset their government's interests."[142]

It would be natural, therefore, for the international law on CVDs to take precautions to minimize or neutralize such biases.[143] Some commentators argue, in fact, that one of the main purposes of the SCM Agreement is to regulate opportunistic abuses of countervailing measures by national governments.[144]

The issue of opportunism was addressed early on in Article 34 of the Havana Charter, which required determination of the value of a subsidy, above which the application of CVDs was prohibited. The GATT, making use of some of the Havana Charter language, stated that nothing should "prevent any contracting party from imposing . . . countervailing duty,"[145] but in terms of regulating potential abuses lacked the detailed rules necessary to establish clear procedures and institutional requirements for CVD application, thus opening the door for their arbitrary and opportunistic use.[146] The GATT revision session was of little assistance, having seemingly avoided any issues of enforcement and leaving the parties with the same CVD rules.[147]

The Tokyo Round agreements regulated the unilateral responses to subsidies, permitting the Contracting Parties to impose countervailing measures in response to subsidized goods up to the amount of the subsidy.[148] This presents an important enforcement issue, in that the imposition of CVDs depended on formal investigations to determine

---

[142] Benvenisti, "Judicial Misgivings Regarding the Application of International Law: An Analysis of Attitudes of National Courts" p. 161.

[143] Caiado and Bär, "Die Rolle von nationalen Behörden im Subventionsregime des WTO-Rechts – wurde der Bock zum Gärtner gemacht?"

[144] Having their origins in the nineteenth century, many trade partners have argued that some of the US's anti-foreign subsidy legislation measures and investigations were made without a clear economic rationale, thus leading to potentially welfare-reducing and protectionist measures.

[145] GATT, Article II2(b).

[146] GATT, Article XXIII.

[147] Luengo, *Regulation of Subsidies and State Aids in WTO and EC Law: Conflicts in International Trade Law* p. 52, notes that the "provisions on trade remedies that Contracting Parties could adopt against countervailable subsidies granted by another Contracting Party were not modified in the reforms of 1955. The Contracting Parties manly continued to use countervailing duties in accordance with Article VI:3 of the GATT and had recourse to Articles XXII and XXIII of the GATT for solving their disputes."

[148] Coppens, *WTO Disciplines on Subsidies and Countervailing Measures: Balancing Policy Space and Legal Constraints* p. 36.

the existence of the subsidy and to establish a causal link between it and a "material injury" suffered by the domestic industry.[149] Determination of material injury required domestic authorities to assess volume of imports, price effects on "like products," and impact on domestic producers. Causality was to be demonstrated according to a non-attribution requirement, by which domestic authorities were required to show that the injury was due to the subsidy and not to other factors.[150] The level of CVD permissible to a Contracting Party was capped at the value of the subsidy, duties being preferably lower than the amount of the subsidy.

Despite the more detailed set of CVD provisions afforded by the Tokyo Round, two problems were left untouched. First, the Code failed to define "subsidy," resulting in uncertainty about precisely what might be subjected to CVDs. Secondly, it provided no clear rule regarding how to determine the monetary amount of a subsidy, giving domestic authorities a great leeway of discretion in that matter.[151]

The SCM Agreement partially addresses these issues. It finally introduces a concept of subsidy, increasing legal certainty in the application of the rules, and now requires detailed investigations prior to imposition of CVDs. In a nutshell, the use of countervailing duties is contingent on the presence of the following prerequisites: (i) a prohibited subsidy (which is always specific), or a countervailable subsidy with demonstrable specificity; (ii) injury, or threat of injury, to domestic industry: (iii) a causal link between the subsidy and the damage; (iv) a countervailing duty not in excess of the estimated amount of the subsidy; (v) limitation of compensatory action to a maximum of five years; and (vi) requirement that the consistency of the measure is subject to analysis by the WTO dispute settlement system.

The imposition of CVDs can be avoided, however, if an amicable solution among the Members is reached through consultations under SCM Agreement Articles 7.1 and 7.3.

---

[149] Before the Tokyo Round, US countervailing measures did not require an injury test, and the simple existence of a subsidy overseas entitled US authorities to impose countervailing duties. The lack of such a test seemed to cause concern in US trading partners, as it potentially left a door open for opportunistic protectionist measures by the US. In this regard, the regulation of CVDs was also an important concern on the mind of Contracting Parties during the negotiations of the Tokyo Round. For a more detailed description of the negotiations on CVD, see Luengo, *Regulation of Subsidies and State Aids in WTO and EC Law: Conflicts in International Trade Law* p. 64.

[150] Ibid. p. 67.

[151] For a more detailed descriptive analysis of the Subsidies Code's rules on CVDs, see ibid.

Like the rules on subsidies, the regulation of countervailing duties has been subject to several changes through the history of the multilateral trading system. A CVD is a unilateral measure designed to offset in the importing market the effects of subsidies conferred by another government. Even though inefficient in economic terms, CVD policy may be justifiable on grounds of welfare. Potential for protectionist iterations of the policy, however, mandates that international legislation establish a coherent set of rules to regulate its use. To this end, the SCM Agreement requires a detailed investigation prior to application of duties, and makes further effort to avoid their use for protectionist purposes by subjecting unilateral decisions to the WTO dispute settlement system.

Criticism of the current system regards both its internal coherence (it is still open to opportunistic use) and its external coherence (a superior strategy would abolish CVDs and focus on multilateral negotiations). To the extent that they are important to the development of this work, these points will be addressed in more detail where appropriate.

4.3.2.5.2 Multilateral In terms of multilateral remedy for subsidies, GATT Article XXIII establishes two different situations in which Members may "make written representations or proposals" to achieve a "satisfactory adjustment of the matter:" (i) where there is a "nullification or impairment of benefits;" and (ii) "situations where the attainment of any objective [. . .] is being impeded." In each situation, any one of three different "causes of action" might be relied on to trigger dispute settlement: (i) the "violation claim," provided by Article XIII:1 (a); (ii) the "non-violation claim," described in Article XXIII:1(b); and (iii) the existence of any other situation, as contemplated by Article XIII:1(c).

Theoretically, therefore, there are six different ways in which states can initiate a dispute in the WTO system.

In practice, however, only "two of the six actions provided in Article XXIII have proven significant in the context of GATT/WTO disputes": (i.) violation claims and (ii). non-violation claims, each in relation to nullification and impairment. *Violation* claims concerning nullification or impairment refers to claims that can "only be leveled at policies that have been contracted over (or that display features, e.g., discrimination, that have been contracted over)."[152] *Non-violation* claims concerning

---

[152] Robert W Staiger and Alan O Sykes, "Non-Violations" (2013) 16 *Journal of International Economic Law* p. 741–75, 746–47.

Table 11: *Rules on CVDs over time.*

	Havana Charter	GATT	Review	Tokyo	SCM
Enforcement	CVDs – Definition and general restrictions on application + NVCs	CVDs – Allowed up to the amount of the affecting subsidy + NVCs	Same as GATT	Application of CVDs to developing countries if not committed to reduce subsidization. Stricter rules on applying CVDs	Application subjected to dispute settlement. Only cases of export, specific and on domestic over imported goods subsidies

Source: Elaborated by the author

nullification or impairment means claims that "can potentially be made against any policies, whether or not those policies have been contracted over (or display features that have been contracted over)."[153]

Violation claims accordingly deal with concrete breaches of obligation, whereas non-violation claims "target policies that have frustrated the legitimate market access expectations of the claimant under the agreement even if these policies have not violated any obligations under the agreement."[154]

4.3.2.5.2.1   Violation Claims

In order to analyze the functioning of the WTO dispute settlement mechanism with regard to subsidies, it is useful to first understand the workings of the dispute settlement under GATT 1947.

The system for resolution of conflicts under GATT 1947 did not have access to the sophisticated mechanisms and perennial institutions offered by WTO dispute settlement today.[155] The dispute resolution provisions of the General Agreement were limited to two main Articles: XII and XIII,[156] according to which if Parties to a dispute were unable to achieve a mutually agreed solution through "consultations under the GATT 1947,"[157] the dispute should be "initially 'handled' by working parties":[158]

> Many provisions of the General Agreement are designed to resolve trade disputes between its Contracting Parties, most of which provide initially, and sometimes exclusively, for consultations. If the contending parties are unable to settle their differences through negotiations, however, they may resort to GATT Article XXIII, the basic provision for GATT dispute settlement.[159]

From this provision, a practical system of dispute settlement, involving small expert groups or so-called "panels," was developed. A panel would be composed "of three to five independent experts from GATT Contracting Parties not involved in the dispute."[160] In essence, "[t]hese

---

[153] Ibid. p. 746.
[154] Ibid.
[155] This will be further explained. For a general overview, see Bossche and Zdouc, *The Law and Policy of the World Trade Organization: Text, Cases, and Materials* p. 176–78.
[156] See ibid.
[157] See ibid.
[158] See ibid.
[159] See William J Davey, "Dispute Settlement in GATT" (1987) 11 *Fordham Int'l LJ* p. 52–109, 53–54.
[160] See ibid.

panels reported to the GATT Council, consisting of all Contracting Parties, which would have to adopt the recommendations and rulings of the panel by consensus before they would become legally binding on the parties to the dispute."[161] It gradually therefore became "the standard practice for the contracting parties to appoint a panel of individuals to consider a dispute and prepare a report so that the contracting parties can take appropriate action."[162]

Over the years the development of the system witnessed an increase in the impartiality of the panelists and in the quality of the reports.[163] The profile of the dispute settlement system changed as a result of this evolution, from a power-based dynamic arising from diplomatic negotiations, "into a system that had many of the features of a rules-based system of dispute settlement through adjudication."[164]

Despite limitations on the dispute settlement provisions and practices under the GATT 1947, they were the only resort for Contracting Parties when conflicts arose between them. These limitations relate to both procedural and enforcement matters. Procedurally, initially open-ended and vague rules were later consolidated by practice. These rules generally required that parties first attempt to resolve a dispute through consultation and negotiation, after which they could request that the GATT Council appoint a panel to adjudicate or "examine the dispute and make such findings as will assist the contracting parties in making recommendations or rulings as provided for in Article XXIII."[165] Even in the absence of an express right to establishment of a panel, panels were "virtually always established if requested, assuming the request [was] vigorously pursued."[166] The Panel, after considering all contingencies, would issue a proposed report. If a breach was found, the Panel would

[161] See ibid.
[162] See ibid. p. 57.
[163] Davey also notes that "[. . .] the Contracting Parties agreed to the addition of legal staff to the GATT Secretariat and, in 1983, to the establishment of a Legal Office within the GATT Secretariat, to help panels, often composed of trade diplomats without legal training, with the drafting of panel reports. Consequently, the legal quality of panel reports improved and the confidence Contracting Parties had in the panel system increased." Ibid.
[164] See ibid. p. 57.
[165] The GATT Council was a body open to all GATT members, which meets every month or so and which has been delegated the authority to act on behalf of the contracting parties as a whole.
[166] Davey, "Dispute Settlement in GATT" p. 53–54.

recommend that the measure be removed, that the harmed party be compensated, or that retaliation be authorized.[167]

On the matter of enforcement, the report proposed by the Panel had to be submitted to and approved by the Council prior to its entry into force. Although the Council did not have the power to re-litigate issues addressed in the report, its decision-making process, by positive "consensus" of all Member states, ensured that the losing Party could block the approval of the report.

With the advent of the WTO, and the institutionalization of multilateral trade, the entire system of dispute settlement was organized and established in the "Understanding on rules and procedures governing settlement of disputes" (Dispute Settlement Understanding, or DSU), which articulated procedures for resolution of WTO controversies. The DSU, by defining a series of formal steps to build up a recognizable procedure, developed and clarified the informal processes of dispute settlement that had emerged during the GATT years.

The DSU also attempted to fix certain problems that had plagued practice under the GATT regarding issues of harmonization, predictability, and enforcement. As will be explained further, the DSU addressed these issues by instituting quasi-compulsory decision-making, which resolved much of the uncertainty that had surrounded dispute settlement prior to the Uruguay Round.

The new DSU procedure is divisible into the following steps. The Parties are first required to engage in consultation, discussing the disputed matter in an attempt to reach a mutually agreeable solution. If no such agreement is reached, the complaining Party may request the establishment of a panel, which, in the absence of consensus to the contrary, is a matter for decision by the WTO Dispute Settlement Body. The Panel, which constitutes three experts, rules on the matter, generally involving conformity of specific measures, within the limits of the terms of reference. If there is a finding of inconsistency with WTO obligations, the Panel will recommend that the measures in question be brought into conformity. The report of the Panel may then be adopted by the DSB or appealed to the WTO Appellate Body (AB). If the decision is not appealed, the report will be adopted by the DSB unless a decision to the

---

[167] Ibid.

contrary is taken by negative consensus: in other words, every Member agrees that the report cannot be approved.[168]

The Appellate Body is a permanent body, comprising seven Members that are appointed by the DSB for a four-year term. The AB, which is competent to review issues of law, "may affirm, modify or reverse panel reports."[169] Adoption of the AB report is again the responsibility of the DSB, subject to the standard decision-making process by the negative consensus rule. Following adoption, the party in breach is given a reasonable period of time to implement the decision, a matter which may be further litigated, after which the complaining party can request authorization to retaliate.[170]

This new and detailed agreement therefore addressed a few criticisms of the previous GATT dispute settlement system. Concerns regarding legal uncertainty and unpredictability gave rise to a set of normative, step-by-step, rules embodied in one specific agreement. Concerns about reliability and independence of panels were addressed by a procedure for their establishment, which also sought to minimize the chances of formation of only a partial panel. The naming of panelists is accordingly to be undertaken by consensus among the parties, and in the absence of consensus by appointment of the Director-General.

Finally, two noticeable improvements were made in relation to concerns about enforcement. First, the change in the consensus rule, from the previous unanimity or majority rule to "consensus to the contrary," makes it more difficult for losing parties to "block" the implementation of decisions. Secondly, the establishment of a full set of procedures for implementation and surveillance of compliance increases the chances that decisions by the Panel and Appellate Body will be effective.

This DSU mechanism, with its Panel and Appellate Body structure, applies to disputes brought pursuant to all "covered agreements," including the SCM Agreement. The nature of the subsidy will, however, determine the specific steps involved in resolution of a controversy caused by subsidy.

As mentioned, a subsidy is prohibited under SCM Agreement Article 3.1(a), if its award is contingent upon exports (export subsidy) or if,

---

[168] There is, thus, "always a result, unlike the situation under GATT, when a consensus (including the losing party) was needed to adopt a report." William J Davey, "The WTO Dispute Settlement System" in The World Bank (ed), *Legal Aspects of International Trade* (Legal Aspects of International Trade, The World Bank 2001) p. 207.

[169] Ibid.

[170] Disputes over the level of retaliation are resolved by arbitration. See ibid.

under Article 3.1(b), it is tied to the consumption of domestic over imported goods (import substitution subsidy). Determination as to whether a prohibited subsidy exists is a decision for the WTO dispute settlement panels and the AB, competent interpreters of WTO law, with the assistance upon request of a "permanent Group of Experts" (SCM Article 4.5).[171]

In the event of a finding of prohibited subsidy, the subsidizing Member is obliged to withdraw it (SCM Agreement, Article 4.7), but this outcome can be avoided if parties are able, through consultations, to find a mutually agreeable solution (SCM Articles 4.1 and 4.3).

An actionable subsidy, although not forbidden, may be challenged if it causes an adverse effect on the interests of other Members (SCM Agreement, Article 5) or seriously prejudices the interests of another Member (SCM Article 5(c) and Article 6). Interests are violated, under SCM Article 5, if there is (a) injury to the domestic industry of another Member; (b) nullification or impairment of GATT 1994 benefits; or (c) serious prejudice to the interests of other members caused by the subsidy. This list is not, however, exhaustive. Remedial measures in relation to actionable subsidies are set out in SCM Agreement, Article 7. The subsidizing Member may either eliminate or withdraw the adverse effects (SCM, Article 7.8).

4.3.2.5.2.2   Non-Violation Claims

The two main avenues for initiation of dispute by GATT/WTO parties, as previously mentioned, are via non-violation and violation claims. The key to the notion of NVCs is a reliance on the capacity of a country to initiate a dispute in the WTO Dispute Settlement System without having to demonstrate a specific violation of the WTO Agreements.

While legal scholars have long criticized NVCs, economists offer a different take on this issue. They have argued that NVCs are covered by the GATT rules on nullification and impairment on grounds that the general rule (that Members are not to nullify or impair benefits of tariff

---

[171] The SCM Agreement foresees the establishment of a "Permanent Group of Experts composed of five independent persons, highly qualified in the fields of subsidies and trade relations. The experts will be elected ... and one of them will be replaced every year. The PGE may be requested to assist a panel, as provided for in paragraph 5 of Article 4." This PGE may also give advisory opinion on "on the existence and nature of any subsidy."

reduction) addresses terms-of-trade concerns: the manipulation of terms-of-trade, which is closely associated with changes in levels of imports, could be perceived as an action that nullifies or impairs trade gains.

The topic is particularly important to the regulation of subsidies, because "the paradigm non-violation case was a new (post-negotiation) subsidy to domestic firms that compete with imports."[172] Even though domestic subsidies are now actionable, "so that the non-violation claim is no longer needed"[173] to facilitate challenges in this regard, analysis of the NVC is helpful for understanding the development of the rules on subsidies.

Direct reference to non-violation mechanisms is found in DSU Article 26 and GATT Article XXIII. This unorthodox legal instrument is routinely justified on the basis of its contractual flexibility, in terms of the need to address those policies impeding market access that were not foreseen by negotiators.[174] An NVC can be used therefore against measures that have not been explicitly regulated, but that might nevertheless impair or nullify the benefits of negotiated tariff reductions. The motivation for this facility is twofold. First, Members "have reasonable expectations that they can benefit from tariff concessions,"[175] and secondly, Members have "by making tariff concessions themselves"[176] already paid for this market access. Should benefits accruing from GATT-negotiated tariff reductions be nullified or impaired, therefore, an NVC could be used to restore this balance "by providing for a compensatory adjustment in the obligations which the contracting party has assumed."[177]

---

[172] Staiger and Sykes, "Non-Violations" p. 754.

[173] Ibid. p. 754.

[174] "Economists have identified a broad range of policy measures that can impede market access, and that are unregulated or weakly regulated by existing GATT/WTO law. As a result, important terms of trade externalities can arise from policies that do not violate the rules." Ibid. p. 758.

[175] Coppens, WTO Disciplines on Subsidies and Countervailing Measures: Balancing Policy Space and Legal Constraints p. 129.

[176] Ibid.

[177] UN document EPCT/A/PV/6 (1947) 5. See also EU Petersmann, The GATT/WTO Dispute Settlement System: International Law, International Organizations and Dispute Settlement (Springer Netherlands 1997) p. 135–70. This purpose remained a valid concern up until the institutionalization of the multilateral trade system, with the advent of the WTO and confirmed by the Panel in Japan – Film: "to protect the balance of concessions under GATT by providing a means to redress government actions not otherwise regulated by GATT rules that nonetheless nullify or impair a Member's legitimate expectations of benefits from tariff negotiations" Panel Report, Japan – Film, para. 1050.

In theory, therefore, if NVCs could be used against subsidies with harmful trade effects, state implementation of trade policy would require closer consideration of its cross border effects, and the GATT would constitute adequate regulation of production subsidies. In a sense, therefore, NVCs were an effective mechanism for internalization of the externalities related to domestic subsidies.[178] Given that domestic subsidies are not restricted generally, but only as to their effects, this "soft" regulation provides some flexibility, giving states a margin of appreciation in which to make use of domestic subsidies that do not result in effects of nullification and impairment.

In fact, certain economists argue that not only were the rules pre-SCM Agreement adequate, but their strengthening during the Uruguay Round has proven to be undesirable, as WTO Members now lack this policy margin and are afraid to commit to further rounds of liberalization.[179]

Legal scholars, however, commonly assert that in practice NVCs cast doubt on the efficacy of the economic perspective on the GATT rules regarding domestic subsidies. Cho argues that NVCs are a "potentially problematic over-expansion of the WTO's jurisdiction,"[180] and in the history of GATT disputes states have proven to be reluctant to make use of this legal remedy,[181] which is only exceptionally applicable.[182]

---

[178] "In principle, a non-violation doctrine might be implemented to require that when nations make policy decisions that affect the terms of trade for others, they must make commensurate adjustments in their trade policies to restore the terms of trade to its original level, thereby eliminating the 'nullification or impairment.' In that way, the nation making the policy choice will 'internalize the externality' from its decisions. Unsurprisingly, policy choices subject to such a rule will tend to be efficient in relation to the policy making government's own welfare metric. The non-violation doctrine thus works much like a Pigouvian tax in neoclassical economics—a trade law equivalent to the 'polluter pays principle.'" Staiger and Sykes, "Non-Violations" p. 759.

[179] Kyle Bagwell and Robert W Staiger, "Will International Rules on Subsidies Disrupt the World Trading System?" (2006) The American Economic Review p. 877–95. For a critical discussion, which is usually shared by legal scholars, see Coppens, WTO Disciplines on Subsidies and Countervailing Measures: Balancing Policy Space and Legal Constraints p. 446.

[180] Sung-joon Cho, "GATT Non-Violation Issues in the WTO Framework: Are They the Achilles' Heel of the Dispute Settlement Process" (1998) 39 Harv Int'l LJ p. 311.

[181] As noted in the literature, "there have been few non-violation complaints," Bossche and Zdouc, The Law and Policy of the World Trade Organization: Text, Cases, and Materials p. 185.

[182] See Panel Report, US – Offset Act (Byrd Amendment), paras. 7.127; and also Coppens, WTO Disciplines on Subsidies and Countervailing Measures: Balancing Policy Space and Legal Constraints p. 128.

Moreover, "[n]one of the non-violation complaints brought to the WTO to date has been successful."[183]

This apparent failure of NVCs in the WTO dispute settlement system is due, in part, to the difficulty of building a *prima facie* case against a measure that does not present as immediately inconsistent with the agreement,[184] but also relates to concern by Members about potential use of NVCs by their trade partners to restrict policies that are not regulated by the multilateral trading system. As stated by Cho, NVCs may result in a "proliferation of harmful cases where Members have yet to establish substantive norms upon which panels can decide cases."[185] While the GATT rules were therefore in principle capable of addressing the substantive issues related to domestic subsidies, their application was subject to a high level of legal uncertainty. As NVCs were, furthermore, "ineffective instruments to protect exporters' interests in third markets,"[186] other legal mechanisms were necessary to address the externalities that arose from subsidized trade with third nations.

4.3.2.6 Subsidies Committee

The "Committee on Subsidies and Countervailing Measures" (Subsidies Committee, or Committee), established in accordance with Article 24 of the SCM Agreement, is composed of representatives from each of the Members, and is required to meet not less than twice a year.[187] Its main function is to supervise the implementation of the Agreement by carrying out "the responsibilities assigned to it under the SCM Agreement."[188] The Committee "is the primary mechanism for monitoring and surveillance of subsidy measures and ensuring compliance."[189]

---

[183] Bossche and Zdouc, *The Law and Policy of the World Trade Organization: Text, Cases, and Materials* p. 185.

[184] Coppens describes that "the burden on formulating a NVC under the GATT era was set high by GATT panels," Coppens, *WTO Disciplines on Subsidies and Countervailing Measures: Balancing Policy Space and Legal Constraints* p. 448.

[185] Cho, "GATT Non-Violation Issues in the WTO Framework: Are They the Achilles' Heel of the Dispute Settlement Process" p. 311.

[186] Coppens, *WTO Disciplines on Subsidies and Countervailing Measures: Balancing Policy Space and Legal Constraints* p. 32.

[187] Bossche and Zdouc, *The Law and Policy of the World Trade Organization: Text, Cases, and Materials* p. 833.

[188] Ibid.

[189] See Rezaul Karim, "Transparency is the Most Important Governance Issue in the WTO Subsidy Control" <http://ssrn.com/abstract=2498863> accessed 07.20.2016, p. 13.

Among other things, the Subsidies Committee is responsible for examination of "all new and full notifications at special sessions,"[190] the design of the "questionnaire for subsidy notifications,"[191] and establishment of "procedures for annual Committee review of notifications."[192] Further, "the ASCM provides for questioning, peer review and other discussion in the Committee for implementation of the subsidy obligations."[193]

As described by Pauwelyn:

> The PGE has three functions: (1) it may be requested to assist a panel 'with regard to whether the measure in question is a prohibited subsidy' (Article 4.5 of the Subsidies Agreement); much like expert review groups, the PGE must submit a report to the Panel, but unlike expert review groups, the PGE's conclusion 'shall be accepted by the Panel without modification'; (2) the Committee on Subsidies may seek an advisory opinion 'on the existence and nature of subsidy'; and (3) any WTO member may consult the PGE and the PGE may give advisory opinions 'on the nature of any subsidy proposed to be introduced or currently maintained by that Member; such advisory opinion are confidential and may not be used in dispute settlement procedures regarding actionable subsidies.[194]

In support of the proper administration and performance of its functions, SCM Article 24, at paragraphs 24.2 and 24.3, establishes that "the Subsidies Committee may set up subsidiary bodies, including the Permanent Group of Experts (PGE),"[195] which is composed of five independent experts.[196] The PGE, therefore, has an important function in relation to clarification and advice regarding the technical information surrounding subsidies policies.

---

[190] See ibid.
[191] See ibid.
[192] See ibid.
[193] See ibid. p. 14.
[194] Joost Pauwelyn, "The Use of Experts in WTO Dispute Settlement" (2002) 51 *International and Comparative Law Quarterly* p. 325–64, 336.
[195] Bossche and Zdouc, *The Law and Policy of the World Trade Organization: Text, Cases, and Materials* p. 833.
[196] "The PGE may be requested to assist panels, in accordance with Article 24.3, or may be consulted by any Member and may give confidential advisory opinions on the existence and nature of any subsidy pursuant to Article 24.4. The Subsidies Committee or its advisory bodies may, as foreseen in Article 24.5, consult with and seek information from any source," ibid.

4.4 Assessing the Current System of Entitlement and Entitlement Protection

A complex system of entitlements and entitlement protection was established by the SCM Agreement to regulate the use of subsidies and their corresponding externalities. Prohibited subsidies are regulated strictly as to both commitments and remedies, although the language of the rules on export subsidies suggests that this subcategory of prohibited subsidy enjoys a higher degree of flexibility than is permitted in relation to the subcategory comprising import substitution subsidies.

Commitments on actionable subsidies are not as strict as those in relation to prohibited subsidies, and remedies grant a greater degree of flexibility. The need to test for specificity and adverse effects[197] and a less stringent protection are coherent with the overall economic understanding of the SCM Agreement. The economic literature indicates that, compared to a prohibited subsidy, an (actionable) domestic subsidy that is not contingent on export performance or import substitution has arguably less direct impact on international trade and greater recognition as a policy instrument.[198] The SCM Agreement requires, therefore, that to successfully challenge such a subsidy a complainant party must prove not only the existence of a discriminatory subsidy, but also that it causes harm. Even if adverse effects are demonstrably caused by the subsidy, the subsidizing WTO Member has the option of preserving the measure and paying compensation. There are mixed reviews, however, as to the impact of this provision on opportunistic use of the measure.

The additional tests for specificity and harm provide, on the one hand, an extra element of good faith to the analysis of the measure, so that if the subsidy is not specific, or it does not cause harm, its use is found to accord with WTO rules. As described in Section 4.3.2.2, however, the specificity test is not equipped to function as a justificatory mechanism,[199] which leaves it to the adverse effects test to introduce a certain degree of flexibility in the use of good faith subsidies. This test is complex and will be analyzed in more detail in Chapter 5.

Evaluation of the effect of a liability rule in the SCM Agreement also suggests that difficulty with assessment by third parties has hindered the full application of the Agreement as a mechanism of flexibility. In contract theory, liability rules are usually the preferred

---

[197] Both additional tests not present in a prohibited subsidies analysis.
[198] WTO, *Exploring the Links between Subsidies, Trade and the WTO* p. 65.
[199] See Section 5.2.2.1.1.

remedy because they give a party discretion to opt for a particular measure if it is willing to compensate the other party, leaving the affected party in a position that is as good as if performance had taken place. Liability rules guarantee contractual gains, while preserving freedom of choice.[200]

In theory, assessing the value of liability or compensation should be a simple task: if State A has lost access to the market of State B, valued at X amount, due to an actionable subsidy, A should be entitled to receive X amount in compensation from B. Assessment of the preferences of a harmed state, however, is a complex task, and it is unclear whether monetary compensation or access to other areas of the market will suffice to balance the harm caused to a (politically) relevant economic sector. The courts might, moreover, have to confront problems in their ability to observe, verify, and quantify the consistency of a measure in an evaluation *ex post*.[201]

The parties themselves might deal with this problem by finding a negotiated solution for disputes, but the approach is subject to a second level of opportunistic behavior. One party might, for example, conceal information about its true preferences, or its evaluation of harms and gains, in an attempt to increase what it extracts from the surplus, which, if the allegedly harmed (opportunistic) party is successful, could prevent the use of legitimate domestic subsidies. If, on the contrary, the subsidizing state is successful, the harmed party will suffer a loss and be left in a worse position than if performance had occurred. This situation calls, once again, for the intervention of courts or external bodies.

In contract theory, the courts offer a relevant vehicle for assessment of the good faith of measures, but it is less clear whether they have the expertise to assess the welfare impact of subsidies and the political impact of a measure on a WTO Member. Alternatively, WTO Members might recall that they have competence to use an expert body, composed of parties appointed by the Members, to assess these issues. A similar body of experts already exists under the SCM Agreement, but has never been fully put into operation.

---

[200] As noted by Pauwelyn: "Here, as well, the remedy is not cessation or specific performance, as there is no violation in the first place, but rather the obligation to 'make a mutually satisfactory adjustment' (DSU Article 26:1b) for which arbitration is made available to objectively assess the level of benefits that have been nullified or impaired (DSU Article 26:1c)," Pauwelyn, *Optimal Protection of International Law* p. 136.

[201] See Section 2.4.2.

To sum up, the balance between commitments and flexibilities in regards to actionable subsidies seems to be more coherent than that evident in relation to prohibited subsidies. Commitments on actionable subsidies require additional tests for determination of specificity (discrimination) and harm, which could be understood as steps towards a good faith evaluation of the measure. With regard to remedies, the Agreement leaves a margin of discretion to the WTO Member to decide, in accordance with its preferences, whether it is worth paying compensation in order to make use of a subsidy.

In contract theory, if the other party is adequately compensated, the preferred remedy will tend to involve liability rules over property rules. The higher flexibility that these afford actionable subsidies finds support in economic theory, as economists have long affirmed that domestic subsidies are an important instrument with which to tackle domestic market failures.[202] The use of a liability rule, however, leaves open the possibility of a second level of opportunistic behavior in relation to compensation. Considering that compensation of states often involves political preferences that courts are not necessarily equipped to deal with, judicial assessment of harms and gains may not always be accurate, leaving the subsidizing party in the position, permitted by a liability rule, to breach the rules.

A better solution would be to ensure that WTO Members act upon their responsibility to undergo such an evaluation. In other international legal fora, the role is delegated to a body of experts appointed by the states. The relevant body, although established by the SCM Agreement, has not yet commenced operations, thus opening the door to misunderstandings in relation to compensation.

The SCM Agreement rules on subsidies, whether prohibited or actionable, impose restrictions on the use of industrial subsidies by WTO Members as a means of avoiding possible opportunistic uses of subsidies. Commitments are but one side of subsidies regulation, and the introduction of flexibility into a treaty is necessary to address the legal and economic realities of international trade relations. The SCM Agreement should, therefore, have included contractual flexibilities that permit the use of good faith subsidies as a means of facilitating policy and addressing emergencies. Legal and economic theory would say that WTO

---

[202] Besides, as argued above, export subsidies are more clearly protectionist and are more difficult to be justified by legitimate reasons. Rubini, *The Definition of Subsidy and State Aid: WTO and EC Law in Comparative Perspective* p. 370.

Members should be given sufficient "policy space" to enable the use of certain subsidies without payment of compensation. The question, therefore, is how to identify the current flexibility mechanisms in the SCM Agreement that facilitate the distinction between opportunistic and good faith subsidies.

5

Defining Uncertainty in the SCM Agreement

The negotiation and drafting of treaties, as discussed in Chapter 2, is generally subject to costs. The implication of "bounded rationality" for the formation of contracts is that rational policymakers cannot be expected to foresee all future contingencies and probabilities, nor to draft complex, consistently bulletproof, clauses. Treaty analysis must therefore take into account that there will be "human contracting errors."[1]

It is, consequently, to be expected that every treaty will be incomplete and that such contractual incompleteness will provide an impetus for parties to make use of flexibility instruments, such as general conceptual standards and default rules.[2]

Uncertainty in contract theory is commonly classified as "uncertainty about the future (unforeseeability), uncertainty about the actions of other players (asymmetrical information), and uncertainty about the meaning and scope of contractual provisions (e.g., textual ambiguity)."[3] In legal theory, the categorization of types of uncertainty has been developed into frameworks that seek to devise specific flexibility mechanisms that address the corresponding incompleteness. The application of these

---

[1] This term is credited to Schropp, *Trade Policy Flexibility and Enforcement in the WTO: A Law and Economic Analysis* p. 64.

[2] WTO, *Exploring the Links between Subsidies, Trade and the WTO* p. 45. Schropp makes a detailed description of the reasons for contract incompleteness, manly focusing on transaction costs, which he defines in temporal terms (*ex ante* or *ex post* the drafting of the contract for the later) and to the relation between the costs and the contract (exogenous and endogenous costs) and on rationality, which as he points out might lead to uncertainties of its own due to the limitations of rational parties, an issue commonly discussed in the literature as bounded rationality, as discussed in Section 2.3.2.2. Also, see Schropp, *Trade Policy Flexibility and Enforcement in the WTO: A Law and Economic Analysis* p. 62–77.

[3] van Aaken, "Delegating Interpretative Authority in Investment Treaties: The Case of Joint Commissions" p. 26.

Table 12: *Contractual outcomes of incompleteness.*

Incompleteness					
Treaty language			Enforcement		
Ambiguous	Insufficient	Too rigid	Detectable	Verifiable	Quantifiable

Source: Based on Schropp[4]

frameworks requires a better understanding of the uncertainties to which policymakers are subject during the negotiation of subsidy rules.

5.1 The Uncertainty in the SCM Agreement

Uncertainty, as discussed in Chapter 2, might result in two sets of problems, one related to treaty language, and the other to enforcement. Treaty language is potentially: (a) ambiguous and ambivalent; (b) insufficient, leading to gaps and loopholes, which can permit harm to victims of *ex post* nonperformance; and (c) overly rigid or restrictive, failing to allow for regret contingencies, and potentially undermining good faith breaches. Enforcement can be deficient because it is not (a) detectable; (b) verifiable; or (c) quantifiable. Parties to a subsidies agreement are expected to make use of flexibility mechanisms, therefore, to promote *ex post* adjustments in the level of commitments.

A critical analysis of the flexibility mechanisms currently employed by the SCM Agreement demands a detailed examination of the uncertainties to which negotiators were subject during the drafting process. The economic analysis and record of negotiations presented in Chapters 3 and 4 offer a comprehensive source of information and insight in support of this investigation. The following analysis, using contract theory, divides uncertainty into three categories: unforeseeability, ambiguity, and information asymmetry.

5.1.1 Unforeseeability

Treaties are the result of a negotiation process, as discussed in Chapter 2, in which states aim to improve their welfare by transacting in

---

[4] Schropp, Trade Policy Flexibility and Enforcement in the WTO: A Law and Economic Analysis.

jurisdiction. To achieve a treaty, states will negotiate until they meet participation constraints: until benefits of the agreement outweigh the costs to each of the parties. The balance thus achieved is, however, unstable, as it is subject to future events that might alter the cost benefit relationship of the agreement.

Such events are "contingencies" if they are not otherwise absorbed, provoking a reaction by the state.[5] For the purpose of this analysis, contingencies can be classified into those that improve welfare (or create conditions conducive to such improvement), and those that diminish welfare.

Several types of economic event are capable of improving welfare within a country.[6] Companies might, for instance, by achieving better labor specialization, gradually become more efficient, and increase their market share in international markets. This will have a positive effect on the terms-of-trade of the country, which could cause harm to competing industries abroad. It is the system of market economy, however, that leads to overall gains in efficiency.

As this analysis is concerned mainly with subsidies, its focus will be the impact of contingencies on governments. As was discussed in Chapter 2, governments have legitimate reasons for using subsidies to prevent market failures. In circumstances of economic development, situations might arise in which it becomes rational for governments to intervene, even though this was not a viable option when provisions for the regulation of subsidies were being negotiated.[7] Government action in regard to increasing concerns about environmentally harmful emissions, for example, may not have been contemplated in prior treaty commitments, due to the absence during negotiations of available technology with which to reduce them.

The effect of contingencies on welfare can also be negative, the obvious example being natural and social disasters. Governments are often

---

[5] Schropp, *Trade Policy Flexibility and Enforcement in the WTO: A Law and Economic Analysis* p. 62.

[6] van Aaken, "Delegating Interpretative Authority in Investment Treaties: The Case of Joint Commissions" p. 29.

[7] For instance, the expansion of firms in new markets might give rise to a shortage in specialized labor force. As the market for education could suffer from imperfections, it could be reasonable to expect that the government subsidizes training to meet this new demand. Similarly, technological advances could enable a state to tackle failures in new markets, for instance, in the generation of renewable energies or in the market for broadband internet access. See WTO, Exploring the Links between Subsidies, Trade and the WTO.

expected, if not obliged by domestic law, to intervene by all available means to redress the severity of negative impacts on the economy caused by natural disasters. Such means may include the subsidization of aid products and services, but also support for the reconstruction of infrastructure and businesses.

Certain negative effects of economic development might also be appropriately ameliorated by subsidies. Should the introduction of a new technology lead to significant unemployment in a labor-intensive industry, for instance, government intervention could be used, if the market is unable to retrain this workforce, to raise education to a socially optimal level.[8]

Despite the divergence of these scenarios, in which one improves welfare and the other controls or prevents its fall, each affects the welfare balance that was agreed *ex ante* by the parties. The difficulty is that, even though some contingencies (such as, for example, susceptibility to earthquakes in certain geographical locations) may be anticipated, parties are generally unable to determine with any precision what the contingencies are, or their likelihood *ex ante*, and will therefore also fail to define with accuracy an effective course of action to be taken should a contingency occur.[9]

The impact on treaty-drafting is thus rather straightforward. Though negotiators might spend considerable resources trying to anticipate all contingencies, there will still be unpredictable future situations that are not regulated by the agreement, thus calling for an *ex post* completion of the rules.

5.1.2   Textual Ambiguity

Textual ambiguity arises when the language of an instrument gives rise, purposefully or not, to ambiguity related to rights and obligations, making it difficult to detect the occurrence of a breach.[10]

---

[8] See the discussion on externalities in Chapter 3, Section 3.3.2.2.2, and also Mankiw, *Principles of Macroeconomics* p. 223; DeRemer, *The Evolution of International Subsidy Rules* p. 2–13; Friederiszick, Röller, and Verouden, "European State Aid Control: An Economic Framework" p. 640; and, for an overview of the trade impacts of externalities, see WTO, *Exploring the Links between Subsidies, Trade and the WTO* p. 55.

[9] The issue of contingencies and its impacts on treaty-making have been addressed in Chapter 2. See for instance Robert E Scott and Paul B Stephan, *The Limits of Leviathan: Contract Theory and the Enforcement of International Law* (1st edn, Cambridge University Press 2011) p. 59–83.

[10] See van Aaken, "Delegating Interpretative Authority in Investment Treaties: The Case of Joint Commissions" p. 28.

A major source of ambiguity specific to agreements regulating subsidies is the variety of definitions that might apply to the concept of subsidy.[11] The problem is not merely semantic, as these definitions reflect divergent conceptions of the permissible role or level of state intervention in the economy.[12]

The complexity of the problem will be apparent, especially to policymakers, with regard to the potential effects of subsidies on sensitive spheres of public policy, as well as the maintenance of the state and its valued constituencies. The definitional problem therefore constitutes a source of acute uncertainty for the regulation of subsidies. Attempts to prevent the use of specific subsidies by other states could reveal to policymakers that whether due to a simple inability to anticipate the reach of the rules, or to difficulties inherent in complex contractual drafting, their hands are tied in particular policy areas. While social programs, such as child allowances or homeowner credit guarantees might, for instance, fall under direct or potential expenses, governmental services also commonly encompass education and public transport, and regulatory policy deals routinely with delicate issues such as security, border controls, and long-term government objectives.

The issue of definition is closely related to the versatility of subsidies as a policy measure capable of reaching multiple objectives through various legal measures. Subsidies are employed in pursuit of a wide range of policy objectives, from industrial innovation and development to social redistribution, the provision of public services, the adjustment of regional imbalances,[13] the mitigation of harmful effects on declining

---

[11] This can be spotted in the records on the use of subsidies and public spending of domestic institutions and governments. See WTO, *Exploring the Links between Subsidies, Trade and the WTO* p. 47.

[12] Economists have not yet managed to achieve one single and unanimous concept of subsidy, but have rather established a few basic consensual elements for its existence. The lack of a unanimous definition has nonetheless not prevented economics from explaining what the basic general effects of subsidies. Economic models have been devised to determine the effects of subsidies in closed markets, in markets opened to international trade, and in several other specific markets, such as the market for innovation.

[13] Germany has provided several measures of economic and social support to deal with issues arising due to the re-unification. A detailed overview of subsidies in Germany at the moment of reunification can be found in Frank Stille and Dieter Teichmann, "German Subsidisation Policy in the Wake of Unification" (1993) 29 *Economic Bulletin* p. 11–18; and a critical view can be found in Hans-Werner Sinn, "Germany's Economic Unification: An Assessment after Ten Years" (2002) 10 *Review of International Economics* p. 113–28.

industries,[14] and the protection of cultural[15] and environmental[16] assets. Governments can, further, direct subsidies to specifically pinpointed domestic actor(s) and choose to benefit them either directly, or in indirect ways by, for instance, giving consumers credit to be used exclusively in the purchase of a certain good in order to benefit its producer. Moreover, once a policy objective has been chosen, innumerable administrative measures, such as tax breaks and monetary transfers, are available to policymakers for implementation of the subsidy.[17] The design of the subsidy to be used as a policy measure is a relevant consideration because subsidies vary with regard to the extent of the distortive effects that they are likely to cause.[18]

The potential for a subsidy to create distortion is related to the design of the subsidy measure. In general terms, "specific" subsidies, which are conferred on a particular subset of companies (selective) or that disproportionately benefit a certain subset of market agents (asymmetric), are most likely to cause distortions.[19]

The effect of the payment timeline on distortion is less straightforward. "Recurrent" subsidies are more likely to preserve, for longer, the presence

---

[14] Schwartz and Sykes argue, for instance, that it might be "politically efficient from the perspective of parties to trade agreements to afford transitory protection to import-competing industries suffering severe dislocation, at the expense of growing and prosperous foreign competitor," Warren F Schwartz and Alan O Sykes, "The Economic Structure of Renegotiation and Dispute Resolution in the World Trade Organization" p. 8.

[15] State policies, also through subsidies, play an important role in culture and arts, and internationally recognized policies might as well conflict with the WTO rules regulating subsidies, as in Mira Burri-Nenova, "Trade versus Culture in the Digital Environment: An Old Conflict in Need of a New Definition" (2009) 12 *Journal of International Economic Law* p. 17–62; and also Michael Hahn, "A Clash of Cultures? The UNESCO Diversity Convention and International Trade Law" (2006) 9 *Journal of International Economic Law* p. 515–52.

[16] For an interesting overview of the use of subsidies as an instrument of environmental policy, see Andrew Green, "Trade Rules and Climate Change Subsidies" (2006) 5 *World Trade Review* p. 377–414; and also for a discussion about the consistency of environmentally friendly subsidies with WTO law, see Rubini, "Ain't Wastin' Time No More: Subsidies for Renewable Energy, The SCM Agreement, Policy Space, and Law Reform."

[17] For an extensive analysis on the application of subsidies and state aid rules to tax incentives, see Claire Micheau, *State Aid, Subsidy and Tax Incentives under EU and WTO Law* (Wolters Kluwer 2014).

[18] UK, Public Subsidies p. 6–7; and Grossman and Mavroidis, "US–Lead and Bismuth II: United States–Imposition of Countervailing Duties on Certain Hot-Rolled Lead and Bismuth Carbon Steel Products Originating in the United Kingdom: Here Today, Gone Tomorrow? Privatization and the Injury Caused by Non–Recurring Subsidies."

[19] See UK, *Public Subsidies* p. 6–7; and WTO, *Exploring the Links between Subsidies, Trade and the WTO* p. 45–54.

of (subsidized) inefficient companies in the market, and to cause corresponding profit reduction to competitors, thus stimulating their exit from the market. One-off subsidies may nevertheless be relevant "when firms' costs are not evenly spread"[20] in cases in which, for instance, a company is entering a new market or developing a new technology, both of which activities which usually require a large upfront dedication of resources.

The amount of a subsidy is also relevant to distortion, because it is the larger grants, especially in relation to the variable costs of production that are most likely to have an impact on the behavior of a firm. Subsidies that are freely used by the firm and not tied to a particular activity tend also, however, to have significant impact on markets, because the targeted subsidy may have only an indirect effect on costs. Subsidies for training activities, for instance, tend to have an impact on costs that is lower than the impact of a tax relief used freely by the firm to offset costs.

To facilitate the analysis, it could be said that judicial determination of the consistency of a measure with international rules will generally, in the absence of clearly applicable exceptions, be confronted by two alternatives. The courts might decide that the measure is outside the scope of application of the SCM Agreement and cannot therefore be deemed inconsistent with it, or that it falls under the Agreement, in which case they have recourse to various rules in the Agreement with which to introduce, within the boundaries of their competence, an appropriate degree of flexibility. These two scenarios are discussed below.

First, only subsidies that are specific, as previously discussed, fall within the scope of the SCM Agreement. Should a measure fail to fulfill any of the elements of Articles 1, 2, or 3 of the SCM Agreement, the measure is outside of its scope and cannot be considered to be inconsistent with it. The second scenario involves analysis of judicial interpretation regarding the remedies to be applied in case of breach. The nature and extent of applicable remedies, as discussed in Chapter 2, are crucial to the assurance of optimum compliance. In contract theory, compliance, it may be recalled, is not the equivalent of complete deterrence of a behavior. On the contrary, where flexibility is required, remedies may provide an important legal instrument with which to foster or prevent behavior, as is appropriate to the various purposes and parts of a treaty. In order to undertake an analysis of the capacity of courts to resolve legal ambiguity in a manner that introduces

[20] See UK, *Public Subsidies* p. 6–7.

flexibility while controlling for opportunistic behavior, it is necessary to first understand the WTO enforcement system as applied to subsidies. The following section will briefly introduce the enforcement system before analyzing the SCM Agreement rules on definition of subsidy, and remedies that apply in the event of breach.

Contracts, as discussed in Chapter 2, make an explicit effort to regulate behavior through the clear definition of rights and obligations of the parties. Given the existence of incentives for parties to defect, however, enforcement is an equally important feature of the law of treaty and contract. Enforcement is an important topic in international studies because, unlike domestic law, the international system lacks clear centralization of enforcement power. In light of this special feature of international law, states will often devise singular rules of enforcement.

In the GATT system, for instance, parties had recourse to a dispute settlement system based on the political consent of all the parties. In regard to subsidies, states have devised unilateral measures capable of handling the undesirable effects of foreign subsidies within their territories. As reviewed in more detail below, not only were these unilateral measures economically inefficient, but they opened the door for opportunistic behavior. It was necessary, therefore, to build a stronger system of enforcement, to deal with both the political components of the dispute settlement system, and the excessive unilateralism promoted by some of the Contracting Parties.

During the initial stages of negotiation of the Havana Charter,[21] enforcement had already become a concern, and the GATT made provision for unilateral and multilateral action, including non-violation claims. Article XVI permitted Contracting Parties to seek consultations, with the intent of limiting subsidization wherever a subsidy caused or threatened to cause serious prejudice. In the absence of a stronger mechanism, Contracting Parties would have had recourse at the multilateral level to the non-violation claim, a remedy of doubtful efficacy, which would have only poorly equipped the courts to interpret the GATT rules for purposes of application in practice. Decisions in the GATT dispute resolution system were, further, contingent upon acceptance by all the parties, subjecting enforcement to political will and compromise among states.

---

[21] Concerning Countervailing Duties, the Havana Charter (article 34) defined its concept as measures exclusively against unfair subsidization, basing the limitations of CVDs on this definition. Havana Charter Article 34.

5.1.3   Asymmetrical Information

Hidden contingencies are not the only uncertainty to which negotiators are subject in the drafting of a subsidies agreement. Even if all contingencies that improve or diminish welfare could be foreseen, their effects may not be apparent: there could be uncertainty about their "real" as opposed to perceived effects on the welfare of various parties, and about the permissibility of measures used to address what a party might construe as an opportunistic behavior.

Insecurity about foreign state intentions is the result of rational fear that the parties may take opportunities to hide relevant information or disguise their real motives in order to appropriate a larger share of contractual gains.[22] Negotiators may feel that it is easy for other states to make use of the regulatory complexity that surrounds such issues, which can make it difficult to evaluate potentially opportunistic behavior. A problematic lack of "observability" arises from limitations on availability of information, which can prevent the harmed party from detection of a failure, independent assessment of its extent, and evaluation of the appropriateness of the subsidizing state response to it. These limitations can also cause verification issues by undermining the ability of parties to generate, at reasonable cost, sufficient factual evidence to convince a third party of the existence of a failure, or the appropriateness or inconsistency of a measure.

Observability has particular relevance for controversies over "how to correct for market failures"[23] because a government, attempting to adequately address a market failure with an effective and welfare-enhancing subsidy, needs to be able to correctly diagnose the problem in order to appropriately tailor its measure.

There are at least three issues that might affect the judgment of a government in its evaluation of the existence and extent of a market failure and preparation of an appropriate response. One such issue is

---

[22] See the discussion on Chapter 1 about cooperation, Section 2.2.2. See also Martin, "The Rational State Choice of Multilateralism" p. 91–93.

[23] In economics, the existence of market failures is widely accepted, and it is "certainly possible to investigate whether a market failure is likely to exist at all and whether it is significant," but establishing parameters for tackling such failures seem to be a less unanimous field. Hans W Friederiszick, Lars-Hendrik Röller, and Vincent Verouden, "EC State Aid Control: An Economic Perspective" in Michael Sánchez Rydelski (ed), *The EC State Aid Regime: Distortive Effects of State Aid on Competition and Trade* (The EC State Aid Regime: Distortive Effects of State Aid on Competition and Trade, Cambridge University Press 2006) p. 160.

"measurability." While economic theory has identified several markets in which failures are prevalent, the task of determining the precise magnitude of a failure can, in practice, be complex and difficult. While it may be feasible, therefore, to conduct a qualitative market assessment related to existence of a failure, a quantitative assessment of the issue is more complicated.[24]

Another problem is that, even if governments could correctly assess the magnitude of the failure, it is difficult to weigh up the "costs and benefits" of intervention. While the benefits that flow from the subsidy might be desirable, subsidies also produce costs that are difficult to measure. If the costs are higher than the benefits, the subsidy will generate inefficiency.

Finally, there is the prospect of "government failure," which is likely to occur when self-interested policymakers face the lobbying of interest groups that favor protection.[25] A further difficulty, given that evaluation of market failure generally refers to domestic effects, is that foreign governments and international courts may not able to access the local information that is available to the subsidizing state.

To conclude, negotiators might reasonably fear opportunistic uses of the information asymmetries, which are due to the regulatory complexity associated with these issues, as well as limitations on availability of information in relation to parties' other than the subsidizing state.

5.2 The SCM Mechanisms to Overcome Uncertainty Problems

In its description of the evolution of the rules on subsidies, this work has already touched upon the legal mechanisms available for tackling the uncertainty to which the SCM Agreement is subject. Somewhat

---

[24] As put by the authors when referring to innovation subsidies, the "exact size of the market failure depends on the difference between the social and the private returns, which in turn depends on a large number of other factors such as market structure, the ability to appropriate intellectual property, the patent system, the importance of the innovation, and the R&D production function," Friederiszick, Röller, and Verouden, "European State Aid Control: An Economic Framework" p. 637.

[25] As discussed by Hoekman and Kostecki, "[n]ecessary conditions for a more efficient allocation of resources to result from intervention are that the problem has been diagnosed correctly and the policy used is targeted appropriately. In practice, governments are prone to fail as often, if not more, than markets- especially if account is taken of the incentives of interest groups to lobby for a subsidy or a tax exemption," Hoekman and Kostecki, *The Political Economy of the World Trading System*. See also Friederiszick, Röller, and Verouden, "European State Aid Control: An Economic Framework" p. 637.

unusually in critical accounts of legal doctrine, the system of flexibility established by the SCM Agreement is sophisticated enough to employ not only exceptions and various types of default rules, but also a complex mechanism for delegation of power to national and multilateral authorities. The Agreement is also demonstrably concerned with opportunistic behavior, establishing mechanisms to improve transparency and monitor the relevant actions of WTO Members.[26]

The following section focuses on three mechanisms that address problems associated with flexibility and opportunistic behavior. The first is "interpretation." Treaty interpretation, as discussed in Chapter 2, can be a powerful instrument for the *ex post* completion of treaties. The SCM Agreement delegates this task to those domestic authorities competent to investigate and apply countervailing duties, and to WTO conflict resolution bodies, being the panels and Appellate Body. The focus here will be the multilateral system, as unilateral decisions of domestic trade authorities are subject to revision and correction by WTO adjudicators. Delegation of power to the courts is usually construed as a means of coping with uncertainty resulting from textual ambiguity in legal instruments, but the interpretative competence of the courts is in fact broader than literal interpretation, extending to issues of good faith and thus questions of opportunistic behavior, as well as application of the law in the event of contingencies. The courts are therefore fully equipped to deal with the uncertainties identified above.[27]

The second mechanism is that of explicit exception. Treaty drafters, as noted earlier, will introduce exceptions as a means of coping *ex ante* with the potential for contingencies to arise *ex post*. This is not only an *ex ante* attempt to limit state behavior to a defined set of actions pre-approved by all the parties, but also provides a guide to the interpretation of the law in the event of a dispute.

---

[26] While the functioning of this system has proved to be below the initial expectation, much of the problem seems to be related to the deadlock in general WTO negotiations, which arguably hindered the reintroduction of exceptions in the SCM Agreement after the lapse of Article 8, as well as the lack of enforcement concerning monitoring rules. It is true, however, that there are problems with the general balance between commitments and flexibilities. This is an issue because of the level of obligations, especially the restrictions imposed on prohibited subsidies, and the limitations to make use of exceptions, caused both to the precise requirements and to the impossibility to apply the justifications to substantive fields other than those explicitly foreseen in Article 8.

[27] Other instruments might, however, be better suited to tackle a specific type of uncertainty. For instance, in order to assess specialized knowledge, transferring competence to other bodies with expertise in the different areas of science may be a superior solution.

A third mechanism is the monitoring system. The production and widespread dissemination of data by this system helps with identification of opportunistic behavior by overcoming barriers to access that would prevent parties from observing and assessing whether other WTO Members' subsidies have been introduced in good faith.

Further qualitative analysis of these three mechanisms will, in the following sections, identify and assess their advantages and deficiencies, laying the groundwork for the proposal of recommendations for improvement of the system.

5.2.1   Treaty Interpretation

Treaty interpretation is an important mechanism for the application of the terms of an incomplete contract to the factual situations of practical cases. Courts and other competent third parties may use interpretation *ex post* to assess the good faith behind a measure, a process that is usually necessary if a treaty adopts broad or ambiguous language. Interpretation might also be important, however, in the event of contingencies or emergency situations that have not been fully articulated in the contract.

The SCM Agreement has delegated interpretative powers to a number of different bodies, as explained in detail in Chapter 4. This analysis will focus on interpretation by panels and the Appellate Body of the WTO, being the bodies that most commonly address international subsidies disputes. It will not discuss the national application of the SCM Agreement by domestic trade authorities to countervailing cases. There are two reasons for this. First, as domestic decisions may be challenged at the WTO, panels and the Appellate Body in effect take priority in relation to interpretation of the rules. Although case reports in WTO law legally binds only the parties to the relevant dispute and creates no formal precedent by which future panels are bound, panels, in practice, take into consideration AB decisions, and WTO Members amend their rules to conform to WTO recommendations. Secondly, scholarship on the application of WTO law by domestic trade authorities is still very limited, and effort needs to be made to generate further data as well as more descriptive and comparative analyses in support of further qualitative research.[28]

---

[28] See Gregory Wells Bowman, Trade Remedies in North America, vol 27 (Kluwer Law International 2010).

The concept of subsidy, as previously described, has particular relevance for the introduction of flexibility by the SCM Agreement. If a measure does not meet the criteria for subsidy in Article 1, it is found to be outside the scope of application of the SCM Agreement and cannot therefore be in violation of its terms. There is, moreover, a long history of disagreement among negotiators regarding definitions of subsidy.

The broad language in elements of the SCM Agreement definition of subsidy, which was a tool used to accommodate differences during the negotiations, ultimately delegated to WTO adjudicators the power to interpret the concept of subsidy in the context of emerging disputes. The language regarding "benefits" is particularly broad, and thus prone to widest interpretation, but other concepts such as "financial contribution" and "specificity" also deserve analysis.

5.2.1.1   Financial Contribution

The financial contribution contemplated by SCM Agreement Article 1 may be the result of either a positive or a negative government action. An action is described as positive if the agent makes a directed or targeted move that qualifies as a financial contribution.

The SCM Agreement conceives of positive action as a direct transfer of funds,[29] a provision of goods or services, or a purchase of goods,[30] with very broad reach. "Fund" has a meaning that extends far beyond "money," and a transfer of funds encompasses grants, loans, equity infusion, debt forgiveness, extension of loan maturity, joint ventures, and other similar transactions that involve financial resources.[31] Within the concept of financial contribution, therefore, a wide range of government measures is captured by the SCM Agreement.

Broadening the notion even further, a transfer of funds may conform to the Article 1 concept of subsidy, whether it is a retrospective or prospective act: whether the financial contribution has already been made or is still a potential act. The case of US – Large Civil Aircraft

---

[29] See Article 1.1(a)(1)(i) of the SCM Agreement.
[30] See Article 1.1(a)(1)(iii) of the SCM Agreement.
[31] This comprehension was adopted by the Appellate Body in the Japan – DRAMS (Korea) dispute: "[i]n our view, the term 'funds' encompasses not only 'money' but also financial resources and other financial claims more generally. The concept of 'transfer of funds' adopted by Korea is too literal and mechanistic because it fails to encapsulate how financial transactions give rise to an alteration of obligations from which an accrual of financial resources results."

defined "potential" in the SCM Agreement to mean the possibility that a fund will be made available for a recipient.[32] In effect, the term "potential," understood as "possibility," ensures the existence of a subsidy in the event that no action occurs to trigger the transfer of funds.

A financial contribution can also take the form of a negative action, in which the agent does not perform as would normally be expected in such conditions. SCM Article 1.1(a)(1)(ii) affirms that there is a financial contribution where government revenue that is otherwise due is "foregone or not collected."[33]

Revenue is foregone or not collected when a company is made exempt from an obligation to pay funds that would normally be due to the government. The act of permitting exemption from payment of dues, such as taxes or fees for public services, is a negative one, in that the government relinquishes an entitlement to raise revenue. Several tax regime privileges[34] come under this provision, but import duties do not, as tariffs are not within the scope of the SCM Agreement. Tariff exemptions were nonetheless in *Indonesia - Autos*[35] classified as foregone revenue, in keeping with the SCM Agreement rules.

A significant issue for this analysis is how to determine the ideal benchmark with which to perform a fair comparison[36] of revenues collected and foregone. Certain WTO solutions to this question serve also to broaden the definition of financial contribution.

---

[32] As noted by a WTO panel, "a potential direct transfer of funds is a 'possibility' due to uncertainty about whether the triggering event will occur, rather than uncertainty about whether the transfer of funds will follow once the predefined event has transpired." Panel Report, United States - Measures Affecting Trade in Large Civil Aircraft (US - Large Civil Aircraft), WT/DS353/R, adopted 23 March 2012, as modified by Appellate Body Report WT/DS353/AB/R, DSR 2012:II, p. 649, para. 7164.

[33] See Article 1.1(a)(1)(ii) of the SCM Agreement. See also Panel Report, Brazil - Taxation, para. 7.391.

[34] See Luengo, *Regulation of Subsidies and State Aids in WTO and EC Law: Conflicts in International Trade Law* p. 108–10.

[35] In this case, it was noted that parties agreed that "tariff and sales tax exemptions in question represent government revenue forgone within the meaning of Article 1.1(a)(1) (ii)." Panel Report, Indonesia - Certain Measures Affecting the Automobile Industry (Indonesia - Autos), WT/DS54/R, WT/DS55/R, WT/DS59/R, WT/DS64/R, Corr.1 and Corr.2, adopted 23 July 1998, and Corr.3 and Corr.4, DSR 1998:VI, p. 2201, para. 14.116.

[36] To analyze a situation that might involve subsidization through foregone revenue, it takes three steps: (i) study of the recipient's tax treatment and any changes it suffers and the reasons why that change happened; (ii) establish a benchmark of tax treatment; and (iii) compare the recipient's tax treatment with the benchmark to define whether any revenue is being foregone or not.

Initially, panels based the benchmark on the national tax regime. They adopted the so-called "but for" test to evaluate "whether the government measure impedes the collection of government revenue that would have been collected otherwise, considering the situation in the absence of ('but for') the government measure."[37] It was noted however, that the "but for" test could be circumvented by certain tax rules and would not be sufficient to address all potential cases.[38]

The solution articulated by the panel was that where there was "but for" test insufficiency, the benchmark should be the "legitimately comparable income." The standard, established from a policy, rather than a normative, point of view, should be based on the structure and principles of the tax regime in question, and not solely on the historic taxation of the specific matter.

A financial contribution may also assume the form of government provision of goods or services other than general infrastructure,[39] in

[37] Luengo, *Regulation of Subsidies and State Aids in WTO and EC Law: Conflicts in International Trade Law* p. 110. A good example of application of this test is related in the Appellate Body Report in Canada – Autos. This case also reinforces the idea reached in Indonesia – Autos that import duties exemptions configured revenue foregone. In the Canadian case, the AB stated that " . . . Canada has established a normal MFN duty rate for imports of motor vehicles of 6.1 per cent. Absent the import duty exemption, this duty would be paid on imports of motor vehicles. Thus, through the measure in dispute, the Government of Canada has, in the words of United states – FSC, 'given up an entitlement to raise revenue that it could 'otherwise' have raised.' More specifically, through the import duty exemption, Canada has ignored the 'defined, normative benchmark' that it established for itself for import duties on motor vehicles under its normal MFN rate and, in so doing, has foregone 'government revenue that is otherwise due.'" Appellate Body Report, Canada – Certain Measures Affecting the Automotive Industry (Canada – Autos), WT/DS139/AB/R, WT/DS142/AB/R, adopted 19 June 2000, DSR 2000:VI, p. 2985, para. 91.

[38] As concluded by the Appellate Body in the US – FSC case: "(. . .) we have certain abiding reservations about applying any legal standard, such as this "but for" test, in the place of the actual treaty language. Moreover, we would have particular misgivings about using a 'but for' test if its application were limited to situations where there actually existed an alternative measure, under which the revenues in question would be taxed, absent the contested measure. It would, we believe, not be difficult to circumvent such a test by designing a tax regime under which there would be no general rule that applied formally to the revenues in question, absent the contested measures. We observe, therefore, that, although the Panel's 'but for' test works in this case, it may not work in other cases." Appellate Body Report, United States – Tax Treatment for "Foreign Sales Corporations" (US – FSC), WT/DS108/AB/R, adopted 20 March 2000, DSR 2000:III, p. 1619, para. 91.

[39] The Appellate Body Report in US – Softwood Lumber IV delineated the scope of the terms "goods" and "provision." "Goods" covers government's possessions and properties, including also immovable properties: "(. . .) we find that the ordinary meaning of the term

fulfillment of some sort of right that generates an advantage to the recipient.

The exclusion of "general infrastructure" from this stipulation is highly significant, probably reflecting an understanding both of the necessity of imposition of limits on the reach of the SCM Agreement, and that provision of infrastructure, commonly seen as an essential function of the state, should not fall within its purview.

The meaning of "general," as it qualifies infrastructure, is, however, difficult to discern. It could perhaps make reference to the public availability of the infrastructure: if the infrastructure is available to only one recipient, clearly it is not "general." The Panel in *US – Large Civil Aircraft*, however, suggests that public availability can be an inadequate "determining factor in analyzing whether a measure is general infrastructure."[40]

In that case, the Panel suggested other complementary analyses, such as the relationship of the project to the need of the company for infrastructural improvement. It found that infrastructure that is crafted for or tailor-made to a specific recipient, in the absence of any public objectives, is within the scope of the agreement.[41]

"goods" in the English version of Article 1.1(a)(1)(iii) of the SCM Agreement should not be read so as to exclude tangible items of property, like trees, that are severable from land." ... "We see no reason why disciplines on subsidies that regulate the provision of non-monetary resources should focus on identifiable physical objects and not on tangible, but fungible, input material." Appellate Body Report, United States – Final Countervailing Duty Determination with Respect to Certain Softwood Lumber from Canada (US – Softwood Lumber IV), WT/DS257/AB/R, adopted 17 February 2004, DSR 2004:II, p. 571, paras. 58–59.

[40] Appellate Body Report, US – Large Civil Aircraft, para. 7431.

[41] The financial contribution may also assume the form of purchases of goods by the government. On the other hand, service purchase is not even mentioned in the legal text, but according to the Appellate Body in US – Large Civil Aircraft it is not exactly excluded from the scope of the SCM Agreement. It was concluded that the purchase of services shares the same characteristics of a joint-venture or an equity infusion, lying on the stipulations of transfer of funds. This was the context of the case (note the approximation to an equity infusion): "Like equity investors, NASA and the USDOD provide funding. This funding is provided in the expectation of some kind of return. In the case of NASA and USDOD funding to Boeing, the return is not financial, but rather takes the form of scientific and technical information, discoveries, and data expected to result from the research performed. Again, like equity investors, NASA and the USDOD have no certainty at the time they commit the funding that the research will be successful. Success will depend on whether any inventions are discovered and the usefulness of the data collected, as well as the scientific and technical information produced. NASA's and the USDOD's risks are limited to the amount of money they contribute and the opportunity cost of the other support they provide to the project, much like an equity investor." Facing this situation, the Appellate Body took this decision: "(. . .) the particular characteristics of the NASA procurement contracts and USDOD assistance instruments before us are such

Financial contribution is, thus, a broad concept that encompasses a myriad of state measures.[42] Mavroidis notes that the "various examples of financial contribution reflected in the SCM Agreement underscore the impression that what matters is that economic value is being transferred."[43] Despite this breadth, however, SCM Article 1 provides an exhaustive list of forms of financial contribution within which a subsidizing measure must fall.[44] The "form" of the measure thus acquires a decisive importance, and unforeseen measures, even if capable of producing similar economic effects, are outside of the scope of application[45] of the Agreement.

Concerns of over-rigidity might be raised by the fact that measures other than those expressly foreseen by the SCM Agreement, despite having the same effect, might, due to the finite list, be left outside the scope of the Agreement. This need not be overemphasized however, because, as discussed, interpretation of the constitutive elements of "financial contribution" has tended to broaden the definition, capturing virtually all state measures that imply a transfer of economic value to a company.

---

that, in our view, they are most appropriately characterized as being akin to a species of joint venture. Furthermore, these joint venture arrangements between NASA/USDOD and Boeing have characteristics analogous to equity infusions, one of the examples of financial contributions included in Article 1.1(a)(1)(i) of the SCM Agreement. We recall that, under subparagraph (i), there is a financial contribution where 'a government practice involves a direct transfer of funds'. Several examples of direct transfers of funds are provided. These examples are not exhaustive. Where, as here, there are measures that have sufficient characteristics in common with one of the examples in subparagraph (i), this commonality indicates to us that the measures fall within the concept of 'direct transfers of funds' in Article 1.1(a)(1)(i). We have identified two contributions by NASA and the USDOD under the respective joint ventures. Both NASA and the USDOD provided payments to Boeing to undertake the research. These payments constitute a direct transfer of funds within the meaning of Article 1.1(a)(1)(i)." Appellate Body Report, US – Large Civil Aircraft paras. 624–25.

[42] As noted by Mavroidis, the concept of financial contribution is "wide enough to function as anti-circumvention device," Petros C Mavroidis, *The Regulation of International Trade: The WTO Agreements on Trade in Goods* (MIT Press 2016) p. 202.

[43] Ibid. p. 203.

[44] Ibid. p. 202, and Luengo, *Regulation of Subsidies and State Aids in WTO and EC Law: Conflicts in International Trade Law* p. 107. See US – Export Restraints, para. 8.69.

[45] In this regard, a measure restraining exports, such as an export tax, it not considered a financial contribution, even though it might benefit domestic downstream producers that acquire an input for less than the world market price. See Mavroidis, *The Regulation of International Trade: The WTO Agreements on Trade in Goods* p. 203.

According to SCM Article 1(a)(2), a subsidy also exists if there is any form of income or price support. Despite the addition of "in the sense of Article XVI of GATT 1994," the absence of any judicial interpretation means that there is still no clear definition of income or price support to refer to. Whatever form it might assume, income or price support broadens the scope of subsidization in the SCM Agreement beyond financial contribution. As the Article 1 reference to income or price support is preceded by "any form," the provision might be construed to include anything that culminates in the raising of prices. The Panel in *China – GOES*, however, affirmed that "price support" necessarily aims to set prices, thus ruling out incidental price effects. Income support follows the same logic.

To constitute a subsidy, income support must be targeted, and not a side effect. To Luengo, export restraint is an example of income support, since governmental action without financial contribution is responsible for income support to domestic purchasers. The Panel in *US – Export Restraint* did not, however, follow this thinking, but rejected a purely effects-based view of subsidization for fear of over-broadening the scope of the SCM Agreement, and placed more importance on financial contribution. It also mentioned the necessity of construing income support "in the sense of Article XVI of the GATT of 1994" which, according to Luengo, should be read to include any form of income or price support that increases exports or reduces imports of any product.

SCM Article 1, through the use of these broad concepts, expands the scope of the SCM Agreement to encompass government activity, much of which transfers value to individuals or has economic impact on firms. Other elements of the definition of subsidy might therefore be expected to act as a filter in relation to this activity, to separate general measures from those that are potentially harmful to international trade.

5.2.1.2 By a Government

Financial contribution, the fundamental element of "subsidy," in the SCM Agreement, is given a broad interpretation by the WTO, and is capable of supporting a large number of measures. Other elements of the definition of subsidy, however, act as filters to reduce the breadth of "financial contribution" and limit its application.

The first filter is the public origin of the measure. SCM Agreement Article 1 authorizes the government, or a public body, to lead the process of subsidization, and addresses the situation in which a private institution acts under the influence of the government.

Subsidization by government or public body, referred to as "direct subsidization,"[46] may be performed at any state level (national, regional, or even local) through positive or negative action.[47] A public body is an entity that possesses, exercises, or is vested with governmental authority.[48]

Evaluation of the subsidizing entity must consider the overall conduct of the institution, and not merely specific or isolated actions. Public ownership is meaningful, but in the view of the Appellate Body is an insufficient basis upon which to conclude that an institution is a public body.[49] To determine whether the actions of a company render it

[46] See Section 5.1.2.

[47] The concept of what a public body is was defined in the caselaw. In accordance with US – Antidumping and Countervailing Duties (China), public body does not have a direct link with government ownership over an enterprise or bank, even less with majority shareholding (view of the Panel in US – Antidumping and Countervailing Duties (China)): "[t]o read 'any public body' in Article 1.1(a)(1) as excusing from a Member government's direct responsibility a wide swathe of government-controlled entities engaging in exactly the sorts of transactions listed in Article 1.1(a)(1)(i)-(iii) of the SCM Agreement would fundamentally undermine the Agreement's logic, coherence and effectiveness, and thus would be at odds with its object and purpose." Panel Report, United States – Definitive Anti-Dumping and Countervailing Duties on Certain Products from China (US – Anti-Dumping and Countervailing Duties (China), WT/DS379/R, adopted 25 March 2011, as modified by Appellate Body Report WT/DS379/AB/R, DSR 2011:VI, p. 3143, para. 7.89.

[48] As noted by the Panel, " . . . the Appellate Body found, in Canada – Dairy, that the essence of government is that it enjoys the effective power to regulate, control, or supervise individuals, or otherwise restrain their conduct, through the exercise of lawful authority. The Appellate Body further found that this meaning is derived, in part, from the functions performed by a government and, in part, from the government having the powers and authority to perform those functions. As we see it, these defining elements of the word 'government' inform the meaning of the term 'public body'. This suggests that the performance of governmental functions, or the fact of being vested with, and exercising, the authority to perform such functions are core commonalities between government and public body." Panel Report, US – Anti-Dumping and Countervailing Duties (China), para. 290.

[49] This was stressed by the Panel, in the sense that " . . . apart from an express delegation of authority in a legal instrument, the existence of mere formal links between an entity and government in the narrow sense is unlikely to suffice to establish the necessary possession of governmental authority. Thus, for example, the mere fact that a government is the majority shareholder of an entity does not demonstrate that the government exercises meaningful control over the conduct of that entity, much less that the government has bestowed it with governmental authority. In some instances, however, where the evidence shows that the formal indicia of government control are manifold, and there is also evidence that such control has been exercised in a meaningful way, then such evidence may permit an inference that the entity concerned is exercising governmental authority."

a "public body" requires a casuistic evaluation of its core features and its relationship with the government.

The Appellate Body in *US – Antidumping and Countervailing Measures (China)* held that a finding of "public body" requires evidence (i) of the statute or legal instrument granting the entity government authority; or evidence (ii) that actions of the entity exert governmental authority, despite that such powers are not legally vested in it.[50] The exercise of governmental authority, even if *de facto* authority, thus seems to be an important element of the definition of "public body."

Even if a corporation is not considered a public body, its actions might nevertheless, according to SCM Article 1.1(a)(1)(iv), amount to indirect subsidization by a "private body." A government may entrust or direct a private body to carry out the types of functions that would normally be vested in the government, including the positive act of financial contribution via transfer of funds, provision of goods or services, or purchase of goods. A private body acting by means of entrustment or direction requirements are then perceived as public bodies. The presence of the government is, therefore, a basic requirement, and the meaning of the

Appellate Body Report, US – Anti-Dumping and Countervailing Duties (China), paras. 317–18. The AB expressed, though, that "just as no two governments are exactly alike, the precise contours and characteristics of a public body are bound to differ from entity to entity, state to state, and case to case. Panels or investigating authorities confronted with the question of whether conduct falling within the scope of Article 1.1.(a)(1) is that of a public body will be in a position to answer that question only by conducting a proper evaluation of the core features of the entity concerned, and its relationship with government in the narrow sense." Appellate Body Report, US – Anti-Dumping and Countervailing Duties (China), paras. 317–18.

[50] The AB already stated that ". . . when a statute or other legal instrument expressly vests authority in the entity concerned, determining that such entity is a public body may be a straightforward exercise. In others, the picture may be more mixed, and the challenge more complex. The same entity may possess certain features suggesting it is a public body, and others that suggest that it is a private body. We do not, for example, consider that the absence of an express statutory delegation of authority necessarily precludes a determination that a particular entity is a public body. What matters is whether an entity is vested with authority to exercise governmental functions, rather than how that is achieved. There are many different ways in which government in the narrow sense could provide entities with authority. Accordingly, different types of evidence may be relevant to showing that such authority has been bestowed on a particular entity. Evidence that an entity is, in fact, exercising governmental functions may serve as evidence that it possesses or has been vested with governmental authority, particularly where such evidence points to a sustained and systematic practice. It follows, in our view, that evidence that a government exercises meaningful control over an entity and its conduct may serve, in certain circumstances, as evidence that the relevant entity possesses governmental authority and exercises such authority in the performance of governmental functions," US – Anti-Dumping and Countervailing Duties (China), paras. 317–19.

terms "entrust" and "direct" and how to demonstrate such ties between a private body and the government deserve further attention.[51]

Evidence of a change in corporate behavior may reasonably be taken to indicate indirect subsidization.[52] Corporate commercial interests have a significant role in this analysis, as companies that have been entrusted or directed to exercise governmental functions may act contrary to their usual private interests. It is well established in the caselaw that such action is an important signal of subsidization by a private entity.[53]

[51] When a government entrusts a private company to perform any kind of subsidization, it is not configured simply as an act of delegation by the government. It refers to a situation in which the government gives to the body a responsibility. When a government directs a company, however, has a different meaning. It makes reference to more than a mere command issued by the government; it is the government exerting its authority over private bodies. These definitions were reached in the Appellate Body Report in US – Countervailing Duty investigation on DRAMS. "In sum, we are of the view that, pursuant to paragraph (iv), 'entrustment' occurs where a government gives responsibility to a private body, and 'direction' refers to situations where the government exercises its authority over a private body. In both instances, the government uses a private body as proxy to effectuate one of the types of financial contributions listed in paragraphs (i) through (iii)." Appellate Body Report, United States – Countervailing Duty Investigation on Dynamic Random Access Memory Semiconductors (DRAMS) from Korea (US – Countervailing Duty Investigation on DRAMS), WT/DS296/AB/R, adopted 20 July 2005, DSR 2005:XVI, p. 8131, para. 116.

[52] The same Appellate Body report warned about the difficulty in this demonstration: "It may be difficult to identify precisely, in the abstract, the types of government actions that constitute entrustment or direction and those that do not. The particular label used to describe the governmental action is not necessarily dispositive. Indeed, as Korea acknowledges, in some circumstances, 'guidance' by a government can constitute direction. In most cases, one would expect entrustment or direction of a private body to involve some form of threat or inducement, which could, in turn, serve as evidence of entrustment or direction. The determination of entrustment or direction will hinge on the particular facts of the case." Appellate Body Report, US – Countervailing Duty Investigation on DRAMS, para. 116.

[53] In this sense, the AB noted that "... the commercial unreasonableness of the financial transactions is a relevant factor in determining government entrustment or direction under Article 1.1(a)(1)(iv) of the SCM Agreement, particularly where an investigating authority seeks to establish government intervention based on circumstantial evidence." Appellate Body Report, Japan – Countervailing Duties on Dynamic Random Access Memories from Korea (Japan – DRAMS (Korea)), WT/DS336/AB/R and Corr.1, adopted 17 December 2007, DSR 2007:VII, p. 2703, para. 138. The Panel had stated that "(...) we agree with the parties that conduct which is contrary to a private body's commercial interests might be indicative of government entrustment or direction." Panel Report, Japan – DRAMS (Korea) WT/DS336/R, adopted 17 December 2007, as modified by Appellate Body Report WT/DS336/AB/R, DSR 2007:VII, p. 2805, para. 7.70. Similarly, it was also stated that "when demonstrated, such non-commercial behavior may well be seen as an indication of possible government entrustment or direction. It can thus be taken into account as an element of evidence that the government was perhaps entrusting

Another factor indicative of indirect subsidization is the degree of government ownership in the private body. It is ownership, rather than whether the entity may be considered a public body,[54] that is relevant to the analysis regarding the direction of a private body by a government.

These indicators are, in themselves, insufficient to infer governmental interference constituting indirect subsidization. Government ownership and irrational commercial behavior merely provide reasons for deepening investigations and searching for more evidence.[55] It is necessary therefore to look to other elements, such as government motives or intentions, or its coercive action or cooperation with investigations, to obtain evidence of the presence of the government.

As not every governmental measure is a subsidy, these additional elements have an important role in distinguishing the subsidizing measures, which confer a benefit to the recipient, from other measures. Governments often act according to market standards, which do not confer a particular advantage on the recipient of the financial contribution, but nonetheless the broad interpretation given to "government or public body" reaches a wide range of governmental activity, whether carried out directly by the state or entrusted to private agents. A direct financial contribution by a government does not necessarily, however, in relation to the economic agents concerned, constitute a subsidizing measure. This is because governments often act as private agents in the market, without granting or intending to grant any advantage to economic agents. Unsurprisingly, therefore, the next element, the existence

---

or directing these private bodies to act in a certain way (. . .)" Panel Report, European Communities – Countervailing Measures on Dynamic Random Access Memory Chips from Korea (EC – Countervailing Measures on DRAM Chips), WT/DS299/R, adopted 3 August 2005, DSR 2005:XVIII, p. 8671, para. 7.59.

[54] Concerning this issue, a panel stated that ". . . the extent of government ownership still remains a very relevant factor in the evaluation of the evidence concerning possible entrustment or direction by the government. It is clear that, as the sole shareholder, it is easier for the government to direct the bank to act in a certain manner than in a situation of no or only minor government involvement." Panel Report, EC – Countervailing Measures on DRAM Chips, para. 7.119.

[55] "However, this does not mean that a finding of entrustment or direction can never be made unless it is established that the financial transactions were on noncommercial terms. A finding that creditors acted on the basis of commercial reasonableness, while relevant, is not conclusive of the issue of entrustment or direction. A government could entrust or direct a creditor to make a loan, which that creditor then does on commercial terms. In other words, as a conceptual matter, there could be entrustment or direction by the government, even where the financial contribution is made on commercially reasonable terms." Appellate Body Report, Japan – DRAMS (Korea), para. 138.

of a "benefit," has been the object of a great deal of attention by interpreters of WTO law.

5.2.1.3 Benefit

"Subsidy," as defined by SCM Agreement Article 1, is a financial contribution by a government that confers a benefit. What, then, is the
definition of a benefit?

In the investigative process related to subsidy, the question as to
whether a benefit has been conferred is secondary to those considering
the existence of a financial contribution and if it was made by
a government.[56] A benefit, if it is to constitute subsidization, as described
by the Appellate Body in *Canada - Aircraft*, must be received and
enjoyed by the recipient[57]. The focus of the analysis, it explained, is not
the government, the one that confers—gives, grants or bestows—the
benefit,[58] but the recipient. The cost of the subsidy to the subsidizing
government, which pertains to the investigation of financial
contribution,[59] is of no concern here. The important question, at this
stage, is whether the contribution confers a benefit[60]: whether it makes
the recipient "better off" than it would be without it.,[61]

A benefit affords the recipient an advantage over its market
competitors[62],. To determine whether a financial contribution by the

---

[56] "The reason why the framers dissociated financial contribution from benefit is that they
did not want to bar WTO members from investing in the market if they acted as private
investors." Mavroidis, *The Regulation of International Trade: The WTO Agreements on
Trade in Goods* p. 216.

[57] Therefore, abstract or potential benefit must not be considered in dispute cases.
"A 'benefit' does not exist in the abstract, but must be received and enjoyed by
a beneficiary or a recipient." Appellate Body Report, Canada - Aircraft, para. 154.

[58] Ibid. para. 154.

[59] It has been noted that "[...] WTO law distinguishes the financial contribution of the
government from the benefit of the recipient. Therefore, the benefit cannot be the mere
net cost of the government. The way to calculate the benefit focuses on the recipient's
situation. Guidelines for the purpose of this calculation are given by the case law,"
Micheau, *State Aid, Subsidy and Tax Incentives under EU and WTO Law* p. 201.

[60] Appellate Body Report, Canada - Aircraft, para. 157.

[61] A Panel found that "Article 14 apply to the calculation of the 'benefit to the recipient
conferred pursuant to paragraph 1 of Article 1' (emphasis added)" and that "this explicit
textual reference to Article 1.1 in Article 14 indicates to us that 'benefit' is used in the same
sense in Article 14 as it is in Article 1.1. Therefore, the reference to 'benefit to the
recipient' in Article 14 also implies that the word 'benefit', as used in Article 1.1, is
concerned with the 'benefit to the recipient' and not with the 'cost to government', as
Canada contends." Ibid. para. 155.

[62] A WTO Panel already stated that "... 'cost to government' is one way of conceiving of
'benefit' is at odds with the ordinary meaning of Article 1.1(b), which focuses on the

government will—in reality—make the recipient "better off," the benchmark for comparison must be the market prices in that market in which the (potential) recipient is present.[63]

Despite analytical differences identified during examination of financial contribution and benefit, these two aspects of subsidy remain interrelated. If a financial contribution is made through a negative act, involving, for example, revenue that is foregone or not collected, the occurrence of a benefit is always implied.[64] Financial contribution through positive action, however (involving direct or potential for direct transfer of funds, provision of goods or services, or purchase of goods), needs to be analyzed more extensively in order to determine whether a benefit has in fact been conferred by a government. This work is, accordingly, dedicated to cases of financial contribution by positive action.

A paradigmatic case of benefit is *EC – Large Civil Aircraft*, in which the Appellate Body reaffirms the guidelines detailed in SCM Agreement Article 14. The decision made certain stipulations concerning loans, loan guarantees and equity investments, all three of which belong to the species of financial contribution involving direct (or potential for direct) transfer of funds.

SCM Article 14 is key to the interpretation of the term "benefit" as reliant on a market benchmark. By affirming that "financial contribution should not be equated to a subsidy,"[65] Article 14 ensures that WTO Members are not prevented from "investing in the market as private investors."[66] The Panel in *EC – Countervailing Measures on DRAM chips* states: "Article 14 of the SCM Agreement thus refers on each occasion to the market place as the appropriate benchmark for determining the existence of a benefit to the recipient of the financial contribution."[67]

recipient and not on the government providing the 'financial contribution'." Ibid. para. 154.

[63] "In our view, the marketplace provides an appropriate basis for comparison in determining whether a 'benefit' has been 'conferred', because the trade-distorting potential of a 'financial contribution' can be identified by determining whether the recipient has received a 'financial contribution' on terms more favourable than those available to the recipient in the market." Ibid. para. 157.

[64] Coppens, *WTO Disciplines on Subsidies and Countervailing Measures: Balancing Policy Space and Legal Constraints* p. 65. See also Panel Report, Brazil – Taxation, para. 7.396 and para. 7.829.

[65] Mavroidis, *The Regulation of International Trade: The WTO Agreements on Trade in Goods* p. 233.

[66] Ibid. p. 216.

[67] Panel Report, EC – Countervailing Measures on DRAM Chips, para. 7.173.

Government decisions regarding equity investments should, under Article 14(a), be compared with the usual investment practice of private investors in the territory of the relevant Member, regarding costs and returns expected from the investment.[68] Regarding loans under Article 14(b), the *DRAM chips* Report affirms that the conditions of the loan granted to the recipient should be compared to the conditions of a commercial loan that could have been obtained at the time of the grant.[69] Article 14(c) ensures that similar disciplines apply to determination of benefit in relation to loan guarantees.[70] Finally, in relation to the provision of goods or services or purchase of goods under Article 14(c), a benefit is conferred if the provision or purchase is inadequately remunerated, adequacy being determined, once again, by market conditions.[71]

The general approach of this market benchmark is illustrated by the following example. Assuming that a government grants a loan at the rate of 4 percent interest, and that the recipient is normally subject to a market-based rate of 6 percent, the benefit is not the 4 percent represented by the financial contribution, but the 2 percent difference between the two rates. Countermeasures or CVDs to a maximal level of 2 percent may therefore be legally applied to the subsidizing WTO member or the product.[72]

---

[68] "Article 14(a) states that equity capital provided by a government shall not be considered to confer a benefit unless it is inconsistent with what is termed the 'usual investment practice' of private investors in the territory of that Member. The two words 'usual' and 'practice' are in a sense reinforcing, with the former signifying '[c]ommonly or customarily observed or practiced' and the latter 'usual or customary action or performance'. Thus, we understand the term 'usual practice' to describe common or customary conduct of private investors in respect of equity investment." Ibid. para. 999.

[69] "Article 14(b) of the SCM Agreement calls for a comparison of the 'amount the firm receiving the loan pays on the government loan' with 'the amount the firm would pay on a comparable commercial loan which the firm could actually obtain in the market'. As we have already discussed in general terms, we read this as suggesting that the comparison is to be performed as though the loans were obtained at the same time. In other words, the comparable commercial loan is one that would have been available to the recipient firm at the time it received the government loan." Appellate Body Report, EC – Large Civil Aircraft, para. 836.

[70] "Article 14(c) requires a comparison between 'the amount that the firm receiving the guarantee pays on a loan guaranteed by the government' with 'the amount the firm would pay on a comparable commercial loan absent the government guarantee'." Ibid. para. 706.

[71] "According to Article 14(d), this benefit is to be found when a recipient obtains goods from the government for "less than adequate remuneration," and such adequacy is to be evaluated in relation to prevailing market conditions in the country of provision." Appellate Body Report, US – Antidumping and Countervailing Measures (China), para. 436.

[72] Example from Mavroidis, The Regulation of International Trade: The WTO Agreements on Trade in Goods p. 233.

The analysis so far reflects that the standard benchmark for determining whether a benefit has been conferred is market conditions or market prices. What if these prices are distorted? What if they do not reflect real market conditions? In either event they should be disregarded as benchmark, lest the whole examination be jeopardized, and an alternative benchmark for determining benefit be found.

At this point, the cases *US – Softwood Lumber III and IV* deserve attention. In these cases, the US Department of Commerce adopted US private market prices as the benchmark for its analysis of the Canadian market because, according to the US, Canadian market prices were substantially influenced by the Canadian government and would not be useful.[73]

The Canadian government claimed in response that, according to SCM Article 14, the benchmark should be established within the borders of the country in issue.[74] The Appellate Body however overruled the decision of the Panel in favor of an expansive interpretation, based on the US argument, finding that an in-country benchmark is not, depending on the circumstances of the case,[75] the only possibility.

---

[73] As noted by the Panel, "According to the US, in this particular case, the provincial governments completely dominate the market in those provincial markets and are virtually the sole providers of timber. In the US' view, the evidence indicates that Canadian provincial governments so dominate the Canadian market for timber that below-market government prices in the small private market for timber in Canada. Therefore, the US submits, in the absence of market prices in Canada, the use of other prices commercially available to Canadian lumber producers on world markets is the only reasonable alternative." Panel Report, US – Softwood Lumber III, para. 7.36

[74] In this dispute, Canada argued that "a cross-border analysis using transactions in another country to determine the existence of a benefit, and to measure it, is inconsistent with Article 1 and Article 14 (d) SCM Agreement." Panel Report, US – Softwood Lumber III, para. 7.31. The Panel shared the Canadian opinion: "In sum, our conclusion on the basis of the text of Article 14 (d) SCM Agreement is that as long as there are prices determined by independent operators following the principle of supply and demand, even if supply or demand are affected by the government's presence in the market, there is a 'market' in the sense of Article 14(d) SCM Agreement. The problem raised by the United states of comparing in certain situations the government price with a market price significantly affected by the government's price, is in our view inherent in the text of Article 14 (d) SCM Agreement. We consider that, if the Members feel the rules as laid down in the WTO Agreements do not address certain situations in what they consider to be a satisfactory manner, they should raise this issue during negotiations. Our task consists of interpreting the Agreement to explain what it means, not what in our view it should mean, nor are we allowed to read words in to the text of the Agreement which are not there, even if we were to consider that the text inadequately addresses certain specific situations." Panel Report, US – Softwood Lumber IV, para. 7.60.

[75] "In sum, the Panel's interpretation of Article 14(d) appears, in our view, to be overly restrictive and based on an isolated reading of the text. To us, such a restrictive reading of Article 14(d) is not supported by the text of the provision, when read in the light of its

The Appellate Body in *Softwood Lumber* thus developed a practical rule that would satisfy, where necessary, the need for alternative benchmarks for determining whether or not a recipient enjoys a benefit.

The case of *US - Antidumping and Countervailing Duties (China)*, however, went further, shaping new considerations regarding situations in which the in-country benchmark is not sufficient. Differentiation by the Appellate Body of three degrees of influence by a government (as sole, predominant, or significant supplier) provided some clarification as to when it is appropriate to use an alternative benchmark. If a government is a sole supplier or regulates prices, distortion of prices is inferred, and an alternative benchmark is required. If the government is a predominant provider, prices are likely to be distorted, requiring little evidence in favor of an alternative benchmark. Lastly, where the government is a significant supplier, greater evidence will be necessary to prove price distortion.[76]

In *US - Antidumping and Countervailing Duties (China)* the issues were whether China was conceding loans on beneficial terms and whether an outside benchmark could be used. A beneficial loan is one that is dissimilar to those granted by the market. As the Chinese banking sector had particular characteristics that made it impossible to establish a benchmark within the Chinese borders, the Appellate Body opted for a broad interpretation of SCM Agreement Article 14(b).[77]

---

context and the object and purpose of the SCM Agreement, as required by Article 31 of the Vienna Convention. Thus, in our view, Members are obliged, under Article 14(d), to abide by the guideline for determining whether a government has provided goods for less than adequate remuneration. However, contrary to the views of the Panel, that guideline does not require the use of private prices in the market of the country of provision in every situation. Rather, that guideline requires that the method selected for calculating the benefit must relate or refer to, or be connected with, the prevailing market conditions in the country of provision, and must reflect price, quality, availability, marketability, transportation and other conditions of purchase or sale, as required by Article 14(d)." AB Report, US - Softwood Lumber IV, para. 97.

[76] Ibid. 73. See also AB Report, US - Antidumping and Countervailing Duties (China), para. 455, where the AB states that "with 96.1 per cent market share, the position of the government in the market is much closer to a situation where the government is the sole supplier of the goods than to the situation where it is merely a significant supplier of the goods. This, in our view, makes it likely that the government as the predominant supplier has the market power to affect through its own pricing strategy the pricing by private providers for the same goods, and induce them to align with government prices. In such a situation, evidence of factors other than government market share will have less weight in the determination of price distortion than in a situation where the government has only a 'significant' presence in the market."

[77] As noted by the AB: "Finally, a benchmark loan under Article 14(b) must be a 'loan which the firm could actually obtain on the market'. The use of the conditional tense, 'could', suggests that a benchmark loan under Article 14(b) need not in every case be a loan that

Having overcome this interpretative issue, the establishment of an alternative benchmark turned on the particular characteristics of the case. The Appellate Body decided that the dispute involved more than the role of ordinary monetary policy in the distortion of loan interest rates.[78] Its specific interpretation, based on the word "could," elaborated the circumstances of the case, making room for alternative benchmarks in cases of direct (potential) transfer of funds.

In a nutshell, the concept of benefit functions as a filter to limit the broad definition and interpretation of other constitutive elements of subsidy under WTO law. The use of a market benchmark against which the measure must be compared is of crucial importance to this function. Should the financial contribution made by the government confer no advantage or benefit to an economic actor, the measure falls outside of the scope of the SCM Agreement. Such a comparison can, nevertheless, be extremely complex, giving rise to difficulties with respect to production of evidence. It may be wise, therefore, to resort to other mechanisms of flexibility in order to safeguard economic and politically sensitive areas of governmental activity from the application of the SCM Agreement.

5.2.2 Explicit Exception

The analysis presented in Chapter 4 introduced the rights and obligations of WTO Members based on a classification of the various types of

exists or that can in fact be obtained in the market. In this respect, we agree with the Panel that this refers 'first and foremost' to the borrower's risk profile, that is, whether the benchmark loan is one that could be obtained by the borrower receiving the investigated government loan. Thus, we consider that Article 14(b) does not preclude the possibility of using as benchmarks interest rates on commercial loans that are not actually available in the market where the firm is located, such as, for instance, loans in other markets or constructed proxies." AB Report, US – Antidumping and Countervailing Duties (China), para. 480.

[78] Coppens, *WTO Disciplines on Subsidies and Countervailing Measures: Balancing Policy Space and Legal Constraints* p. 76. In this regard, the AB noted that "China accepts the proposition that, notwithstanding governments' role in setting and implementing monetary policy, a competitive commercial lending market may exist. Indeed, China argues that despite the role of the Chinese Government in setting interest rates, the Chinese market for commercial lending is competitive. In our view, therefore, the central issue in applying Article 14(b) is not whether a 'clear distinction' exists in the roles of government, but rather, whether there is evidence and reasoning demonstrating that the Chinese Government, by participating in the RMB-lending market and by intervening in that market (beyond its monetary policy role), is able to and does in fact distort interest rates." AB Report, US – Antidumping and Countervailing Duties (China), para. 501.

subsidies. It explained that while actionable subsidies are submitted to an "effects-test," prohibited subsidies are prohibited *per se*. A *per se* prohibition is a stringent restriction on behavior that is commonly complemented by exceptions.

Also discussed in Chapter 4 were potential justifications for certain uses of subsidies. The economic literature suggests that there is a legitimate use for domestic subsidies in counteracting market failures, and that even export and import substitution subsidies might, on occasion, be helpful in addressing specific issues, such as information asymmetry around an exported product, and economic crises in certain sectors.

No generalizations can be made, therefore, regarding the application of exceptions to the WTO rules in disputes over subsidies. General exceptions could have been, but are not, included in either the text of the SCM Agreement itself or in any related treaty, such as the GATT, that could apply to the SCM Agreement.

Instead, the literature identifies two sets of rules that may be used to justify subsidies: the rules on non-actionable subsidies contained in SCM Agreement Article 8, and the specific exceptions provided by GATT Articles XX and XXI.

5.2.2.1   Non-Actionable Subsidies

The SCM Agreement, in Article 8, contemplates a class of subsidies that are considered to be non-actionable. Such subsidies are not subject to legal remedy and are therefore permitted.[79]

This "green" category of subsidies is, however, more theoretical than practical, as Article 8 has been partially emptied of its substance, and further negotiations regarding content have so far been unsuccessful.[80]

---

[79] The adoption of countervailing measures was not allowed, and non-actionable subsidies could not be subject to discussion at the WTO dispute settlement mechanism. See Rubini, *The Definition of Subsidy and State Aid: WTO and EC Law in Comparative Perspective* pp. 73–74; Bossche and Zdouc, *The Law and Policy of the World Trade Organization: Text, Cases, and Materials* p. 561; and Gary N Horlick and Peggy A Clarke, 'The 1994 WTO Subsidies Agreement' (1993) 17 *World Competition* pp. 41–54.

[80] The validity of Article 8 of the SCM Agreement should have been expressly renewed at the end of 1999, according to Article 31 of the SCM Agreement. This renewal never took place. Therefore, subsidies falling under Article 8 of the SCM Agreement automatically form part of the category of actionable subsidies as of 2000 and they can be subject to multilateral or unilateral trade remedies. See, for instance, Alan O Sykes, "Subsidies and Countervailing Measures" in Patrick Macrory, Arthur Appleton, and Michael Plummer (eds), *The World Trade Organization: Legal, Economic and Political Analysis* (The World Trade Organization: Legal, Economic and Political Analysis, Springer 2005) p. 101–03.

As an understanding of Article 8 is nevertheless important for general comprehension of the SCM Agreement, it will be analyzed here.

5.2.2.1.1   First Case: Non-specific   SCM Agreement Article 8.1 provides that there are two main types of non-actionable subsidy. The first category, described in Article 8.1(a), comprises subsidies that are not "specific" within the meaning of SCM Article 2,[81] which requires that non-prohibited subsidies be tested for their "specificity" or discriminatory application to particular economic sectors. If a non-prohibited subsidy is non-specific, it will fall outside the regulatory scope of the SCM Agreement, and as such be permissible. If a non-prohibited subsidy is specific, it will be tested for adverse effects.

The SCM Article 2 criterion for specificity is that the subsidy is exclusively or predominantly available to an enterprise or industry, to a group of enterprises or industries, or to certain enterprises in a defined geographic region of a WTO Member.

Nothing in the language of Article 2, however, allows for the use of subsidies on the basis of public policy preferences, to correct market failures, or in response to situations of social or economic crisis. Further, as externalities are usually associated with particular industries (such as policies to foster renewable energy that subsidize credit for the generation of solar energy), the current specificity test raises concern that measures targeting externalities might be specific by nature.

The specificity test, as a means of introduction of flexibilities, is therefore insufficient or inadequate to deal with the most prominent issue in relation to the balance between commitment and flexibility in the SCM Agreement, the difference between good faith and opportunistic uses of subsidies. One legal commentator has said that the specificity requirement "cannot be reasonably treated as a normative proxy for potential non-trade-related rationales for subsidies that have unavoidable trade spill-overs."[82] The primary focus is therefore on the second category of non-actionable subsidies.

5.2.2.1.2   Second Case: Substantive Exceptions   The second category of non-actionable subsidies, defined by SCM Agreement Article 8.1(b), encompasses subsidies that provide assistance: (i) for R&D activities; (ii)

---

[81] See Seung Wha Chang, "WTO Disciplines on Fisheries Subsidies: A Historic Step towards Sustainability?" (2003) 6 *Journal of International Economic Law* p. 879–921.

[82] Michael J Trebilcock, *Advanced Introduction to International Trade Law* (Edward Elgar Publishing 2015) p. 88.

to disadvantaged regions; and (iii) for adaptation of existing infrastructure to new environmental requirements.[83] Justification for this category of "green light" subsidies is generally found in an economic perspective on market failures[84] that suggests that its purpose is to give "nations the policy space to correct market distortions."[85]

This perspective reinforces the economic rationale for non-actionable subsidies.[86] The inherent danger, however, is that Members could, in bad faith, use subsidies available for correction of market failures in order to opportunistically distort international trade.[87] In other words, the green light category opens the door to opportunistic behavior.

Scholars propose various mechanisms to control for opportunism, including exception clauses, which have long been associated with the regulation of such behavior. One option is to make use of a good faith test, such as the "necessity" or "trade restrictiveness" tests of GATT Article XX. A second, reflected in the SCM Agreement, is to subject the use of the exception to a series of specific requirements with which the party must comply *ex ante.*

---

[83] Although these three exceptions are considered non-actionable subsidies and cannot be subject to countervailing duties at the national level, it is possible to initiate against them a procedure before the SCM Committee to establish their conformity with the Agreement. Furthermore, it should be noted that in order to benefit from the non-actionable status, these subsidies must be notified to the SCM Committee before their adoption.

[84] See Section 3.3.2.2.2.

[85] Francisco Aguayo Ayala and Kevin Gallagher, *Preserving Policy Space for Sustainable Development: The Subsidies Agreement at the WTO* (International Institute for Sustainable Development 2005) p. 10. As noted by these authors, based on the economics of subsidies as a means to tackle market failures, "Research and development efforts are essential to building domestic capacities through knowledge creation. Subsidizing regions in or across countries is a key form of redistributing economic growth benefits to raise living standards. Subsidizing firms and communities for environmental protection and providing environmental services is important to achieve environmental sustainable development. Subsidies of this type are sound in economic theory."

[86] There have been suggestions for amendments in the SCM Agreement so as to reintroduce and improve the category of green light subsidies, mainly covering classical externalities examples such as environment and innovation subsidies. See Gary N Horlick and Peggy A Clarke, "WTO Subsidies Discipline During and After the Crisis" (2010) 13 *Journal of International Economic Law* p. 859–74, 870–72. See also Trebilcock, *Advanced Introduction to International Trade Law* p. 86.

[87] See Chapter 3 for references; see specially Bhagwati and Ramaswami, "Domestic Distortions, Tariffs and the Theory of Optimum Subsidy" p. 50; WTO, *Exploring the Links between Subsidies, Trade and the WTO* p. 55–65; and Trebilcock and Howse, *The Regulation of International Trade* p. 291.

Before proceeding with the analysis, the following sections examine the provisions of SCM Article 8. The first subcategory of (specific) non-actionable subsidy, established by SCM Agreement Article 8.2(a), refers to innovation subsidies.

5.2.2.1.2.1 Innovation Subsidies

Proceedings documenting the negotiations reflect that the parties understood R&D subsidies to be an essential mechanism for the development of a national economy, but they also indicate awareness that this kind of assistance could lead to artificial increases in production and create trade distortions.[88] The final text of the Article is a compromise, therefore, which permits innovation subsidies, while imposing certain barriers to prevent their protectionist use. These barriers take the form of several requirements or criteria for non-actionability, all of which must be fulfilled by a WTO Member if it is to make use of Article 8 in defense of its assistance.

First, under SCM Article 8.2(a), the subsidized research must be conducted by firms, or by higher education or research establishments that are under contract to firms. Secondly, the assistance must cover not more than 75 percent of the costs of industrial research, or 50 percent of the costs of pre-competitive development activity. Finally, the assistance must be limited exclusively to: (i) costs of personnel (researchers, technicians and other supporting staff employed exclusively in the research

---

[88] This view is demonstrated by Michael Doane, who explains that there was: "[...] a conflict between two different perspectives on research and development subsidies. The international trade policy perspective of the trade negotiators held that any subsidy was a trade distortion and should be subject to the GATT provisions. Technology policy advocates asserted that non-actionability was necessary to permit government support for pre-competitive research." Michael L Doane, "Green Light Subsidies: Technology Policy in International Trade" (1995) 21 *Syracuse J Int'l L & Com* p. 155, 165. Also, as noted in previous work, "R&D policies are considered an essential instrument for the enhancement of productivity. However, due to the specifics of knowledge, such as the possibility of being copied by competitors, many economists recognize private investments in innovation not to be fully undertaken by companies. This is because the social benefits of newly produced knowledge can exceed those that private investors in innovation might be able to individually enjoy. . . . In this sense, scholars claim the situation of a market failure to be apparent and usually justify the use of public financial support in order to create incentives for further—and, at its best, the socially optimal amount of – innovation investments by domestic private companies. In that sense, governmental participation through R&D policies plays an essential role in innovation." Caiado and Berghaus, *R&D Subsidies: A Law & Economics Analysis of Regional and International Rules* p. 2.

activity); (ii) costs of instruments, equipment, land and buildings used exclusively and permanently (except when disposed of on a commercial basis) for the research activity; (iii) costs of consultancy and equivalent services used exclusively for the research activity, including bought-in research, technical knowledge, patents, etc.; (iv) additional overhead costs incurred directly as a result of the research activity; or (v) other running costs (such as those of material, supplies and the like) incurred directly as a result of the research activity.

Notably, it is only subsidies directed toward innovation in R&D that are considered to be non-actionable, while the SCM Article 8.2(a) exception steers clear of activities that could have a direct impact on the production process.

5.2.2.1.2.2   Regional Subsidies

The second subcategory of (specific) non-actionable subsidy relates to assistance given to "disadvantaged regions." During the Uruguay Round, Canada and the European Community pushed for the acceptance of assistance to disadvantaged regions as a way of ensuring regional development and social cohesion. The United States, however, took a different approach. It considered that since regional subsidies were conferring specific subsidies on certain companies, they should be actionable and subject to countervailing duties.

Agreement was again reached by compromise, ultimately delineating the kind of region that is to be considered disadvantaged and the forms of subsidies that may be adopted.

Under Article 8.2(b): (i) each disadvantaged region must be a clearly designated contiguous geographical area with a definable economic and administrative identity; (ii) the region is considered as disadvantaged on the basis of neutral and objective criteria indicating that the region's difficulties arise out of more than temporary circumstances; such criteria must be clearly spelled out in law, regulation, or other official document, so as to be capable of verification; (iii) the criteria shall include a measurement of economic development which shall be based on at least one of the following factors—(1) one of either income per capita or household income per capita, or GDP per capita, which must not be above 85 percent of the average for the territory concerned; (2) unemployment rate, which must be at least 110 percent of the average for the territory concerned.

Article 8.2(b) also mandates that assistance be given pursuant to a regional subsidy program that is part of an internally consistent and generally applicable regional development policy. Further, regional development subsidies are not to be granted in isolated geographical points that have no, or virtually no, influence on the development of such region.

Article 8.2(b) has been a target of controversy. Those who would discourage the use of subsidies for enhancement of regional development policies argue that there are limitations on the extent to which quantitative criteria may be used to determine the degree of development. David Schorr, commenting on the criteria for fisheries subsidies, states that:

> [...] the numerical terms for GDP and unemployment in this provision are somewhat arbitrary. There could be regions that reasonable observers would agree are "disadvantaged" but that do not fit this precise quantitative mold. Conversely, there may be regions whose "disadvantaged" status would be highly debatable but where these statistical tests could easily be met. Still, the drafters of this provision preferred to draw a clear if somewhat arbitrary line rather than leave the definition of "disadvantaged" to the interpretation of WTO dispute panelists.[89]

A contrary position would affirm that regional subsidies are an essential tool for the promotion of regional equality, and that reinvesting the WTO atmosphere with such incentives would have an overall beneficial effect.

5.2.2.1.2.3   Environmental Subsidies

The third subcategory of (specific) non-actionable subsidy focuses on subsidies with environmental objectives. Like Article 8.2(b), the language of SCM Agreement Article 8.2(c) is very precise, ensuring that only those environmental subsidies that meet several criteria may be considered non-actionable.

Assistance to promote adaptation of existing facilities to new environmental requirements may for example, according to Article 8.2(c), be considered non-actionable, but only if the facilities in question have been operating for at least two years, and the new requirements imposed by law or regulations increase constraints and the financial burden on firms.

Compliance with a further set of criteria is required. The assistance will be considered non-actionable only if it (i) is a one-time non-recurring

---

[89] David K Schorr, Sustainability Criteria for Fisheries Subsidies: Options for the WTO and Beyond (UNEP/Earthprint 2007) p. 11.

measure; (ii) is limited to 20 percent of the cost of adaptation; (iii) does not cover the cost of replacing and operating the assisted investment, which should be fully borne by firms; (iv) is directly linked to and proportionate to a firm's planned reduction of nuisances and pollution, and it should not cover any manufacturing cost savings which may be achieved; and (v) is available to all firms that could adopt the new equipment and/or production processes.

Despite economic rationales for each of the three types of specific subsidy described in SCM Article 8.2, none of them have been found to be non-actionable. The only uncontestably non-actionable (green light) subsidies to have been recognized to date are non-specific subsidies, as defined by SCM Agreement Article 8.1 and validated by Article 1.2 of the SCM Agreement. The other R&D, regional, and environmental subsidies established by Article 8.2 have, since January 1, 2000, been actionable, by force of SCM Agreement Article 31.

5.2.2.2   Special and Differential Treatment for Developing Countries

The flexibilities afforded by the SCM Agreement also include special and differential treatment for developing countries. SCM Article 27 "provides for some rules and disciplines for developing country Members that are less strict than the general rules and disciplines."[90] These special rules encompass not only subsidies within the prohibited and actionable categories, but also differential treatment in the application of counter-vailing duties and certain domestic measures targeting privatization plans.[91]

SCM Agreement Article 27 on differential treatment, recognizing that subsidies may play an important role in economic development,

---

[90] Bossche and Zdouc, *The Law and Policy of the World Trade Organization: Text, Cases, and Materials* p. 604. For a brief historical overview and the contextualization of special treatment to developing countries as flexibilities, see Benitah, *The Law of Subsidies under the GATT/WTO System* p. 35–44.

[91] As noted by the WTO Secretariat, "Article 27 of the SCM Agreement include[s] a specification of conditions under which some developing countries are permitted to apply export subsidies to manufactured goods, longer phase-out periods for non-complying export subsidies and subsidies contingent on the use of domestic inputs, restrictions on use of multilateral remedies against developing Members' subsidies, special minimum thresholds for subsidy levels and trade volumes in the context of countervailing duty actions against developing country exports, and exemption from the provisions of Part III of the Agreement (actionable subsidies) in respect of debt forgiveness, subsidies to cover social costs and liability transfers, when associated with privatization," WTO, *Exploring the Links between Subsidies, Trade and the WTO* p. 202.

provided in 27.2(a) that the general prohibition on export subsidies would not apply to the least developed and other low income Members[92] for specified periods of time from the date of entry into force of the WTO Agreement. This exemption was conditional upon demonstration, by economic indicators such as a low level of international competitiveness, that the developing Member country had met certain requisite conditions established by SCM Article 27.4. Once the export competitiveness of a product reached a specified threshold, being a 3.25% share of world trade, the Member was obliged to phase out the export subsidy within a two-year period. There were also special rules on local content subsidies but, due to other WTO restrictions on import substitution policies, these had a lower impact than the special rules on export subsidies.[93]

Regarding actionable subsidies, SCM Article 27.13 provides that certain otherwise actionable subsidies granted by developing countries are non-actionable in the "context of privatization programs," such as "direct forgiveness of debts and subsidies to cover social costs."[94] Further, SCM Article 27.8 overrides the bases of presumption of serious prejudice established by SCM Article 6.1, so that there can be no action or complaint of serious prejudice against a developing country subsidy unless it is demonstrated by positive evidence.[95] In addition, the SCM rules established favorable thresholds for countervailing investigations against developing countries.[96]

Although the rules on special and differential treatment give WTO Members flexibility with regard to how they might use subsidies to

---

[92] These are listed in Annex VII of the SCM Agreement. LDCs are identified by the UN designation, and other low-income countries are identified based on a gross national income threshold established by the SCM Agreement. See Coppens, *WTO Disciplines on Subsidies and Countervailing Measures: Balancing Policy Space and Legal Constraints* p. 223.

[93] See ibid. p. 233.

[94] Bossche and Zdouc, *The Law and Policy of the World Trade Organization: Text, Cases, and Materials* p. 604–05. See also WTO, *Exploring the Links between Subsidies, Trade and the WTO* p. 202–05.

[95] There is currently a doctrinal discussion regarding whether developing countries may be subjected to claim arguing for serious prejudice. See Coppens, *WTO Disciplines on Subsidies and Countervailing Measures: Balancing Policy Space and Legal Constraints* p. 233.

[96] A CVD investigation must be terminated so long as "the overall level of subsidies granted upon the product in question does not exceed 2 per cent ad valorem"; or "the volume of subsidised imports represents less than 4 per cent of the total imports of the like product of the importing Member," Bossche and Zdouc, *The Law and Policy of the World Trade Organization: Text, Cases, and Materials* p. 604–05.

address development issues,[97] there are, nonetheless, significant constraints, especially in comparison with a more general flexibility tool, such as GATT Article XX.

Doctrinal narratives on this topic have identified additional issues with the language and application of SCM Article 27. First, WTO Members seem to have focused on export subsidies exceptions, requesting dozens of extensions for export subsidies programs.[98] Flexibilities might, as discussed earlier, enable export subsidies to play a relevant role in addressing market failures, but need to be analyzed more carefully as potential failures are usually dealt with by domestic subsidies. This suggests that political economy could be a large part of the equation and, as it is not fully regulated by Article 27,[99] could give rise to opportunistic uses of subsidies.

Secondly, the rules on special and differential treatment were subject to temporal limitation and may no longer be available to Members. In regard to Article 27.4, for instance, developing countries were given until 2001 to request an extension of the period of application of special treatment to certain of their domestic programs.[100] It may not be possible to reconcile this temporal limitation with the economic rationale for subsidies. Although subsidies should be used in the presence of a market failure (and, arguably, while the corresponding failure exists), a Member will not necessarily be in a position to address all such failures by a particular deadline.

Thirdly, it seems at odds with economic theory that the SCM Article 27 rules should cover only a portion of the WTO membership. Although developing countries might have greater need than other Member States for leeway in relation to economic policy, developed economies are also challenged by market failures and opportunistic behaviors that might necessitate the use of subsidies or countervailing measures.

---

[97] The SCM Agreement also foresaw flexibilities for countries going through economic transformation from a centrally planned into a market economy. See Article 29 of the SCM Agreement, and also Benitah, *The Law of Subsidies under the GATT/WTO System* p. 46–49.

[98] See a table with the summary of these requests in WTO, *Exploring the Links between Subsidies, Trade and the WTO* p. 204.

[99] On the economics of export subsidies, see especially Green and Trebilcock, "The Enduring Problem of World Trade Organization Export Subsidies Rules" p. 127–30. See also WTO, *Exploring the Links between Subsidies, Trade and the WTO* p. 205–06.

[100] WTO, *Exploring the Links between Subsidies, Trade and the WTO* p. 203.

5.2.2.3   *De Minimis* and Negligible Subsidies

Another flexibility is established by SCM Agreement Article 11.9, which provides for termination of investigations and measures against subsidies "in cases where the amount of a subsidy is *de minimis* (i.e. less than 1 per cent ad valorem), or where the volume of subsidized imports, actual or potential, or the injury, is negligible."[101]

This rule does not presume that such subsidies are consistent with the SCM Agreement, nor does it assume that they are incapable of producing negative externalities. Rather, it simply excludes the application of administrative measures to *de minimis* and negligible subsidies,[102] as

---

[101] Bossche and Zdouc, *The Law and Policy of the World Trade Organization: Text, Cases, and Materials* p. 588 (footnote omitted). As noted by Coppens, "an application to investigate should be rejected and an investigation should be terminated as soon as the authorities are satisfied that there is not sufficient evidence of either subsidization of injury. It should be terminated (i) when the amount of the subsidy is *de minimis* which is the case if it is less than 1 percent ad valorem, or (ii) where the volume of the subsidized imports or the injury is negligible, but this concept is not defined," Coppens, *WTO Disciplines on Subsidies and Countervailing Measures: Balancing Policy Space and Legal Constraints* p. 202.

[102] As noted by Steger, raising the level of *de minimis* subsidies has been one of the tools under negotiation so as to afford more policy space to WTO Members: "several proposals have been made in the Doha Round dealing with countervailing duty investigations and measures. They can be separated into two main types: (1) proposals to prevent abuses in the administration of countervailing duty laws (or to constrain the use of them), and (2) proposals to strengthen countervailing duty laws (or to make them easier to use)." Examples of the first are "increasing the threshold for standing to initiate investigations; clarification of the rules relating to the product under investigation; increasing the thresholds for *de minimis* subsidization and negligible subsidized import volumes; clarifying and expanding the guidelines for calculating the benefit to the recipient under Article 14 of the SCM Agreement; improving the rules relating to cumulation; making the provisions relating to undertakings more workable; developing improved procedures for administrative reviews and sunset reviews; ensuring that measures are not continued longer than necessary; and making 'lesser duty' rules or 'public interest' provisions mandatory"; of the second, "eliminating the requirement for an injury test for export subsidies; expansion and clarification of the concept of government 'direction' of private action in the definition of subsidy; anti-circumvention procedures and measures; rules and procedures for 'persistent' subsidization; expanding the prohibited subsidy category to include the 'dark amber' category in Article 6.1; improving and clarifying the provisions dealing with sampling methods and verification procedures; expanding the scope for retroactive application of duties; improving and clarifying the mechanisms for dealing with perishable, seasonal and cyclical products; and adding procedures to deal with large, fragmented industries." Steger, "The WTO Doha Round Negotiations on Subsidies and Countervailing Measures: Issues for Negotiators" p. 5.

well as those in relation to which thresholds are set "higher in case CVDs are initiated against developing countries."[103]

5.2.3   The Use of GATT Exceptions

Commentators have often suggested that, due to the absence of any general exception from the SCM Agreement, it should be possible to apply to subsidies the justifications contained in Article XX of the GATT. The use of the GATT general exception to justify a breach of the SCM Agreement is a controversial issue on which there has not yet been a clear decision by the WTO bodies.

Jurisprudential and doctrinal reasoning offer arguments both for and against the application of GATT Article XX to the SCM Agreement.[104] Careful scrutiny is therefore necessary to elicit reasons why Article XX may or may not apply to the SCM Agreement.

5.2.3.1   GATT Article XX

Article XX of the GATT sets out a general exception to all the obligations contained in the GATT. This means that, whenever a provision of the GATT is violated, the exception provided by Article XX may be invoked by the violating Member to justify its violation and obtain exemption from compliance with the obligation.[105]

---

[103] Coppens, *WTO Disciplines on Subsidies and Countervailing Measures: Balancing Policy Space and Legal Constraints* p. 202. See also Benitah, *The Law of Subsidies under the GATT/WTO System* pp. 44–45.

[104] In view of the decision, Brazil – Desiccated Coconut, which highlighted that "the relationship between the GATT 1994 and the other goods agreements in Annex 1A is complex and must be examined on a case-by-case basis." Appellate Body Report, Brazil – Measures Affecting Desiccated Coconut, WT/DS22/AB/R, adopted 20 March 1997, DSR 1997:I, p. 14.

[105] The Appellate Body in US – Shrimp reverted the Panel's decision that Article XX cannot be used to justify internal policies implemented unilaterally by a country: "Conditioning access to a Member's domestic market on whether exporting Members comply with, or adopt, a policy or policies unilaterally prescribed by the importing Member may, to some degree, be a common aspect of measures falling within the scope of one or another of the exceptions (a) to (j) of Article XX. Paragraphs (a) to (j) comprise measures that are recognized as exceptions to substantive obligations established in the GATT 1994, because the domestic policies embodied in such measures have been recognized as important and legitimate in character. It is not necessary to assume that requiring from exporting countries compliance with, or adoption of, certain policies (although covered in principle by one or another of the exceptions) prescribed by the importing country, renders a measure a priori incapable of justification under Article XX. Such an interpretation renders most, if not all, of the specific exceptions of Article XX inutile,

Article XX has, on several occasions, been subject to review in the dispute settlement system. Regarding its scope, the Appellate Body decided, in *US – Gasoline*, that Article XX applies to all of the obligations contained in the GATT.[106] This is so because Article XX uses (differently than the SCM Agreement exceptions) broad language that covers issues related to external matters (such as environment and health), as well as internal concerns (such as internal policies and public morals).

The use of less precise language increases the potential for opportunistic use of exceptions. To control for good faith, Article XX establishes two legal tests: the "necessity" test and the "less trade restrictive" test. While controlling for opportunistic behavior, these tests attempt to define a point of equilibrium at which the rights of Members are balanced against the restrictions imposed by others. In *US – Shrimp*, the Appellate Body described the nature and purpose of Article XX as creating a balance between rights and duties[107] brought about by the structure of Article XX and the application of its two-tier test.

5.2.3.1.1   **Two-Tier Test**   The caselaw concerning the incidence of an Article XX exception requires a two-tier analysis: (i) first, as to whether a measure falls within the scope of one of the specified situations constituting a violation of a substantial obligation under the GATT; and (ii)

---

a result abhorrent to the principles of interpretation we are bound to apply." Appellate Body Report, United States – Import Prohibition of Certain Shrimp and Shrimp Products (US – Shrimp), WT/DS58/AB/R, adopted 6 November 1998, DSR 1998:VII, p. 2755, para. 121.

[106] In the words of the AB: "The chapeau says that 'nothing in this Agreement shall be construed to prevent the adoption or enforcement by any contracting party of measures ... ' The exceptions listed in Article XX thus relate to all of the obligations under the General Agreement: the national treatment obligation and the most-favoured-nation obligation, of course, but others as well." Appellate Body Report, United States – Standards for Reformulated and Conventional Gasoline (US – Gasoline), WT/DS2/AB/R, adopted 20 May 1996, DSR 1996:I, p. 3, para. 24.

[107] The AB also decided that " ... interpreting and applying the chapeau is, hence, essentially the delicate one of locating and marking out a line of equilibrium between the right of a Member to invoke an exception under Article XX and the rights of the other Members under varying substantive provisions (e.g., Article XI) of the GATT 1994, so that neither of the competing rights will cancel out the other and thereby distort and nullify or impair the balance of rights and obligations constructed by the Members themselves in that Agreement. The location of the line of equilibrium, as expressed in the chapeau, is not fixed and unchanging; the line moves as the kind and the shape of the measures at stake vary and as the facts making up specific cases differ." Appellate Body Report, US – Shrimp, para. 159.

secondly, as to whether, taking into account the *chapeau*, the measure has been applied in a manner that would constitute neither an arbitrary or unjustifiable discrimination in countries where the same conditions prevail, nor a disguised restriction on trade. Justification of a measure under Article XX requires that both elements of the test be satisfied.[108]

The two-tier analysis requires that if a Member is to invoke its right to exception under Article XX, it must first prove that the measure falls within one of the categories of subject matter described by Article XX in subparagraphs (i) to (j). A breach of a GATT violation may be justified if it relates to, or is necessary to protect, (among other things) public morals, human, animal or plant life, and exhaustible natural resources.[109]

---

[108] The Appellate Body confirmed that examination of a measure under Article XX is two-tiered. "In order that the justifying protection of Article XX may be extended to it, the measure at issue must not only come under one or another of the particular exceptions – paragraphs (a) to (j) – listed under Article XX; it must also satisfy the requirements imposed by the opening clauses of Article XX. The analysis is, in other words, two-tiered: first, provisional justification by reason of characterization of the measure under XX(g); second, further appraisal of the same measure under the introductory clauses of Article XX." Appellate Body Report, US – Gasoline, p 3 at 20.

[109] Subparagraphs of Article XX: "(a) necessary to protect public morals; (b) necessary to protect human, animal or plant life or health; (c) relating to the importations or exportations of gold or silver; (d) necessary to secure compliance with laws or regulations which are not inconsistent with the provisions of this Agreement, including those relating to customs enforcement, the enforcement of monopolies operated under paragraph 4 of Article II and Article XVII, the protection of patents, trade marks and copyrights, and the prevention of deceptive practices; (e) relating to the products of prison labour; (f) imposed for the protection of national treasures of artistic, historic or archaeological value; (g) relating to the conservation of exhaustible natural resources if such measures are made effective in conjunction with restrictions on domestic production or consumption; (h) undertaken in pursuance of obligations under any intergovernmental commodity agreement which conforms to criteria submitted to the CONTRACTING PARTIES and not disapproved by them or which is itself so submitted and not so disapproved; (i) involving restrictions on exports of domestic materials necessary to ensure essential quantities of such materials to a domestic processing industry during periods when the domestic price of such materials is held below the world price as part of a governmental stabilization plan; Provided that such restrictions shall not operate to increase the exports of or the protection afforded to such domestic industry, and shall not depart from the provisions of this Agreement relating to non-discrimination; (j) essential to the acquisition or distribution of products in general or local short supply; Provided that any such measures shall be consistent with the principle that all contracting parties are entitled to an equitable share of the international supply of such products, and that any such measures, which are inconsistent with the other provisions of the Agreement shall be discontinued as soon as the conditions giving rise to them have ceased to exist. The CONTRACTING PARTIES shall review the need for this sub-paragraph not later than 30 June 1960." Article XX GATT.

In relation to the application of subparagraphs (a), (b), and (d), which require measures to be "necessary," the Dispute Settlement Body has developed the so-called "necessity test"[110]. In such situations, the defendant country must prove that the application of the measure is indeed necessary in order to reach a certain policy objective; "necessary" meaning that there can be no alternative, less trade-restrictive, measure available.[111]

5.2.3.1.2 *Chapeau*   After a measure has been provisionally justified by reason of one of the subparagraphs of GATT Article XX, the analysis proceeds to examination of the *chapeau* of the provision. The scope of the

---

[110] It is important to mention that a different language was used for different subparagraphs: "necessary," "relating to," "in pursuance of," "essential," "for the protection of and involving." Each of these terms have a different meaning, therefore, depending on the subparagraph invoked, the argumentation will be different (sometimes requiring a higher level of demonstration and sometimes not too much). This decision was confirmed by the Appellate Body in US – Gasoline: "Applying the basic principle of interpretation that the words of a treaty, like the General Agreement, are to be given their ordinary meaning, in their context and in the light of the treaty's object and purpose, the Appellate Body observes that the Panel Report failed to take adequate account of the words actually used by Article XX in its several paragraphs. In enumerating the various categories of governmental acts, laws or regulations which WTO Members may carry out or promulgate in pursuit of differing legitimate state policies or interests outside the realm of trade liberalization, Article XX uses different terms in respect of different categories: (ii) 'necessary' – in paragraphs (a), (b) and (d); 'essential' – in paragraph (j); 'relating to' – in paragraphs (c), (e) and (g); 'for the protection of' – in paragraph (f); 'in pursuance of' – in paragraph (h); and 'involving' – in paragraph (i). It does not seem reasonable to suppose that the WTO Members intended to require, in respect of each and every category, the same kind or degree of connection or relationship between the measure under appraisal and the state interest or policy sought to be promoted or realized." Appellate Body Report, United states – Standards for Reformulated and Conventional Gasoline, WT/DS2/AB/R, adopted 20 May 1996, DSR 1996:I, p. 17.

[111] This decision was confirmed by the Appellate Body in Korea – Beef: "In sum, determination of whether a measure, which is not 'indispensable', may nevertheless be 'necessary' within the contemplation of Article XX(d), involves in every case a process of weighing and balancing a series of factors which prominently include the contribution made by the compliance measure to the enforcement of the law or regulation at issue, the importance of the common interests or values protected by that law or regulation, and the accompanying impact of the law or regulation on imports or exports." Appellate Body Report, Korea – Measures Affecting Imports of Fresh, Chilled and Frozen Beef (Korea – Various Measures on Beef), WT/DS161/AB/R, WT/DS169/AB/R, adopted 10 January 2001, DSR 2001:I, p. 5, para. 164. See also Gabrielle Zoe Marceau and Joel P Trachtman, "The Technical Barriers to Trade Agreement, the Sanitary and Physanitary Measures Agreement, and the General Agreement on Tariffs and Trade: A Map of the New World Trade Organization Law of Domestic Regulation of Goods" (2002) 36 Journal of World Trade p. 811–81.

chapeau is broader than that of the subparagraphs, since it addresses the overall rationality and reasonableness of the measure. While subparagraphs (i) to (j) facilitate identification and analysis of the objective of the measure, the *chapeau* elicits evaluation of the manner of application of the measure, and in particular whether or not it constitutes an arbitrary or unjustifiable discrimination or a disguised restriction on international trade.[112]

The Appellate Body in *US – Gasoline* opined that the *chapeau* is more relevant to a *de facto* than to a *de jure* analysis, and determined that the purpose of the *chapeau* is to avoid the "abuse of exceptions."[113] This idea of preventing the abuse of rights is confirmed by the AB in *US – Shrimp*, which refers to Article XX as an expression of good faith.[114]

As exceptions of a general nature are prone to open a door to opportunism, it is necessary to incorporate controls into an agreement to

---

[112] This broader scope is confirmed by the decision of the Appellate Body in US – Shrimp: "The standards established in the chapeau are, moreover, necessarily broad in scope and reach: the prohibition of the application of a measure 'in a manner which would constitute a means of arbitrary or unjustifiable discrimination between countries where the same conditions prevail' or 'a disguised restriction on international trade.' When applied in a particular case, the actual contours and contents of these standards will vary as the kind of measure under examination varies." Appellate Body Report, US – Shrimp, para. 120.

[113] In this sense, the AB has already decided that: "The chapeau by its express terms addresses, not so much the questioned measure or its specific contents as such, but rather the manner in which that measure is applied. It is, accordingly, important to underscore that the purpose and object of the introductory clauses of Article XX is generally the prevention of 'abuse of the exceptions of [what was later to become] Article [XX].' This insight drawn from the drafting history of Article XX is a valuable one. The chapeau is animated by the principle that while the exceptions of Article XX may be invoked as a matter of legal right, they should not be so applied as to frustrate or defeat the legal obligations of the holder of the right under the substantive rules of the General Agreement. If those exceptions are not to be abused or misused, in other words, the measures falling within the particular exceptions must be applied reasonably, with due regard both to the legal duties of the party claiming the exception and the legal rights of the other parties concerned." Appellate Body Report, US – Gasoline, para. 22.

[114] Similarly, the AB stated that: "The chapeau of Article XX is, in fact, but one expression of the principle of good faith. This principle, at once a general principle of law and a general principle of international law, controls the exercise of rights by states. One application of this general principle, the application widely known as the doctrine of abus de droit, prohibits the abusive exercise of a state's rights and enjoins that whenever the assertion of a right 'impinges on the field covered by [a] treaty obligation, it must be exercised bona fide, that is to say, reasonably.' An abusive exercise by a Member of its own treaty right thus results in a breach of the treaty rights of the other Members and, as well, a violation of the treaty obligation of the Member so acting." Appellate Body Report, US – Shrimp, para. 158.

prevent opportunistic measures.[115] This is generally achieved by the assignment of powers to courts, to facilitate the conduct of legal and economic tests that act as yardsticks of good faith and non-discrimination to control for opportunistic measures. As van Aaken put it, a measure taken in good faith "is unlikely to be the result of an opportunistic behavior by the government but rather a demand of evolving factual and legal circumstances, that is, it is to be assumed that a purpose enhancing the welfare of the citizens is behind the measure."[116] Accordingly, "a measure taken in good faith should be more readily accepted by tribunals." After all, had the parties foreseen the contingency *ex ante*, they might have regulated the matter differently, probably excluding the need for compensation. Even if the parties had explicitly agreed on compensation in advance, however, the complaining party bears the burden of proving that it should be compensated.[117]

Discriminatory measures, on the other hand, are usually presumed to be in breach of a trade agreement, because "from a political economy point of view [...] there is reasonable suspicion that the motivation behind the policy measure is a protective one."[118] The legal consequences are twofold. First, "[a]s with the good faith review, nondiscriminatory conduct should not lead to a finding of a violation"[119] except in exceptional circumstances contemplated by the agreement. Secondly, even though discrimination is considered a strong indicator of opportunism, the intent behind the measure may have an "exculpatory role since even discriminatory conduct may be permissible if the effect is discriminatory but the intent is benevolent."[120] The legal burden should lie therefore with the defendant to prove that a discriminatory measure does not give rise to a need for compensation.

---

[115] See Schropp, *Trade Policy Flexibility and Enforcement in the WTO: A Law and Economic Analysis* p. 85–93.

[116] van Aaken, "Smart Flexibility Clauses in International Investment Treaties and Sustainable Development" p. 852.

[117] As a result, if a measure is taken in good faith, the complaining party should not be compensated unless explicitly foreseen in the agreement, and even in such case the complaining party would bear the burden of proof to demonstrate that it should be compensated. See ibid. p. 837–39.

[118] Ibid. p. 853–54.

[119] Ibid.

[120] Ibid.

5.2.3.2   GATT Article XXI

A further GATT clause introduces flexibilities in the context of security issues. Article XXI allows WTO members to "breach their GATT obligations for national security reasons,"[121] providing that a WTO Member can take essentially "any action which it considers necessary for the protection of its essential security interests."[122]

It may be noted that, despite the proximity of GATT Articles XX and XXI, and that both are exceptions to the rules, they are used in remarkably different ways. Article XXI has rarely been employed as a justification mechanism in WTO jurisprudence and, so far, there are very few examples of interpretation available for analysis. This provides an interesting contrast to the extensive use that has been made of Article XX, as well as the different type of language employed. The text of Article XXI, "which it considers necessary," is commonly understood as a "self-judging" clause.

Self-judging clauses are:

> provisions in international legal instruments by means of which states retain their right to escape or derogate from an international obligation based on unilateral consideration and based on their subjective appreciation of whether to make use of and invoke the clauses vis-à-vis other states or international organizations.[123]

By limiting the scope of review by the courts, self-judging clauses increase the level of discretion held by states with respect to the way that they implement their policies.

---

[121] Peter Lindsay, "The Ambiguity of GATT Article XXI: Subtle Success or Rampant Failure?" (2003) 52 *Duke Law Journal* p. 1277–313, 1278.

[122] The precise wording of the Article reads as following: "Article XXI Security Exceptions Nothing in this Agreement shall be construed (a) to require any contracting party to furnish any information the disclosure of which it considers contrary to its essential security interests; or (b) to prevent any contracting party from taking any action which it considers necessary for the protection of its essential security interests (i) relating to fissionable materials or the materials from which they are derived; (ii) relating to the traffic in arms, ammunition and implements of war and to such traffic in other goods and materials as is carried on directly or indirectly for the purpose of supplying a military establishment; (iii) taken in time of war or other emergency in international relations; or (c) to prevent any contracting party from taking any action in pursuance of its obligations under the United Nations Charter for the maintenance of international peace and security."

[123] The definition of self-judging clauses is not yet pacified in the international law doctrine. This work will make use of the definition used above proposed by Schill and Briese in "'If the State Considers': Self-Judging Clauses in International Dispute Settlement" p. 68.

To employ such clauses, states determine which policy areas will be subject to stringent review and establish requirements for policy implementation in those areas. States thereby obtain greater discretion over the use of measures covered by the self-judging clause, but only "within the scope of application of the clause."[124] They thus retain a great degree of flexibility because they are able to reserve to themselves the power to apply and interpret the law whenever an unforeseen event takes place.

This might, ideally, lead to a situation in which a state party to (an incomplete) treaty has the *ex post* opportunity to exercise regret in good faith and adjust its behavior to a new event or set of circumstances, by abstaining from performance of a certain obligation. This is in keeping with the notion that, could the state have anticipated the event, it would have contracted differently.

The possibility of misuse, and thus a need for control, is not in fact a prerogative of self-judging clauses.[125] In reality, there is, however, a concern that self-judging clauses may "invite the state that is invoking such a clause ex post . . . to make use of its discretion in a manner that is beyond what the Contracting states had originally anticipated."[126] In other words, self-judging clauses might permit states to behave opportunistically once an unanticipated event has occurred.

This narrative is especially important for purposes of international law. There are certain areas of state sovereignty, such as matters of national security, that states might be unwilling to delegate to the courts, as previously discussed, thus restricting the competence of the judiciary to review certain aspects of a measure.

It is not difficult to see that protectionist measures could be embedded in self-declared national security measures, but that is not to say that parties might not be willing to subject such measures to good faith control. It simply means that states might choose to limit the power of courts on certain sensitive matters. In its evaluation of the consistency of self-judging clauses, such as GATT Article XXI with WTO rules, the WTO dispute settlement system is expected to control for opportunistic behavior by monitoring good faith limits defined by legality, rather than expediency. In practice, for instance, indication of good faith would be strong in cases in which a state is merely implementing obligations

[124] Ibid. p. 65.
[125] Though they might arguably more easily hide opportunistic intent due to the greater discretion given to states.
[126] Schill and Briese, "'If the State Considers': Self-Judging Clauses in International Dispute Settlement" p. 64.

arising from other international agreements. This could also apply to decisions under non-self-judging Article XX.[127]

5.2.3.3   The Relationship of GATT to Other Covered Agreements

The significance of the GATT throughout WTO history is indisputable. Since its creation in 1947 as a result of the Bretton Woods Agreement, the GATT has been the main, and possibly the only, source of law to guide trade relationships between countries.

With rounds of negotiation during the second half of the twentieth century culminating in the creation of the WTO, however, a wide range of specific agreements came into existence to complement the GATT. New subject matter expanded the WTO sphere on themes related to: services, intellectual property, agriculture, subsidies, technical barriers, anti-dumping, and many more.

Having broadened its reach, it was inevitable that WTO law and especially the WTO Agreements would overlap and conflict with each other. The issue, therefore, is how this process of overlapping and conflicting norms works, and how the dispute settlement agreement has dealt with it.

5.2.3.3.1   Single Undertaking   Fundamental to this analysis is the idea of a "single undertaking."[128] As a principle of negotiation in WTO law, the single undertaking means that "every item of the negotiation is part of a whole and indivisible package and cannot be agreed separately."[129]

The single undertaking may be understood from two perspectives. It is both (i) a "single political undertaking," which motivates the WTO negotiation method ("nothing is agreed until everything is agreed"); and (ii) a "single legal undertaking," meaning that "results of the negotiations would form a 'single package' to be implemented as one single treaty."[130] In the case of conflicting rules, therefore, it must be

---

[127] See van Aaken, "Control Mechanisms in International Investment Law" p. 422–24.

[128] Para. 47, Doha Ministerial Declaration, WT/MIN/DEC/1 20 November 2001. Available in: https://www.wto.org/english/thewto_e/minist_e/min01_e/mindecl_e.htm #organization.

[129] Available in: https://www.wto.org/english/tratop_e/dda_e/work_organi_e.htm (accessed 05.09.2015).

[130] Marceau and Trachtman, "The Technical Barriers to Trade Agreement, the Sanitary and Physanitary Measures Agreement, and the General Agreement on Tariffs and Trade: A Map of the New World Trade Organization Law of Domestic Regulation of Goods" p. 812, fn 5.

acknowledged that all the agreements aim to be read as a whole, or as one single, agreement. Gabrielle Marceau and Joel Trachtman explain that the provisions of the WTO Agreements were "originally negotiated through fifteen different working groups, which may not have been sufficiently coordinated with one another."[131] As there may, accordingly, be contradictions within the WTO Agreements, the concept of a "single undertaking" emphasizes their coherence.

5.2.3.3.2   Lex Specialis Principle   The principle of *lex specialis derrogat generali* is a general principle aimed at reconciling rules that are in conflict with one another. This principle states that where a more specific rule is present, it prevails over the general one.

In WTO law, the WTO Agreement establishes, in regard to the relationship between the GATT and agreements identified in its Annex 1A that:

> In the event of conflict between a provision of the General Agreement on Tariffs and Trade 1994 and a provision of another agreement in Annex 1A to the Agreement Establishing the World Trade Organization (referred to in the agreements in Annex 1A as the 'WTO Agreement'), the provision of the other agreement shall prevail to the extent of the conflict.[132]

This is an example of the principle of *lex specialis*, since the provisions of the other agreements from Annex 1A, which are more specific than the GATT, prevail over the GATT provisions. There are, however, certain important premises on which the principle operates: (i) *lex specialis* will apply only when provisions of the GATT and provisions of the other agreements conflict—which is difficult to demonstrate on the basis of WTO caselaw; and (ii) the scope of application of the principle is limited to the extent of the conflict.

Hence, a divergence from the principle, in its original form, is already perceptible: while the *lex specialis derrogat generali* causes a deviation from the general rule by application of the specific, in WTO law the applicability of the general law (the GATT) is not compromised by this because the GATT will only be dismissed where there is a contradiction with a specific rule, and only to the extent of the conflict. To fully understand the use of the *lex specialis derrogat generali*, therefore, it is necessary to know when provisions are considered to be "in conflict"

[131] Ibid. p. 812.
[132] General interpretative note to Annex 1A, WTO Agreement.

with one another, and what contribution the "extent of the conflict" makes to this analysis.

5.2.4 Monitoring

SCM Agreement Article 26.1 gives the Subsidies Committee responsibility for surveillance, mandating "that emphasis should be placed on new and full subsidy notification being submitted every two years, while updating notifications in the interim years is de-emphasized."[133]

In keeping with the rules established in Article 25.11, Members are not only to notify the Committee of any new countervailing measures, but must also "submit, on a semi-annual basis, reports on any countervailing duty actions taken within the preceding six months." The Committee is to regularly examine these reports.

Given that "transparency is essential for the effective operation of the SCM Agreement,"[134] the procedure of notification—under the authority of the Subsidies Committee—is significant in its enhancement of a pillar principle of the WTO.

The notification requirement applies to every specific subsidy "granted or maintained within" a Member's territory, and "shall be submitted not later than 30 June of each year." The content of the notification "should be sufficiently specific to enable other Members to evaluate the trade effects and to understand the operation of notified subsidy programmes." SCM Article 25.3 itemizes five specific pieces of information, all of which must be provided; in the absence of any one of them "an explanation shall be provided." If subsidies "are granted to specific products or sectors, the notifications should be organized by product or sector." Should Members consider that there is no need to notify, they must "inform the Secretariat in writing" about this decision.

SCM Article 25.7 indicates recognition by Members that notifications do not alter the status, effects, or nature of the measure itself under either the GATT 1994 or the SCM Agreement. This was affirmed by the Appellate Body in Brazil – Aircraft, which stated that "Article 25 aims to promote transparency by requiring Members to notify their subsidies, without prejudging the legal status of those subsidies."[135] The Panel in

---

[133] Bossche and Zdouc, The Law and Policy of the World Trade Organization: Text, Cases, and Materials p. 832.

[134] Ibid.

[135] Appellate Body Report, Brazil – Export Financing Programme for Aircraft (Brazil – Aircraft), WT/DS46/AB/R, adopted 20 August 1999, DSR 1999:III, p. 1161, para. 149.

Canada – Aircraft states, further, that "the mere notification by Canada of the programme under these subsidiary agreements was an insufficient basis for a finding of a prima facie case that subsidiary agreement assistance was provided in the form of non-repayable contributions."[136]

Under SCM Article 25.8 concerning notifications by other Members, "Any Member may, at any time, make a written request for information on the nature and extent of any subsidy granted or maintained by another Member (including any subsidy referred to in Part IV), or for an explanation of the reasons for which a specific measure has been considered as not subject to the requirement of notification." SCM Article 25.10 stipulates, further, that "Any Member which considers that any measure of another Member having the effects of a subsidy has not been notified in accordance with the provisions of paragraph 1 of Article XVI of GATT 1994 and this Article may bring the matter to the attention of such other Member. If the alleged subsidy is not thereafter notified promptly, such Member may itself bring the alleged subsidy in question to the notice of the Committee."

Notifications, along with the Subsidies Committee, also play an important role with regard to countervailing duties. Article 25.11 requires that these duties be reported without delay to the Subsidies Committee and be available to all the Members. Members must also notify the Committee about the domestic authority and procedure of the imposition of countervailing duties within their territories.

The so-called Trade Policy Review (TPR), which complements the mechanism of notification, is also fundamental to assurance of transparency in the WTO.[137] The TPR "was an early result of the Uruguay Round, established during the negotiation period in December 1988. Later, Annex 3 of the Marrakesh Agreement placed the TPR on an equal footing with other WTO agreements."[138] The main objective of the mechanism is

---

[136] Panel Report, Canada – Aircraft, para. 9.256.
[137] WTO, *Understanding the WTO* (WTO 2015) p. 53. Individuals and companies involved in trade have to know as much as possible about the conditions of trade. It is therefore fundamentally important that regulations and policies are transparent. In the WTO, this is achieved in two ways: governments have to inform the WTO and fellow Members of specific measures, policies, or laws through regular "notifications"; and the WTO conducts regular reviews of individual countries' trade policies—the trade policy reviews.
[138] Julien Chaisse and Debashis Chakraborty, "Implementing WTO Rules through Negotiations and Sanction: The Role of Trade Policy Review Mechanism and Dispute Settlement System" (2007) 28 *University of Pennsylvania Journal of International Economic Law* p. 158–59.

"facilitating the smooth functioning of the multilateral trading system by enhancing the transparency of members' trade policies."[139]

The Trade Policy Review Body, which is an "*alter ego* of the General Council,"[140] is responsible for production of the Trade Policy Review Reports. This is evident from Article IV:4 of the Marrakesh Agreement, which states that:

> The General Council shall convene as appropriate to discharge the responsibilities of the Trade Policy Review Body provided for in the TPRM. The Trade Policy Review Body may have its own chairman and shall establish such rules of procedure as it deems necessary for the fulfilment of those responsibilities.

Notably, "the TPR examines every national policy adopted to check their compatibility with the WTO agreements"[141] and "implementation of WTO agreements clearly remains one of the most important issues discussed within the TPR."[142] Ensuring compatibility with WTO obligations is therefore a cornerstone of the publication of Trade Policy Reports.

A trade policy review differs from a decision of the Dispute Settlement Body, in that it is "performed independently of any litigation and its results have no binding effect. This function was underlined by the Ministerial Conference,"[143] which states that, because of the policy character of the TPR mechanism, it cannot "serve as a basis for the enforcement of specific WTO obligations or for dispute settlement procedures, or to impose new policy commitments on Members."[144] The Trade Policy Reports, despite having no binding effect on Members, play an important role in influencing the actions of Members because "diplomatic pressure is sometimes so severe that a country will have to conform to the report, if only to avoid a potential litigation."[145]

---

[139] Ibid. p. 159.
[140] Bossche and Zdouc, *The Law and Policy of the World Trade Organization: Text, Cases, and Materials* p. 124.
[141] Chaisse and Chakraborty, "Implementing WTO Rules through Negotiations and Sanction: The Role of Trade Policy Review Mechanism and Dispute Settlement System" p. 159.
[142] Ibid.
[143] Ibid. p. 160–61.
[144] Ministerial Conference of Nov. 30–Dec. 3, 1999.
[145] Chaisse and Chakraborty, "Implementing WTO Rules through Negotiations and Sanction: The Role of Trade Policy Review Mechanism and Dispute Settlement System" p. 160–61.

With respect to procedural issues, the periodicity required of such reports varies depending "on the members' share of world trade,"[146] and is less frequent in relation to developing and least developed Members. The review also results in the production of and independent report written by the WTO Secretariat.[147] This report then may highlight concerning policy areas and serves, therefore, as a source of information for WTO Members to exercise peer pressure.

5.3   Remarks on the Level of Flexibility

This chapter used elements of contract theory with which to analyze the flexibilities and monitoring mechanisms of the SCM Agreement. The analysis concludes that drafters of the SCM Agreement attempted to set up a complex system of rules capable of coping with various types of uncertainty to which the Agreement is subject.

First, language was used in the Agreement with various levels of precision. Broad language was used to delegate powers to third parties, and to delineate the scope of the Agreement through the definition of subsidy, and especially the definition of benefit. Under contract theory, this may be understood as a response to contingencies, or as a mechanism to ensure *ex post* that the treaty is adequate to address events that were not foreseen by the drafters.

Very precise language was on the other hand used in Article 8 (exceptions) to restrict the competence of the courts and set a very clear road map for WTO Member use of permitted subsidies. Even though it is debatable whether this is the best way to address uncertainties related to the behavior of parties, contract theory suggests that imposition of very specific requirements is a legitimate method of controlling for opportunistic behavior.

Secondly, the system of monitoring is, in relation to control of opportunistic behavior, an important element in fostering transparency and avoiding the bad faith use of subsidies. The system should ensure that WTO Members disclose certain subsidizing measures in order to allow

---

[146] Ibid. p. 161. "Indeed, the Annex mandates that the four members with the largest share of world trade (currently the EC, the United states, Japan, and Canada) be reviewed every two years, the next sixteen members be reviewed every four years, and others be reviewed every six years. A longer period may be fixed for least-developed members. The idea is to carry on a regular review of the import polices in major import destinations so as to ensure minimum trade diversion."

[147] Ibid. p. 162.

others to better understand and evaluate its functions and objectives, and to assess its potential effects within their borders.

Thirdly, the SCM Agreement also makes use of various default rules. Prohibited subsidies are prohibited *per se* and are protected by a property rule, whereas actionable subsidies face an effects test, and any inconsistency with the WTO rules can be remedied by compensation under a liability rule.

This complex system of flexibility is emphasized here because legal scholars commonly assess the level of flexibility in the SCM Agreement solely by a focus on the availability of exceptions. The focus on exception clauses, given that contract theory provides negotiators with many other instruments of flexibility, suggests that legal theory has an inadequate grasp of the concept of contractual flexibility.

In spite of the efforts involved in the establishment of such a complex system of flexibility, certain problems remain. The flexibilities in the current SCM Agreement are limited, in terms of coverage and substance, and several economic areas that might be subject to market failure are left out. Moreover, many of the exceptions were subject to temporal limitations and have already been phased out, or they have been applied only to certain countries (mainly developing countries) despite economic rationale to suggest that they have relevance for the whole WTO membership.

There are, nevertheless, ways of overcoming these difficulties. One solution would be to redesign the rules. A second would be to interpret the SCM Agreement in a manner that affords more flexibility to Member States, while controlling for opportunistic behavior.

6

Final Remarks and Policy Recommendations

Employing an analytical framework based in contract theory, this work indicates that the SCM Agreement has instituted a set of mechanisms designed to foster completion of its rules. The current system may not be entirely adequate to its task, but clearly the flexibility of the SCM Agreement should not be judged solely on the availability of exemption clauses, as most legal scholars do. In many cases, results similar to those achieved by use of explicit exceptions, such as GATT Article XX, could be obtained by a more detailed description of obligations and the use of appropriate default rules. By identification of such alternative means of flexibility, this work facilitates examination of the adequacy of mechanisms other than exceptions, and a better comprehension of levels of flexibility overall.

Potential for improvement of this complex system of flexibility has been demonstrated, therefore, through a broader analysis involving both amendment and interpretation of the rules. Even though there is an apparent economic rationale for their more stringent regulation, the current rules leave virtually no margin of flexibility in the use of certain prohibited subsidies. Import substitution subsidies are not only prohibited *per se*, but are also protected by a property rule, leaving no available justification for their use. The pressure that this places on interpreters of the rules results in solutions that may not always be optimal.[1]

Secondly, the SCM Agreement fails to provide clear rules for use in moments of crisis. While such rules are not a *sine qua non* of adequate contractual flexibility, they have proven to be useful in the regulation of international trade.[2] A clear set of rules in regard to subsidies, for

---

[1] See discussion on Canada – Renewables in Section 4.3.2.3.1.
[2] See GATT Article XXI. See also Lindsay, "The Ambiguity of GATT Article XXI: Subtle Success or Rampant Failure?"

instance, might have better dealt with measures taken during the recent global financial crisis. Scholars suggest that although rules on export subsidies were mostly complied with, a series of import substitution subsidies were employed by WTO Members, many in potential contradiction of Article 3 of the SCM Agreement.[3]

Thirdly, unnecessary gaps may be observed in the current SCM Agreement. Several important rules of the SCM Agreement, for example, have expired because the further negotiation among WTO Members necessary to ensure they remained in force was prevented by the gridlock of the Doha Round. The current level of legal uncertainty or ambiguity regarding the Agreement is, as a result, particularly high, and the WTO dispute settlement bodies have, in some cases, been reluctant to make use of their general role as treaty interpreters. The applicability of GATT Article XX to the SCM Agreement is, for example, an issue that, had it been clearly addressed, would by now have contributed much to legal security and predictability.

6.1 Interpretation Solutions

A rather straightforward solution that could add a considerable degree of flexibility to the SCM Agreement is offered by interpretation because, while negotiations to amend treaties are at a general impasse, the WTO dispute settlement system has been very active.

Currently at issue is the question of the application of GATT flexibilities to the SCM Agreement. The use of the GATT offers a plausible solution to the need for flexibility, because there is no clear rule in the SCM Agreement regarding the application of GATT rules, resulting in legal ambiguity that it would be suitable for courts and legal experts to resolve. Had there been an express veto over the use of GATT rules, courts would be obliged not to rule *contra legem*, and it would therefore have been necessary to amend the treaty.

As a matter of treaty interpretation, however, there are arguments against the application of GATT rules to the SCM Agreement.

From the knowledge that the SCM Agreement is a development of GATT Articles VI and XVI, it may be extracted that the Agreement is a *lex specialis* of the GATT.[4] As such, it has been said that, "Prima facie,

---

[3] In fact, many of these measures are now being contested. See the Request for Consultations by the EU (WT/DS472/1), and the Request for Consultations by Japan (WT/DS497/1).

[4] This critic is connected to the idea of maintenance of the "inner balance of the rights and obligations of the SCM Agreement," Rubini, "Ain't Wastin' Time No More: Subsidies for

applying the *lex specialis* maxim of interpretation, when dealing with subsidies, attention should be given to the SCM Agreement first and foremost, rather than applying the GATT and its Art XX exceptions."[5]

It is necessary therefore, before reaching for Art. XX exceptions, to determine whether the SCM Agreement itself does not provide an exception.[6] The Agreement used to provide a category of justifications —the non-actionable subsidies—that have since expired[7] because Members were unable to reach the requisite consensus regarding their permanence. Ingrid Jegou and Luca Rubini explain that "The absence of an extension of these rules could be seen as a decision that exceptions should not exist under the SCM Agreement."[8] From this perspective, the intention of the Members in eliminating the non-actionable subsidies of Article 8.2 was clearly to abolish exceptions from the SCM Agreement, not to resort to more justifications for breach of its obligations through the application of GATT Article XX.[9] There would be no logic in

Renewable Energy, The SCM Agreement, Policy Space, and Law Reform" p. 38. According to the decision of the Appellate Body in US – Anti-Dumping and Countervailing Duties (China), there seems to be a preoccupation concerning the broad interpretation of the SCM Agreement: "As we see it, however, too broad an interpretation of the term 'public body' could equally risk upsetting the delicate balance embodied in the SCM Agreement (...)." Appellate Body Report, US – Anti-Dumping and Countervailing Duties (China), paras. 301–03. This understanding is also perceived in the Appellate Body Report of US – Countervailing Duty Investigation on DRAMS, which states that the SCM "reflects a delicate balance between the Members that sought to impose more disciplines on the use of subsidies and those that sought to impose more disciplines on the application of countervailing measures," Appellate Body Report, US – Countervailing Duty Investigation on DRAMS, para. 115. Therefore, the entire idea of the arguments against the application of GATT Article XX is based on the fact that broadening the justification for countries to breach their obligations under the SCM Agreement would undermine the inner functioning of the SCM Agreement.
5 Christopher Tran, "Using GATT, Art XX to Justify Climate Change Measures in Claims under the WTO Agreements" (2010) 27 *Environmental and Planning Law Journal* p. 346, 356.
6 Christopher Tran explains that: "Art 8.2(c) already provided an environmental 'exception' in the form of a non-actionable environmental subsidy, albeit that provision has since sunsetted." Ibid. Therefore, as will be further explained, it is possible to see that the SCM does regulate its exceptions and such provision shall be considered before recurring to the general rule under GATT Article XX.
7 Rubini, "Ain't Wastin' Time No More: Subsidies for Renewable Energy, The SCM Agreement, Policy Space, and Law Reform" p. 38.
8 Ingrid Jegou and Luca Rubini, "The Allocation of Emission Allowances Free of Charge: Legal and Economic Considerations" (2010) ICTSD Global Platform on Climate Change, Trade Policies and Sustainable Energy p. 40.
9 When the SCM disciplined its exceptions, it was clear that the provision in Article 8 was not a development of Article XX of the GATT: "The negotiating record strongly indicates

eliminating one exception to reintroduce it again—along with many others.

Such a view, however, fails to take into account the type of uncertainty to which negotiators were exposed during the drafting of the SCM Agreement. As argued throughout this entire work, treaties require flexibility mechanisms. Exceptions, though not the only available mechanism, provide an instrument for the definition *ex ante* of certain policy areas and measures which, if adopted in good faith, will be exempt from compliance with the relevant obligations. If the SCM Agreement negotiators had anticipated the political deadlock at the WTO negotiations, it might be assumed, on the basis of contract theory, that they would have established instruments capable of striking an appropriate balance between obligations and flexibilities. The rules currently in place however, as noted in Chapters 4 and 5, are not capable of addressing the rigidity of certain rules, a problem that could be remedied by the introduction of an exception.

The language of the *chapeau* itself provides arguments against the application of GATT Article XX. It expressly states that:

> Subject to the requirement that such measures are not applied in a manner which would constitute a means of arbitrary or unjustifiable discrimination between countries where the same conditions prevail, or a disguised restriction on international trade, **nothing in this Agreement** shall be construed to prevent the adoption or enforcement by any contracting party of measures [...]

Some authors assert that when a GATT text uses the expression "this agreement," it does not refer to all of the WTO Agreements generated by the Uruguay Round, but only to the GATT. This textual construction restricts the scope of application of the GATT rules to breaches of the GATT itself.[10]

that the idea was to examine 'green' subsidies in a self-contained manner in the SCM context: documents by the Secretariat, the Chairman of the Negotiating Group on Trade Environment, as well as by various WTO Member belonging to different alliances, such as New Zealand, India, and Austria on behalf of EFTA (European Free Trade Association) strongly support the conclusion that Article 8 SCM was not thought of as an add-on to Article XX GATT, but rather as the only provision dealing with subsidies not bound by the disciplines embedded in the SCM Agreement." Mavroidis, *The Regulation of International Trade: The WTO Agreements on Trade in Goods* p. 479.

[10] As noted by Christopher Tran: "The chapeau of GATT, Art XX expressly refers to 'this Agreement', and this means, according to the cases, the GATT. Tran, "Using GATT, Art XX to Justify Climate Change Measures in Claims under the WTO Agreements" p. 356.

As the SCM Agreement does not, moreover, make any express reference to the GATT or its Article XX, it might be understood that it was not the intention of the Members to make GATT Article XX an available justification. According to Luca Rubini, "when members wanted a justification to be available, they made this clear."[11]

This interpretation, however, fails to provide for the introduction of alternative flexibility mechanisms and, more importantly, ignores the fact that the subsidies rules developed from the general rules on goods regulated by the GATT. The significance of this will be addressed in more detail below.

It is important, for now, to note that as Article XX of the GATT "occupies a central position in the GATT,"[12] its effects could arguably extend to other goods-related agreements. Given that the principle of a single undertaking is a cornerstone of treaty interpretation, the effects of GATT Article XX could extend to the SCM Agreement in order to ensure that the system remains harmonious and functions well as a whole.

In keeping with this argument, the General Interpretative Note to Annex 1A of the WTO Agreement demonstrates how the GATT is developed in other Agreements,[13] supporting the notion that the applicability of the GATT may not depend on any express reference to it. The development, through the entire SCM Agreement, of obligations contained in GATT Articles VI (Anti-Dumping and Countervailing Measures) and XVI (Subsidies) is clear evidence of a material connection between them. What can be taken from this is that the General Interpretative Note to Annex 1A permits the application of the GATT to the extent of the conflict, and it would apply therefore to conflicts under the SCM Agreement only to the extent that they relate to subsidization of industrial goods.[14]

A second line of argument for the application of Article XX focuses on the relationship between the GATT and the SCM Agreement. The GATT

---

[11] Rubini, "Ain't Wastin' Time No More: Subsidies for Renewable Energy, The SCM Agreement, Policy Space, and Law Reform" p. 38. This view can be defended departing from the reading of Article 2.4 of the SPS Agreement, which states that: Sanitary or phytosanitary measures which conform to the relevant provisions of this Agreement shall be presumed to be in accordance with the obligations of the Members under the provisions of GATT 1994 which relate to the use of sanitary or phytosanitary measures, in particular the provisions of Article XX(b).

[12] Ibid. p. 38.

[13] Ibid.

[14] Ibid.

makes an express appearance in SCM Agreement Article 32.1: "No specific action against a subsidy of another Member can be taken except in accordance with the provisions of GATT 1994, as interpreted by this Agreement."[15] According to Trachtman, "the SCM is, [...] in the language of Article 32.1, an interpretation of GATT."[16] That idea is in line with decisions by both the *Appellate Body in China – Publications* and *China – Raw Materials*. As explained by Danielle Spiegel Feld and Stephanie Switzer, "the Appellate Body established that GATT Article XX can be invoked outside of the GATT, when, and only when, the breached provision includes a direct reference to Article XX or language alluding to a general 'right to regulate.'"[17]

The one general reference to the GATT that is identifiable in the SCM Agreement, and the fact that all the provisions contained in the SCM are an integral part of the Agreement, may suggest that it was impractical to ensure that each provision made direct reference to GATT Article XX. The express GATT reference in the text of the SCM Agreement would seem to imply an intention by the Members to make all GATT provisions available to the SCM Agreement, including GATT Article XX.

Affirmation for this connection between the GATT and the SCM Agreement is found in the international law of treaty interpretation. The Vienna Convention on the Law of Treaties, at Article 31.3(c), determines that "any relevant rules of international law applicable in the relations between the parties" shall be taken into consideration in the interpretation of treaties. The fact that the principle of sustainable development must be considered in relation to green subsidies, and that the GATT provides incentives for sustainable development, as will be explained further, strengthens the argument for applicability of GATT Article XX to the SCM Agreement.[18]

Article 32 of the Vienna Convention on the Law of Treaties also affirms that the interpretation of a treaty shall consider the history of its negotiation. The negotiating history of Article XX can be understood to support a broad application of the general exceptions, because one

[15] Article 32.1 of the SCM Agreement
[16] Joel P Trachtman, "SCM and GATT Article XX – A Quick Question" (2014) *World Trade Law* <http://worldtradelaw.typepad.com/ielpblog/2014/11/scm-and-gatt-article-xx-a-quick-question.html> accessed 09.24. 2016.
[17] Danielle Spiegel Feld and Stephanie Switzer, "Whither Article XX? Regulatory Autonomy Under Non-GATT Agreements After China—Raw Materials" (2012) 38 *Yale Journal of International Law Online* p. 30.
[18] Canada – Certain Measures Affecting the Renewable Energy Generation Sector (DS412): IISD, CELA, Econjustice – Amicus Curiae Brief. 2012, 16.

might view the WTO negotiations as meant to broaden, "rather than to limit the application of the Article XX exceptions."[19] The negotiating history of the SCM Agreement is also indicative of an intention to broaden the scope of the GATT exceptions, according to developments during the *travaux préparatoires*, because negotiations of subsidies were intended to improve GATT disciplines on the topic.[20]

The Ministerial Declaration from 1986 reinforces the idea that there is a strong link between the GATT 1994 and the SCM Agreement, on the basis of which it could be argued that the "intention of the parties was to leave room for non-trade objectives."[21] The intention of WTO Members may also support this connection between the GATT and the SCM Agreement. The Appellate Body in *China - Audiovisuals* affirmed the importance of the right of Members to regulate, being an inherited right that can only be modified by an express agreement.[22] Further, in *"EC - Hormones*, the Appellate Body affirmed that it cannot be lightly assumed 'that sovereign states intended to impose upon themselves the more onerous, rather than the less burdensome, obligation.'"[23] The green light subsidies provision can, similarly, be read from this perspective.[24]

---

[19] For instance, "in the London draft, Article 37 of what later became the chapeau of Article XX of the GATT 1994 did not yet refer to 'this Agreement' but to 'undertakings in Chapter IV of this Charter relating to import and export restrictions'. The formulation 'this Agreement' was introduced in the Geneva Conference by the Benelux and French delegations to generalize the application of Article XX of the GATT including to disciplines in GATT Articles III, VI and XVI. In other words, the term 'this Agreement' was introduced to broaden." Ibid.

[20] "At the very beginning of the Uruguay Round the participants explicitly specified the objective of the talks, namely: 'Negotiations on subsidies and countervailing measures shall be based on a review of Articles VI and XVI and the MTN Agreement on Subsidies and Countervailing Measures with the objective of improving GATT disciplines,'" General Agreement on Tariffs and Trade (GATT): Punta del Este Declaration, Ministerial Declaration of 20 September 1986.

[21] "'The travaux préparatoires clarify that the intention of the parties was to leave room for non-trade objectives including environmental protection within the SCM Agreement. Subsidies and countervailing measures were not a new topic for negotiators (they were already regulated by Articles III, VI and XVI of the GATT and the Subsidies Code of 1979). The predecessor of the SCM Agreement, the Subsidies Code, states in its preamble that 'subsidies are used by governments to promote important objectives of national policy.' Such a position was reiterated several times during the Uruguay Round," as in Ecojustice - Amicus Curiae Brief, 16.

[22] Ibid. p. 11.

[23] Ibid.

[24] As explained by the amicus curiae brief in Canada - Renewable Energy: "By including Article XX into the GATT 1947 (and incorporating the provision unchanged into the GATT 1994) Members clarified the manner in which they can exercise their inherent

According to Coppens: "Under the original SCM Agreement, an action-able subsidy claim could not be undertaken against a limited group of subsidies. This group of green light subsidies could also not be countervailed."[25]

An inference that might be drawn from these non-actionable sub-sidies, therefore, is that they act in a way similar to that of the environmental exception contained in certain subparagraphs, such as (b) and (g), of GATT Article XX. This category of subsidies, however, expired on December 31, 1999, because "pursuant to Article 31 of the [SCM] Agreement, [this category] could be extended by consensus of the SCM Committee. As of 31 December 1999, no such consensus had been reached."[26] The non-actionable subsidies prescribed in SCM Article 8 were therefore only valid for a provisional period of five years.

Apart from this expiration, arguments can be made both for and against the application of Article XX to the SCM Agreement. The argument in favor consists of the fact that, due to the principle of *lex specialis*, and in the absence of a specific rule concerning exceptions to the SCM Agreement, the general rule of GATT Article XX can be applied.[27] Luca Rubini explains that "Article XX could actually be invoked to justify any breach of the SCM Agreement due to the General Interpretative Note to Annex 1A of the WTO Agreement and the negotiation history does not give clear

---

right to protect important public interests such as the conservation of exhaustible natural resources and the health of human, animal and plant life. [...] Accordingly, it cannot lightly be assumed that Members have diminished this autonomy with regard to subsidies by adopting the SCM Agreement. The relevant question is not whether the drafters of the SCM Agreement explicitly confirmed the application of Article XX of the GATT 1994; rather, it is whether the drafters expressed any intention to not apply GATT Article XX. They did not. As a result, Article XX of the GATT 1994 continues to apply to subsidies both under the GATT 1994 and the SCM Agreement." Ibid.

[25] Coppens, *WTO Disciplines on Subsidies and Countervailing Measures: Balancing Policy Space and Legal Constraints* p. 164.

[26] Available in: <https://www.wto.org/english/tratop_e/scm_e/subs_e.htm> accessed 05.25.2015.

[27] This point has already been made in the literature: "[...] with the expiry of this provi-sional category of subsidies, only the special discipline of exceptions of the SCM Agreement has disappeared, giving way to the applicability of the general exceptions of the GATT. The crux of this argument is that the general exceptions of the GATT should apply to rules that, as seen, find their origin within the GATT itself." Jegou and Rubini, "The Allocation of Emission Allowances Free of Charge: Legal and economic Considerations" p. 40.

evidence that members wanted Article 8 to be the only justification of certain 'good' subsidies." [28]

Considering the intentions of the parties expressed in the aforementioned negotiating history, it would be unreasonable to suppose that the aim of the parties, in the drafting of SCM Article 8, was to narrow the scope of the GATT Article XX exceptions. Rather, the Article 8 exceptions are better understood in light of the fact that they were designed to address specific subsidies situations without being prejudiced by the broad exceptions contained in GATT Article XX.[29]

Several commentators also point to risks associated with refraining from the application of GATT Article XX to the SCM Agreement. They explain that to choose the non-application approach would lead to an unjustifiable internal inconsistency in the WTO Agreements due to the fact that the measures that are more distorting would be justifiable, while other less distorting measures would not.[30]

Measures such as quotas would perhaps be justifiable in relation to breaches of the GATT, for example, while subsidies, though less distorting, would not, simply because they belong to the SCM Agreement rather than to the GATT. According to Rubini, it would be unreasonable to draw a distinction between measures that pursue the same objective based solely on their form, thus corroborating an incoherent system, since measures that have the same effect would in some cases be justifiable and in other cases not. Neither are subsidies the most trade restrictive measures available to governments.[31]

It is also clear that barriers preventing application of GATT Article XX to the SCM Agreement may be political rather than textual. Those who argue against expansion of the scope of Article XX tend to focus on the

---

[28] Rubini, "Ain't Wastin' Time No More: Subsidies for Renewable Energy, The SCM Agreement, Policy Space, and Law Reform" p. 39.

[29] As explained by the amicus curiae brief in Canada – Renewable Energy: "The Article 8(c) environmental carve-out was intended to cover a very specific situation: where governments might want to defray the costs of new environmental regulations on existing facilities. It defined as 'non-actionable' one-time payments of up to 20% of adaptation costs for existing facilities, provided those costs were 'directly linked to and proportionate to a firm's planned reduction of nuisances and pollution,' and with the provisos that such payments not cover the actual costs of replacement, that they not cover any manufacturing cost savings that might be achieved, and that the payments be available to 'all firms which can adopt the new equipment and/or production processes." Ecojustice – Amicus Curiae Brief. 2012, 12.

[30] Rubini, "Ain't Wastin' Time No More: Subsidies for Renewable Energy, The SCM Agreement, Policy Space, and Law Reform."

[31] Ibid.

idea that the "inner balance of rights and obligations would be altered," and defend the view that to change this inner balance would "breach the WTO bargain."[32]

Analysis of the decisions concerning application of GATT Article XX reveals a significant rigidity of approach by the panels and the Appellate Body in relation to the granting of exceptions. A subsidy that does not meet the requirements of the subparagraphs or the *chapeau*, therefore, they will not allow to prevail in the WTO system.[33]

The analysis developed in this work, however, provides some new arguments for the application of GATT Articles XX and XXI. It will be apparent by now that the SCM Agreement suffers, like any other treaty, from incompleteness, and that its current mechanisms are not adequately designed to overcome this problem. Due to the deadlock in WTO negotiations, the application of GATT Articles XX and XXI through treaty interpretation would appear to put WTO Members in a better position than they are currently in given the rigidity of the SCM Agreement. These Articles not only offer policy space, but also control for opportunistic behavior, thus addressing several levels of uncertainty to which the SCM Agreement is exposed.

6.2 Negotiated Solutions

A potential solution for some of the issues of incompleteness to which the SCM Agreement is exposed is the interpretation of the SCM Agreement in a manner that would increase the extent of the flexibility it affords Member states. Whereas interpretation might contribute to the regulation of good faith subsidies, it is less clear whether it is capable of addressing other problems, such as those related to burden of proof and to monitoring. The main alternative would be to amend the SCM Agreement.

Amendment of the rules of the SCM Agreement should consider the mechanisms discussed in Chapters 4 and 5. There are interesting differences between the explicit exceptions established by the SCM Agreement and the GATT. While GATT Article XX adopts broad language, that of the SCM Agreement is very precise, defining with a great degree of detail the criteria for exemption with which a measure must comply. This type

---

[32] Ibid. p. 40.
[33] Ecojustice – Amicus Curiae Brief, 19.

of legal structure, as already discussed, is a rules-based mechanism used ideally in the presence of low transaction costs.

The use of such a high level of detail is arguably an attempt by negotiators of the SCM Agreement to deal with the potential for opportunistic behavior by WTO Members, given that, if not properly regulated, exceptions open a door to protectionist measures. At the same time, however, precise rules can impose costly conditions on the interested party and are less prone to offer flexibility with which to address unforeseen events.

The variety of situations that subsidies are capable of addressing suggests that it might have been better had SCM negotiators made use of broader language, such as the standard-type clause adopted by GATT Article XX. This assertion is supported not only by the economic theory of subsidies (the variety in means and forms of subsidies, and of possible market failures), but also by the aversion of WTO Members to the use of SCM Agreement Article 8 during the period in which the justification clause was in force.

The failure to apply Article 8 raises three main concerns. First, Article 8 imposed too many hurdles for its use. Secondly, WTO Members were afraid that disclosure of information could result in its use against them in a dispute (and even "reveal" to the other party an otherwise unidentifiable measure). Thirdly, the SCM Agreement lacked proper incentives to encourage WTO Members to overcome this fear of "revelation" of a measure that would only be evaluated for its consistency at the end of a dispute.

A better incentive for disclosure would be evaluation of the consistency of the measure *ex ante* to a dispute, in such a way that a measure in good faith would be granted "immunity" exempting it from challenge. Such immunity could also be extended to the evaluation period, giving WTO Members an extra incentive to adequately tailor and report their measures in accordance with the SCM Agreement.

It is doubtful, moreover, that SCM Article 8 has the substantive scope to address all potential market failures. This problem is compounded by the precise language of Article 8, which leaves little room for its application to economic areas other than those that receive explicit mention in the SCM Agreement: innovation, environment, and integration. Think, for example, of *Brazil – Aircraft*, in which there was development of a claim that the private financial market of developing countries suffered from market failures in the financing the export of goods.

This suggests that a broadly worded exception might have been a better way to grant the necessary flexibility, permitting control of opportunistic

---

BOX 1: Proposed amendment of SCM Agreement Article 26.

Article 26
Surveillance

26.1   The Committee shall examine new and full notifications submitted under paragraph 1 of Article XVI of GATT 1994 and paragraph 1 of Article 25 of this Agreement at special sessions held every third year. Notifications submitted in the intervening years (updating notifications) shall be examined at each regular meeting of the Committee.

26.2   The Committee shall examine reports submitted under paragraph 11 of Article 25 at each regular meeting of the Committee.

26.3   The Committee shall, within a reasonable period of time, determine whether the subsidy is being used in good faith, according to whether the subsidy was necessary to achieve a legitimate policy objective, and whether other less trade restrictive measures were not available to the party notifying the subsidy.

26.4   Should the Committee decide that the subsidy complies with the requirements of Article 26.3, there shall be a rebuttable presumption that the subsidy does not cause adverse effects in the terms of Article 6.

Source: Elaborated by the author

---

behavior by the courts *ex post* through good faith analysis, such as in GATT Article XX.

Even more striking, perhaps due to its political sensitivity, is the absence of any clear exception for use of subsidies in response to crisis situations and issues of defense. While GATT Articles XX and XXI can be invoked in such situations, the precise language of SCM Article 8 leaves little margin for discretion, even in the presence of extreme situations such as imminent economic crisis and external conflict. The issue has been tested somewhat during the recent financial crisis, and the SCM Agreement has been much disregarded by WTO Members, at least in terms of actionable subsidies.[34]

---

[34] See Gary N Horlick and Peggy A Clarke, "WTO Subsidies Discipline During and After the Crisis" (2010) 13 *Journal of International Economic Law* p. 859–74.

BOX 2: Proposed amendment of SCM Agreement Article 8.

PART IV: NON-ACTIONABLE SUBSIDIES

Article 8

Identification of Non-Actionable Subsidies

8.1 The following subsidies shall be considered as non-actionable:

(a) subsidies which are not specific within the meaning of Article 2;

(b) subsidies which are specific within the meaning of Article 2 but which meet all of the conditions provided for in paragraphs 2(a), 2(b) or 2(c) below;

(c) subsidies that can be justified under GATT Articles XX and/or XXI.

Source: Elaborated by the author

In the face of such rigidity and incompleteness, WTO adjudicators are naturally under pressure to take matters into their own hands. As the WTO has instated a fairly decent system for ensuring impartiality of its adjudicators, however, the issue has more to do with the interpretative margin granted to these adjudicators within the boundaries of a WTO Agreement. The interpretation of the definition of subsidy, for example, could function as explained previously as a flexibility.

Due to the restrictive SCM Agreement obligations on prohibited subsidies, however, the interpretative margin has resulted in some controversial decisions that could threaten legal certainty and throw the impartiality of WTO adjudicators into question. The case of *Canada – Renewable Energy*, for instance, established a sophisticated interpretation of the subsidy definition that placed a Canadian measure (alleged to be a prohibited import substitution subsidy) outside the scope of the SCM Agreement.

Apart from other motivations for taking the Canadian measure outside of the SCM Agreement, the SCM Article 3 prohibition *per se* of import substitution subsidies left adjudicators with only one option for granting flexibility that would permit such a measure to target environmental concerns.

If the drafters of the SCM Agreement had used less stringent language, the court would not have had to turn to a "creative" interpretation. A contract theory analysis of flexibility mechanisms suggests that drafters did in fact have less restrictive alternatives for regulation of the matter. A simple option would have been to regulate import substitution subsidies by application of an effects test similar to the one used in disputes related to actionable subsidies.

Even if drafters feared this type of subsidy to be more harmful than other actionable subsidies, they could have shifted the burden of proof to the defendant, leaving the complaining party to establish the *prima facie* existence of the measure. Once existence is established, it would be for the defendant to prove that no adverse effects have been produced, or that the measure has been used to address a market failure, or both. If the defendant can prove that the subsidy was, under the necessity test, used in good faith, then the complainant must prove the adverse effects, which could then be reimbursed.

This "rebuttable" type of presumption is widely adopted by other legal instruments and might have contributed to a greater balance of obligations in the SCM Agreement. Combined with a notification requirement, by which a measure notified to the WTO can be given a green light, the rebuttable presumption rule, which gives WTO Members incentive to report their measures, might improve the agonizing monitoring system currently in place.

Proof of good faith, however, also requires, besides procedural tests such as the unavailability of less restrictive measures, a substantive benchmark against which it can be measured. What is needed is either a broad, cross-sector definition of those emergency and market failure situations in which a subsidy can be considered to be used in good faith, or a more specific "policy area" definition, such as that found in GATT Article XX. This again calls for introduction of new SCM Agreement language similar to GATT Article XX, or the preamble of the GATT, that is capable of at least informing the interpretation of the rules.

6.3   Final Remarks

The study of law and economics related to treaty is commonly undertaken within the theoretical framework of contract. Parties use contracts to solve cooperation problems, often related to negative externalities, through the exchange of entitlements. The aim of each party in such exchange is to limit the authority or capacity for unilateralism of the others, thus making decision-making, especially when it relates to domestic policies with

---

BOX 3: Proposed amendment of SCM Agreement Article 3.

Article 3 *Prohibition*

===

3.1   Except as provided in the Agreement on Agriculture, the following subsidies, within the meaning of Article 1, shall ~~be prohibited~~, be presumed to cause adverse effects in the terms of Article 5:

(a)   subsidies contingent, in law or in fact, whether solely or as one of several other conditions, upon export performance, including those illustrated in Annex I5;

(b)   subsidies contingent, whether solely or as one of several other conditions, upon the use of domestic over imported goods.

3.2   A Member shall neither grant nor maintain subsidies referred to in paragraph 1, unless such subsidies have been duly notified and authorized.

3.3   The burden of proof shall be upon the complainant to establish a prima facie case regarding the existence, de jure or de facto, of the subsidies identified in paragraph 3.1.

3.4   If a subsidy is determined by a panel to exist, the burden of proof shall fall upon the defendant to demonstrate that the subsidy was necessary in order to overcome a domestic market failure, and that the subsidy was the least trade restrictive instrument reasonably available for such use.

3.5   The panel shall consider the burden of Article 3.4 to be met if:

(a)   the challenged subsidy has been duly notified and authorized; and

(b)   taking into account all other relevant evidence, the subsidy has been used in good faith.

3.6   If it is determined that a subsidy was not used in good faith, the subsidy shall be deemed to have caused adverse effects.

===

Source: Elaborated by the author

---

potential spillover effects, a more predictable process for everyone. In this sense, contracts are mutually welfare enhancing.

Once within a contract, however, a state might be able to achieve higher individual welfare if it is in a position to receive the expected benefit of the contract without complying with the treaty. In a world of

---

BOX 4: Proposed amendment of SCM Agreement Article 7.

7.11.   The assessment of the necessity of a subsidy shall take into account
its net effect, including its effects on consumers in both domestic
and foreign markets. If the net effect of the measure is positive, there
shall be a rebuttable presumption of necessity in favor of the
measure.

Source: Elaborated by the author

"full information," all possible welfare-maximizing behaviors, including noncompliance, would be described in the contract, so that every potential breach is identified as opportunistic behavior that is subject to sanction.

Despite the efforts employed by contracting parties however, certain limitations prevent the preparation of complete contracts. Various types of difficulty in the negotiation and drafting of treaties, reflected in transaction costs and incompleteness, can add considerably to the cost of the process. Nor can policymakers, due to the bounds of rationality, be expected to foresee every future contingency and the probability of their occurrence, or to draft complex clauses in a consistently bullet-proof manner. In other words, treaty analysis must take into account "human contracting error."[35] It is to be expected therefore that, like every other treaty, a subsidies agreement will be incomplete.

As incompleteness permits opportunistic behavior, parties might introduce mechanisms that enable the efficient completion of the contract *ex post*. Treaty parties can then adopt more or less specific language to carve out exceptions to the agreement, and to provide guidance regarding its interpretation.

Introduction of flexibility into a contract can also be achieved by the delegation of competence to third parties, such as the courts. The powers of the courts, for example, enable them to act as gap fillers, with a capacity to interpret or complete the contract after emergence of a contingency or occurrence of an event that causes disagreement among the parties.

---

[35] This term is credited to Schropp, *Trade Policy Flexibility and Enforcement in the WTO: A Law and Economic Analysis* p. 64.

Finally, states can also resort to default rules: "rules that define the parties' obligations in the absence of any explicit agreement to the contrary" and that serve to "resolve disputes that are not settled by the terms of the document itself."[36] Default rules, if appropriately designed and fully informed, could encourage parties to mimic, *ex post*, the behavior they would have chosen *ex ante* if they had been in a position at that time to write a complete contract.

Contract theory suggests that certain flexibility mechanisms might be better able than others, depending on the source of the uncertainty, to address incompleteness. In reality, however, because contracts make use of a variety of flexibility mechanisms, an evaluation would require the legal analysis of a particular area of substantive law in order to identify the corresponding uncertainty and compare the results of the various flexibility mechanisms under current law.

The treaties that comprise the multilateral trading system exhibit various levels of flexibility throughout. Take, for example, the current rules regulating tariffs found in GATT Articles II, XX, and XXI. Article II prohibits WTO Members from raising tariffs above a mutually agreed level, which enables all parties to maximize welfare by increasing trade. The provision thus gives legal expression to the cooperation issue that the parties attempt to address in the treaty.

The exceptions contained in GATT Articles XX and XXI enable parties to respond to public policy needs and crises while, at the same time, mandating a series of tests that control for opportunistic uses of trade measures. If a measure passes the Article XX and XXI tests, even if it is inconsistent with Article II, it will be justified and no compensation will be payable. In other words, if a measure is both (i.) taken in good faith; and (ii.) non-discriminatory, it is justifiable and the WTO Member that imposed the measure will not be subject to retaliation.[37]

---

[36] Craswell, "Contract Law: General Theories" p. 1–2.

[37] The most considerable difference between Articles XX and XXI, however, is on the level of scrutiny delegated to the courts to examine a measure. As mentioned above, measures implementing public policies and also those taken during severe crises might have opportunistic intent and are thus regulated. As it deals with issues of severe crises and security, however, Article XXI covers a more sensitive area of state behavior than Article XX, and negotiators have limited the scope of review assigned to courts. Article XXI is a so-called essential security and self-judging clause and once the justification for the measure arises, such as national security, WTO Member states "are free to choose the means and the third party adjudicator may not review their measures." van Aaken, "Smart Flexibility Clauses in International Investment Treaties and Sustainable Development" p. 843–44.

Like the GATT, the SCM Agreement is also reliant upon a complex system of flexibility. It has, however, been less well-researched than the GATT flexibilities, and much of the literature focuses on the lack of explicit exceptions. As this study has concluded, however, there is much more to SCM Agreement flexibility than justification clauses. Even if the drafters of the SCM Agreement were careful to ensure a detailed system of substantive flexibility, certain contingencies will have escaped their efforts, no matter how diligent they were.[38] This means that rules, therefore, might not sufficiently separate bad faith from good faith measures, thus permitting opportunistic behavior by the parties and reinforcing the need for *ex post* interpreters.

As flexibility mechanisms can be introduced into a treaty through substantive and procedural rules reflected in layers of language, interpretation, and remedies, a systematic analysis of SCM Agreement flexibility demands a comprehensive analysis of the treaty as a whole, in an attempt to connect the rationale behind its commitments to the currently available flexibility.[39]

The SCM Agreement defines a subsidy as a financial contribution by a government, which confers a benefit to the recipient. The SCM Agreement is restricted in scope to specific subsidies: those subsidies that are granted *de jure* or *de facto* to a limited number of enterprises, within a particular region. In practice, the effect of this definition, when allied with the specificity test, was to remove from the scope of application of the SCM Agreement general regulatory policies.[40] The arguable

---

[38] One interesting example arose in the Shrimp dispute, in which the WTO interpreters were called upon to decide whether the term "exhaustible natural resources" should be read so as to include living animals, such as sea turtles. Despite the efforts of the drafters of the GATT to include a detailed provision with exceptions, there were (and there will still be) questions that need to be addressed by courts due to ambiguous or outdated language.

[39] At the commitment level, critics have focused on lack of contractual language, such as a preamble and exceptions that could preclude actions by harmed parties in circumstances deemed economically, legally, and socially appropriate, such as support to R&D activities, fulfillment of other international obligations, such as environmental agreements, and policies to preserve employment in economically turbulent times. At the enforcement level, critics have cast doubt on the rationale for having a mixed regime of default rules, i.e. a property rule for prohibited, and a liability rule for actionable subsidies. There is also criticism regarding the appropriateness of the rules regulating the level of damages and their temporal scope. This work thus defines, identifies, and analyzes the legal mechanisms (substantive, procedural, and remedial rules) available in the SCM Agreement that should lead to an optimum differentiation between opportunistic behavior and good faith measures.

[40] Specificity is often seen as having a mixed (economic and political) rationale because pure economic reasons often fail to describe the concept, as, for instance, in Rubini,

result of this was to reduce uncertainty about the scope of the SCM Agreement and pave the way for policymakers to negotiate more detailed commitments for the regulation of subsidies.[41] A specific subsidy is subject to legal action only if it is the cause of an adverse effect on trading partners. Any subsidy will however be prohibited *per se* if it is associated with export commitments or designed to foster import substitution, in which case there is a presumption of specificity.

At first glance, this distinction between prohibited and actionable subsidies supports the idea that the treaty was an attempt to regulate the opportunistic use of subsidies, while leaving some policy space for WTO Members. This aligns with economic theory suggesting that because export-contingent and import substitution subsidies can have direct effects on market access commitments, they are more commonly used as an opportunistic tool to deviate from tariff concessions.[42] In a WTO dispute, if a complainant is able to demonstrate that a subsidy is prohibited, there is a conclusive presumption of discrimination and the subsidizing government has no alternative but to either remove the subsidy or face retaliatory measures. The use of prohibited subsidies generates a remedy according to a property rule, with the effect that governments do not have the option to breach and pay.

While the protection of this commitment with a property rule reinforces the perception that prohibited measures are the most harmful type of subsidy, it leaves WTO Members with no flexibility for their use.

Some authors have criticized this regulation of export promotion and import substitution subsidies as overly strict, arguing that such policies might be relevant for protection of crucial economic sectors in times of crisis, and for the promotion of economic diversification and growth.[43] They suggest that WTO negotiators should therefore have left some margin of flexibility for their use. Given this clear ban *per se* and inalienable or property remedies, the most obvious alternative form of flexibility

The Definition of Subsidy and State Aid: WTO and EC Law in Comparative Perspective p. 376. Under contract theory, however, specificity can be understood as an instrument to reduce uncertainties about the scope of the agreement, assuring policymakers that general regulatory policies would not be constrained by the SCM Agreement.

[41] As noted by Rubini "[...] it is sometimes quite difficult to determine whether the measure should be regarded as a general measure [...] or as a specific measure" with the difficulty arising from the "fact that virtually all measures have a differential impact and affect the position of some subjects more than others," ibid. p. 373.

[42] See DeRemer, *The Evolution of International Subsidy Rules* p. 2–4.

[43] Petros C Mavroidis, Patrick A Messerlin, and Jasper M Wauters (eds), *The Law and Economics of Contingent Protection in the WTO* (Cambridge University Press 2010).

for facilitation of the use of such measures is legal interpretation by the WTO courts.

The use of broad treaty language with which to delegate judicial competence expands the scope of review available to the courts[44] and increases the power of interpreters. With regard to prohibited subsidies, however, such delegation only happens in part. Import substitution subsidies are not subject to exception, and are therefore strictly regulated. The "green light" category of non-actionable subsidies has, moreover, been revoked[45] and the treaty currently contains no clear policy or security exceptions.

There has been much discussion about the reformulation and reintroduction of the category of non-actionable subsidies. Some scholars defend the reintroduction of exceptions on economic grounds. Ibáñez Marsilla argues that "it would probably make sense to reinstate non-actionable subsidies, that is, to explicitly establish some purposes that legitimize government intervention in the economy, based in the economic theory on market failure."[46] Others adopt a policy rationale. For Rubini, for example, the absence of exceptions "may affect the conclusion as to the role of public policy objectives and alter the structure of the SCM Agreement as it was designed [. . .] [as] the current discipline does not provide for any justification of important policy objectives."[47]

---

[44] In law and economic theory this is usually framed under the concepts of rules (more specific language) and standards (more broad language). Interpreters have more discretion when negotiators make use of standards and can introduce flexibility by tailoring the standard to a concrete situation.

[45] These non-actionable subsidies (green light) comprise to date only the subsidies contained in Article 8.1, i.e. the non-specific subsidies, whose contestability is set aside by Article 1.2 of the SCM Agreement. The other subsidies present in Article 8.2, such as regional, environmental, and R&D subsidies are, since January 1, 2000, actionable, by force of Article 31 of the SCM Agreement.

[46] See Santiago Ibáñez Marsilla, "Recent Stimulus Packages and WTO Law on Subsidies" (2009) 3 *World Customs Journal* p. 63–78, 72; for Steger, "[a]lthough it will be difficult to achieve a multilateral consensus on which subsidies should be classified as non-actionable, a serious effort should be made to reinstitute such a category. The focus should be on developing generic rules which apply to all WTO Members. The search should be to identify certain types of subsidies that do not cause adverse trade effects." Steger, "The WTO Doha Round Negotiations on Subsidies and Countervailing Measures: Issues for Negotiators" p. 16.

[47] For a policy approach, see Howse, "Do the World Trade Organization Disciplines on Domestic Subsidies Make Sense? The Case for Legalizing Some Subsidies" p. 86; for a mention that Canada has already requested its reinstatement see Kap-You Kim, "Issues and Arguments in Trade Dispute Cases against Korean Industries on Countervailing Measures" (2003) 3 *J Korean L* p. 55–76, 73; for its pertinence for developing countries, see Ayala and Gallagher, *Preserving Policy Space for Sustainable Development:*

This disagreement over introduction of exceptions into the SCM Agreement reflects economic and policy concerns by WTO Members and scholars.[48] In practice, in the absence of a consensus among WTO Members, the category of non-actionable subsidies was considerably diminished at the end of 1999, and now comprises only non-specific subsidies. The SCM Agreement therefore establishes no clear policy exception that could justify the use of any (specific) subsidy.[49]

In the absence of an integral SCM Agreement exception to facilitate subsidy use, an alternative for Member States is to make use of the general exceptions established by the GATT. GATT Article XX provides that a domestic measure found to be inconsistent with the agreement might nevertheless be justified if the measure both passes a necessity test and is used to promote pre-established values, such as health and environment.

Whether GATT Article XX can be invoked to justify a violation under the SCM Agreement[50] has generated much debate. Howse argues in favor of such application on grounds that the SCM Agreement is itself a *lex specialis* of the GATT. Rubini takes a similar position on the basis of a holistic interpretation of the SCM Agreement.[51] Critics, however, raise several arguments against the application of GATT Article XX to the SCM Agreement. First, the SCM Agreement, by its provision on "non-actionable" subsidies, has already established its own exception and should be considered "a specific regime with its own exceptions and flexibilities."[52] Secondly, recent WTO caselaw suggests that GATT

The Subsidies Agreement at the WTO p. 20; see also Rubini, *The Definition of Subsidy and State Aid: WTO and EC Law in Comparative Perspective* p. 255.

[48] Economically, there was a view that due to the fungible nature of money, the green light category opens the door for abuses as subsidized firms could simply reallocate resources for other purposes. Politically, there were countries, such as Brazil and India, which argued for changes in the category to better reflect the needs of developing countries. Coppens, *WTO Disciplines on Subsidies and Countervailing Measures: Balancing Policy Space and Legal Constraints* p. 164–66.

[49] For a brief overview on the background of this provision, see ibid. and Rubini, *The Definition of Subsidy and State Aid: WTO and EC Law in Comparative Perspective* p. 73–74.

[50] If so, Article XX could arguably provide for flexibility to WTO Members to make use subsidies that violate Article 3 and 5 of the SCM Agreement, if such measures are associated to one of the values protected by Article XX and also pass the necessity test.

[51] Rubini seems to favor the application of Article XX to the SCM from a holistic view of the WTO agreements (see Rubini, *The Definition of Subsidy and State Aid: WTO and EC Law in Comparative Perspective* p. 195).

[52] For a discussion on whether the general exceptions in Article XX of the GATT are applicable to the SCM Agreement see Rubini, for whom the only justification for

Article XX is only available to other covered agreements if, as in the TRIPS agreements,[53] its application is explicitly called for. Thirdly, recourse to Article XX in multilateral subsidies disputes would create incongruent defense mechanisms, because countervailing measures may still be applied at the domestic level. Fourthly, the negotiating history of the WTO, at least in the Uruguay Round, is silent about the application of Article XX to the SCM Agreement.[54]

The question of the application of GATT Article XX (and Article XXI) to the SCM Agreement was examined in detail in Chapter 5. In light of recent caselaw, it seems unlikely that recourse to Article XX will be granted by the WTO courts.

Preambular language provides a further interpretative instrument with which the courts can contribute to the introduction of flexibilities. International legal interpretation is governed by Article 31 of the Vienna Convention on the Law of Treaties, which mandates that treaties be interpreted in light of, among other things, their object and purpose. Purpose should be determined by reference to not only the main treaty text, but also its annexes and preamble. Panels and the AB have routinely relied on the preamble of the WTO Agreement in their interpretation of WTO provisions, and interpreters and scholars have used it to argue for more "policy space," thus increasing flexibility that enables governments to address the social, environmental, and developmental issues related to certain measures that affect trade and are subject to the rules of the GATT.[55] The SCM Agreement, on the other hand, has no preamble,

---

a measure examined under subsidy rules is the category of non-actionable subsidies under the SCM. Nevertheless, Rubini argues that the general justifications under GATT Article XX might be relevant in those cases in which both GATT and SCM rules are "held to apply cumulatively." Ibid. p. 194–98. See also Coppens, *WTO Disciplines on Subsidies and Countervailing Measures: Balancing Policy Space and Legal Constraints* p. 170.

[53] For a consideration of the application of Article XX to non-GATT agreements after the decision in Raw Materials supporting the view that Article XX "cannot be invoked outside the GATT unless the breached provision specifically incorporates a reference to Article XX or wording of similar import," thus not being applicable to the SCM Agreement; see Feld and Switzer, "Whither Article XX? Regulatory Autonomy Under Non-GATT Agreements After China—Raw Materials" p. 18. Also, see Coppens, *WTO Disciplines on Subsidies and Countervailing Measures: Balancing Policy Space and Legal Constraints* p. 194–95, for a view defending the understanding that the WTO rules as currently interpreted by the AB do not permit the justification of subsidies under Article XX of the GATT.

[54] Coppens, *WTO Disciplines on Subsidies and Countervailing Measures: Balancing Policy Space and Legal Constraints* p. 171.

[55] Debra Steger, "The Culture of the WTO: Why It Needs to Change" (2007) 10 *Journal of International Economic Law* p. 483–95, 486.

perhaps because of a "considerable disagreement"[56] on the definition of subsidy, or simply because "drafters did not consider a preamble necessary."[57] Whatever the reason, the absence of a GATT-like preamble that frames the purpose of the Agreement in terms of broad social and economic objectives and deprives the courts of the potential to interpret the SCM Agreement in such terms, thus arguably reducing the flexibility with which WTO Members are able to pursue such objectives through measures considered to be subsidies under the SCM Agreement.

The SCM Agreement, in essence, misses out on traditional flexibility mechanisms such as exceptions. The legal test of specificity, requisite for actionable subsidies, also seems incapable of making a clear separation between good and bad faith subsidies.[58] This lack of flexibility provides an open door for opportunistic behavior, such as the hold-out of entitlements, and fosters legal uncertainty about the consistency of measures used by states to overcome legitimate economic problems. This creates an incentive for WTO Members to withhold disclosure of these policies, making it even harder for other Members and interpreters to assess the existence and treaty compatibility of a measure. New legal and economic research to provide clarification of the problem, and proposals to overcome it, is therefore imperative.

There are a few ways in which elements of flexibility may be introduced into the SCM Agreement. The most obvious is through legal interpretation, especially of the concept of subsidy, and its sub-elements, because if a measure is not a subsidy, it is outside of the scope of the SCM Agreement. Developments in the jurisprudence suggest a move by the WTO courts towards a more policy friendly interpretation. In *Canada Renewable Energy*, for instance, the AB stated that measures targeting an as yet non-existent market (such as the Canadian market in solar energy) should not be considered a subsidy. Such developments may demonstrate a preoccupation of the AB with policy concerns, but it is unclear whether and how they might be applied in relation to other policy areas or to measures taken in emergency situations.

One suggestion for tailoring the interpretation of "subsidy" to improve the flexibility system of the SCM Agreement is to use the preamble of the Marrakech Agreement Establishing the World Trade Organization to, for

[56] Rubini, *The Definition of Subsidy and State Aid: WTO and EC Law in Comparative Perspective* p. 146.
[57] Wouters and Coppens, "An Overview of the Agreement on Subsidies and Countervailing Measures Including a Discussion on the Agreement on Agriculture" p. 13.
[58] Trebilcock, Advanced Introduction to International Trade Law p. 88.

example, give a policy orientation to the term. This idea has been proposed by the legal literature, but has not yet been fully explored. Howse, for instance, calls for the interpretation of the term "economic" in the footnote to SCM Agreement Article 2.1(b), in light of the "objective of sustainable development and its connection to economic development as articulated in the preamble of the WTO Agreement," so as to "include criteria and conditions ... to sustainable development including biodiversity and protection of the environment."[59]

Given their limitations, as previously discussed, the WTO courts might not be in a position to evaluate a certain preferred policy objective addressed by the measure of a WTO Member. Similarly, the fact-finding capacity of panels might be severely restricted by the incentives created by the SCM Agreement for WTO Members to report subsidies.

The first issue could be addressed by permitting the Members to establish a body of authorities identified by the Members. In theory, courts are an appropriate instrument with which to assess whether measures are taken in good faith, but it is less clear whether they have the expertise to assess the political relevance of a measure to a WTO Member. An alternative would be for WTO Members to recall their competence and to assess these issues through an expert body composed of parties appointed by the WTO Members. A similar body of experts already exists under the SCM Agreement, but has never been put into operation. For an organization that is Member driven, the WTO has so far expressed little interest in establishing a fully functioning body of experts.

The system of reporting and monitoring also needs improvement. Currently, due to uncertainty about the flexibility offered by the SCM Agreement, there are strong incentives for WTO Members not abstain from compliance with the obligation to report subsidies. A way to make this commitment self-enforcing would be to adjust the reporting system in order to grant advantages, such as a stronger presumption of good faith, to reported subsidies. Alternatively, new reporting mechanisms could require that WTO Members undergo a serious analysis of the impact of the subsidy. Like a necessity test, this would help to ensure that the subsidy is positively linked to a legitimate policy objective, and that it is no more harmful than is necessary.

[59] See Howse, "Do the World Trade Organization Disciplines on Domestic Subsidies Make Sense? The Case for Legalizing Some Subsidies" p. 99.

BIBLIOGRAPHY

Abbott KW and others, "The Concept of Legalization" (2000) 54 *International Organization* p. 401–19

Allen D, "Transaction Costs" (1999) 14 *Research in Law and Economics*

Atkinson R, Ezell S, and Wein M, *Localization Barriers to Trade: Threat to the Global Innovation Economy* (Information Technology and Innovation Foundation 2013)

Ayala FA and Gallagher K, *Preserving Policy Space for Sustainable Development: The Subsidies Agreement at the WTO* (International Institute for Sustainable Development 2005)

Bacchetta M and Ruta M (eds), *The WTO, Subsidies and Countervailing Measures*, vol 19 (Critical Perspectives on the Global Trading System and the WTO, Edward Elgar 2011)

Baeumler J, Caiado J, and DeRemer D, "How Do the WTO Articles on Actionable Subsidies Function as Liability Rules?" (Unpublished paper 2014)

Bagwell K and Mavroidis P, "Too Much, Too Little, . . . Too Late?" in Bagwell K and others (eds), *Law and Economics of Contingent Protection in International Trade* (Law and Economics of Contingent Protection in International Trade, Cambridge University Press 2010)

Bagwell K and Staiger RW, "Will International Rules on Subsidies Disrupt the World Trading System?" (2006) *The American Economic Review* p. 877–95

Bagwell K and Staiger RW, "An Economic Theory of GATT" (1999) 89 *The American Economic Review* p. 215–48

Bagwell K and Staiger RW, "The Role of Export Subsidies When Product Quality Is Unknown" (1989) 27 *Journal of International Economics* p. 69–89

Baldwin R, "Politically Realistic Objective Functions and Trade Policy PROFs and Tariffs" (1987) 24 *Economics Letters* p. 287–90

Baylis K, "Countervailing Duties" in William A Kerr and James D Gaisford (eds), *Handbook of International Trade Policy* (Handbook of International Trade Policy, Edward Elgar Publishing Limited 2007)

Begg D, Fischer S, and Dornbusch R, *Economics* (10th edn, McGraw-Hill Higher Education 2011)

Benitah M, *The Law of Subsidies under the GATT/WTO System* (Kluwer Law International 2001)

Benvenisti E, "Judicial Misgivings Regarding the Application of International Law: An Analysis of Attitudes of National Courts" (1993) 4 *European Journal of International Law* p. 159

Bowman GW, *Trade Remedies in North America*, vol 27 (Kluwer Law International 2010)

Bhagwati J and Ramaswami VK, "Domestic Distortions, Tariffs and the Theory of Optimum Subsidy" (1963) *The Journal of Political Economy* p. 44–50

Bossche PVD and Zdouc W, *The Law and Policy of the World Trade Organization: Text, Cases, and Materials* (3rd edn, Cambridge University Press 2013)

Bown CP, "Taking Stock of Antidumping, Safeguards and Countervailing Duties, 1990–2009" (2011) 34 *The World Economy* p. 1955–98

Brou D and Ruta M, "A Commitment Theory of Subsidy Agreements" (2013) 13 *The BE Journal of Economic Analysis & Policy* p. 239–70

Broude T, "Behavioral International Law" (2013) *University of Pennsylvania Law Review* p. 1099–2131

Burri-Nenova M, "Trade versus Culture in the Digital Environment: An Old Conflict in Need of a New Definition" (2009) 12 *Journal of International Economic Law* p. 17–62

Burton SJ, "Breach of Contract and the Common Law Duty to Perform in Good Faith" (1980) 94 *Harvard Law Review* p. 369–404

Caiado J, "From Coordination to Collaboration: Explaining International Disputes over Tariff Classification" (2012) 3 *Economic Analysis of Law Review* p. 95–108

Caiado J and Bär C, "Die Rolle von nationalen Behörden im Subventionsregime des WTO-Rechts – wurde der Bock zum Gärtner gemacht?" in Brändli S and others (eds), *Multinationale Unternehmen und Institutionen im Wandel – Herausforderungen für Wirtschaft, Recht und Gesellschaft Schriften der Assistierenden der Universität St Gallen (HSG)*, vol 8 (Multinationale Unternehmen und Institutionen im Wandel – Herausforderungen für Wirtschaft, Recht und Gesellschaft Schriften der Assistierenden der Universität St Gallen (HSG), Bern Stämpfli 2013)

Caiado J and Berghaus T, R&D Subsidies: A Law & Economics Analysis of Regional and International Rules (2012)

Calabresi G and Melamed AD, "Property Rules, Liability Rules, and Inalienability: One View of the Cathedral" (1972) 85 *Harvard Law Review* p. 1089–128

Chaisse J and Chakraborty D, "Implementing WTO Rules through Negotiations and Sanction: The Role of Trade Policy Review Mechanism and Dispute Settlement System" (2007) 28 *University of Pennsylvania Journal of International Economic Law*

Chang SW, "WTO Disciplines on Fisheries Subsidies: A Historic Step towards Sustainability?" (2003) 6 *Journal of International Economic Law* p. 879–921

Cho S-J, "GATT Non-Violation Issues in the WTO Framework: Are They the Achilles' Heel of the Dispute Settlement Process" (1998) 39 *Harvard International Law Journal* p. 311

Cohen GM, "Implied Terms and Interpretation in Contract Law" in Bouckaert B and De Geest G (eds), *Encyclopedia of Law and Economics*, vol III *The Regulation of Contracts* (Encyclopedia of Law and Economics, Edward Elgar 2000)

Cohen GM, "The Negligence-Opportunism Tradeoff in Contract Law" (1992) 20 *Hofstra Law Review* p. 941–1016

Cooter R and Ulen T, *Law and Economics* (International Edition, New York: Pearson Addison Wesley 2008)

Coppens D, *WTO Disciplines on Subsidies and Countervailing Measures: Balancing Policy Space and Legal Constraints* (Cambridge International Trade and Economic Law, Cambridge University Press 2014)

Craswell R, "The Incomplete Contracts Literature and Efficient Precautions" (2005) 56 *Case Western Reserve Law Review* p. 151

Craswell R, "Contract Law: General Theories" in Bouckaert B and De Geest G (eds), *Encyclopedia of Law and Economics*, vol III *The Regulation of Contracts* (Encyclopedia of Law and Economics, Edward Elgar 2000)

Davey WJ, "The WTO Dispute Settlement System" in The World Bank (ed) *Legal Aspects of International Trade* (Legal Aspects of International Trade, The World Bank 2001)

Davey WJ, "Dispute Settlement in GATT" (1987) 11 *Fordham International Law Journal* p. 52–109

de Moor A, *Key Issues in Subsidy Policies and Strategies for Reform* (Economic Commission for Latin America and the Caribbean 1997)

DeRemer D, *The Evolution of International Subsidy Rules* (Working Paper ECARES 2013)

DiMatteo LA and others, *Visions of Contract Theory: Rationality, Bargaining, and Interpretation* (Carolina Academic Press 2007)

Doane ML, "Green Light Subsidies: Technology Policy in International Trade" (1995) 21 *Syracuse Journal of International Law & Commerce* p. 155

Dunoff JL and Trachtman JP, "Economic Analysis of International Law" (1999) 24 *Yale Journal of International Law* 1

Editorial, Bedingt bereit zum Export (2016)

Fearon JD, "Bargaining, Enforcement, and International Cooperation" (1998) 52 *International Organization* p. 269–305

Feld DS and Switzer S, "Whither Article XX? Regulatory Autonomy Under Non-GATT Agreements After China—Raw Materials" (2012) 38 *Yale Journal of International Law Online*

Feld LP and Voigt S, "Economic Growth and Judicial Independence: Cross-Country Evidence Using a New Set of Indicators" (2003) 19 *European Journal of Political Economy* p. 497–527

Friederiszick HW, Röller L-H, and Verouden V, "European State Aid Control: An Economic Framework" in Buccirossi P (ed) *Handbook of Antitrust Economics* (Handbook of Antitrust Economics, The MIT Press 2008)

Friederiszick HW, Röller L-H, and Verouden V, "EC State Aid Control: An Economic Perspective" in Rydelski MS (ed) *The EC State Aid Regime: Distortive Effects of State Aid on Competition and Trade* (The EC State Aid Regime: Distortive Effects of State Aid on Competition and Trade, Cambridge University Press 2006)

Global Subsidies Initiative <http://www.iisd.org/gsi/> accessed 07.29.2016

Global Trade Alert <http://www.globaltradealert.org/> accessed 07.29.2016

Goetz CJ, Granet L, and Schwartz WF, "The Meaning of 'Subsidy' and 'Injury' in the Countervailing Duty Law" (1986) 6 *International Review of Law and Economics* p. 17–32

Good Jobs First <http://www.goodjobsfirst.org> accessed 07.29.2016

Green A, "Trade Rules and Climate Change Subsidies" (2006) 5 *World Trade Review* p. 377–414

Green A and Trebilcock M, "The Enduring Problem of World Trade Organization Export Subsidies Rules" in Bagwell K and others (eds), *Law and Economics of Contingent Protection in International Trade* (Law and Economics of Contingent Protection in International Trade, Cambridge University Press 2009)

Grossarth J, "Die Milch macht die müden Bauern nicht mehr munter" (04.18.2016) Frankfurter Allgemeine Zeitung

Grossman GM and Mavroidis PC, "US–Lead and Bismuth II: United States–Imposition of Countervailing Duties on Certain Hot-Rolled Lead and Bismuth Carbon Steel Products Originating in the United Kingdom: Here Today, Gone Tomorrow? Privatization and the Injury Caused by Non-Recurring Subsidies" (2003) 2 *World Trade Review* p. 170–200

Guzman A, *How International Law Works: A Rational Choice Theory* (Oxford University Press 2008)

Guzman A and Meyer TL, "Explaining Soft Law" (2010) *Berkeley Program in Law & Economics* p. 1–45

Hadfield GK, "Judicial Competence and the Interpretation of Incomplete Contracts" (1994) 23 *The Journal of Legal Studies* p. 159–84

Hafner-Burton EM, Hughes DA, and Victor DG, "The Cognitive Revolution and the Political Psychology of Elite Decision Making" (2013) 11 *Perspectives on Politics* p. 368–86

Hahn M, "A Clash of Cultures? The UNESCO Diversity Convention and International Trade Law" (2006) 9 *Journal of International Economic Law* p. 515–52

Hancher L, Ottervanger T, and Slot PJ (eds), *EU State Aids* (Sweet & Maxwell 2012)

Hausman DM, "Philosophy of Economics" in Zalta EN (ed) *The Stanford Encyclopedia of Philosophy*, vol Winter 2013 (The Stanford Encyclopedia of Philosophy, Stanford University 2013) <http://plato.stanford.edu/entries/economics/> accessed 07.29.2016

Hayo B and Voigt S, "Explaining De Facto Judicial Independence" (2007) 27 *International Review of Law and Economics* p. 269–90

Hoekman BM and Kostecki MM, *The Political Economy of the World Trading System* (Oxford University Press 2009)

Horlick GN and Clarke PA, "WTO Subsidies Discipline during and after the Crisis" (2010) 13 *Journal of International Economic Law* p. 859–74

Horlick GN and Clarke PA, "The 1994 WTO Subsidies Agreement" (1993) 17 *World Competition* p. 41–54

Horn H, Maggi G, and Staiger RW, "Trade Agreements as Endogenously Incomplete Contracts" (2010) 100 *The American Economic Review* p. 394–419

Howse R, "Do the World Trade Organization Disciplines on Domestic Subsidies Make Sense? The Case for Legalizing Some Subsidies" in Bagwell KW and others (eds), *Law and Economics of Contingent Protection in International Trade* (Law and Economics of Contingent Protection in International Trade, Cambridge University Press 2009)

Irwin DA, Mavroidis PC, and Sykes AO, *The Genesis of the GATT* (The American Law Institute Reporters' Studies on WTO Law, Cambridge University Press 2008)

Jackson J, *The Perplexities of Subsidies in International Trade*, Chapter 11 (The World Trading System, MIT Press 1997)

Jegou I and Rubini L, "The Allocation of Emission Allowances Free of Charge: Legal and Economic Considerations" (2010) ICTSD Global Platform on Climate Change, Trade Policies and Sustainable Energy

Johnson HG, *Optimal Trade Intervention in the Presence of Domestic Distortions* (Rand McNally 1963)

Johnson HG, "Optimum Tariffs and Retaliation" (1953) 21 *The Review of Economic Studies* p. 142–53

Jolls C and Sunstein CR, "Debiasing through Law" (2006) 35 *The Journal of Legal Studies* p. 199–242

Kaplow L, "Rules versus Standards: An Economic Analysis" (1992) 42 *Duke Law Journal* p. 557–629

Karim R, "Transparency is the Most Important Governance Issue in the WTO Subsidy Control" <http://ssrn.com/abstract=2498863> accessed 07.20.2016

Kathy B, "Countervailing Duties" in Kerr WA and Gaisford JD (eds), *Handbook of International Trade Policy* (Handbook of International Trade Policy, Edward Elgar Publishing Limited 2007)

Katz AW, "Contractual Incompleteness: A Transactional Perspective" (2005) 56 *Case Western Reserve Law Review* p. 169

Keck A and Schropp S, "Indisputably Essential: The Economics of Dispute Settlement Institutions in Trade Agreements" (2008) 42 *Journal of World Trade* p. 785–812

Kim K-Y, "Issues and Arguments in Trade Dispute Cases against Korean Industries on Countervailing Measures" (2003) 3 *Journal of Korean Law* p. 55–76

Kirchner C, "The Power of Rational Choice Methodology in Guiding the Analysis and the Design of Public International Law Institutions—Concluding Remarks" (2008) *University of Illinois Law Review* p. 419–28

Knop K, "Here and There: International Law in Domestic Courts" (1999) 32 *New York University Journal of International Law & Politics* p. 501

Kohler B, "Das Schicksal der Bauern" (May 18, 2016) Frankfurter Allgemeine Zeitung p. 1

Koplow D and Dernbach J, "Federal Fossil Fuel Subsidies and Greenhouse Gas Emissions: A Case Study of Increasing Transparency for Fiscal Policy" (2001) 26 *Annual Review of Energy and the Environment* p. 361–89

Koremenos B, "Institutionalism and International Law" in Dunoff JL and Pollack MA (eds), *Interdisciplinary Perspectives on International Law and International Relations: The State of the Art* (Interdisciplinary Perspectives on International Law and International Relations: The State of the Art, Cambridge University Press 2013)

Kovacic WE and Shapiro C, "Antitrust Policy: A Century of Economic and Legal Thinking" (2000) 14 *The Journal of Economic Perspectives* p. 43–60

Krugman PR, Obstfeld M, and Melitz M, *International Trade: Theory and Policy* (The Pearson Series in Economics, Pearson Education Limited 2014)

Laan T, "Gaining Traction: The Importance of Transparency in Accelerating the Reform of Fossil-Fuel Subsidies" in Initiative GS (ed) Untold Billions: Fossil-Fuel Subsidies, Their Impacts and the Path to Reform (Untold Billions: Fossil-Fuel Subsidies, Their Impacts and the Path to Reform, International Institute for Sustainable Development and United Nations Environment Programme 2010)

Lauterpacht H, *The Development of International Law by the International Court* (Cambridge University Press 1982)

Lester S, "The Problem of Subsidies as a Means of Protectionism: Lessons from the WTO EC—AIRCRAFT Case" (2011) 12 *Melbourne Journal of International Law* p. 2–28

Lindsay P, "The Ambiguity of GATT Article XXI: Subtle Success or Rampant Failure?" (2003) 52 *Duke Law Journal* p. 1277–313

Luengo G, *Regulation of Subsidies and State Aids in WTO and EC Law: Conflicts in International Trade Law* (Kluwer Law International 2006)

Mackaay E, "History of Law and Economics" in Bouckaert B and De Geest G (eds), *Encyclopedia of Law and Economics*, vol I *The History and Methodology of Law and Economics* (Encyclopedia of Law and Economics, Edward Elgar 2000)

Maggi G and Staiger RW, "Trade Disputes and Settlement" (2013) Department of Economics—Yale University

Maggi G and Staiger RW, "Optimal Design of Trade Agreements in the Presence of Renegotiation" (2015) 7 *American Economic Journal: Microeconomics* p. 109–43

Mankiw G, *Principles of Macroeconomics* (7th edn, Cengage Learning 2014)

Marceau GZ, *Anti-dumping and Anti-trust Issues in Free-trade Areas* (Clarendon Press 1994)

Marceau GZ and Trachtman JP, "The Technical Barriers to Trade Agreement, the Sanitary and Physanitary Measures Agreement, and the General Agreement on Tariffs and Trade: A Map of the New World Trade Organization Law of Domestic Regulation of Goods" (2002) 36 *Journal of World Trade* p. 811–81

Marsilla SI, "Recent Stimulus Packages and WTO Law on Subsidies" (2009) 3 *World Customs Journal* p. 63–78

Martin L, "The Rational State Choice of Multilateralism" in Ruggie JG (ed) *Multilateralism Matters: The Theory and Praxis of an Institutional Form* (Multilateralism Matters: The Theory and Praxis of an Institutional Form, Columbia University Press 1993)

Mavroidis PC, "Licence to Adjudicate: A Critical Evaluation of the Work of the WTO Appellate Body So Far" in Hartigan JC (ed) *Trade Disputes and the Dispute Settlement Understanding of the WTO: An Interdisciplinary Assessment*, vol 6 (Trade Disputes and the Dispute Settlement Understanding of the WTO: An Interdisciplinary Assessment, Emerald Group Publishing Limited 2009)

Mavroidis PC, *The Regulation of International Trade: The WTO Agreements on Trade in Goods* (MIT Press 2016)

Mavroidis PC, Messerlin PA, and Wauters JM (eds), *The Law and Economics of Contingent Protection in the WTO* (Cambridge University Press 2010)

Merrill TW, "Judicial Prerogative, The" (1992) 12 *Pace Law Review* p. 327

Micheau C, *State Aid, Subsidy and Tax Incentives under EU and WTO Law* (Wolters Kluwer 2014)

Muris TJ, "Opportunistic Behavior and the Law of Contracts" (1980) 65 *Minnesota Law Review* p. 521

OECD, *Competition, State Aids and Subsidies* (Policy Roundtables, 2010)

Oeter S, "Legitimacy of Customary International Law" in Eger T and others (eds), *Economic Analysis of International Law* (Economic Analysis of International Law, Mohr Siebeck 2014)

Office of Fair Trading of the UK, *Public Subsidies* (UNCTAD's Seventh Session of the Intergovernmental Group of Experts on Competition Law and Policy 2004) p. 15

Pauwelyn J, "The Use of Experts in WTO Dispute Settlement" (2002) 51 *International and Comparative Law Quarterly* p. 325–64

Pauwelyn J, *Optimal Protection of International Law* (Cambridge University Press 2008)

Petersmann EU, *The GATT/WTO Dispute Settlement System: International Law, International Organizations and Dispute Settlement* (Springer Netherlands 1997)

Posner EA and Sykes AO (eds), *Economic Foundations of International Law* (Harvard University Press 2013)

Price TM, "Negotiating WTO Fisheries Subsidy Disciplines: Can Subsidy Transparency and Classification Provide the Means towards an End to the Race for Fish" (2005) 13 *Tulane Journal of International and Comparative Law* 141

Przeworski A, "On the Design of the State: A Principal-Agent Perspective" in Pereira LCB and Spink P (eds), *Reforming the State: Managerial Public Administration in Latin America* (Reforming the State: Managerial Public Administration in Latin America, Lynne Rienner Publishers 1999)

Ray D, *Development Economics* (Princeton University Press 1998)

Reinert KA, Rajan RS and Glass AJ (eds), *The Princeton Encyclopedia of the World Economy*, vol 2 (Princeton University Press 2009)

Ribeiro GF and Caiado J, "Why an Economic Analysis of International Public Law: Challenges and Perspectives in Brazil" (2015) 12 *Braz J Int'l L* p. 246

Rodrik D, "The Economics of Export-Performance Requirements" (1987) 102 *The Quarterly Journal of Economics* p. 633–50

Rowley CK, "Public Choice and the Economic Analysis of Law" in Mercuro N (ed) *Law and Economics* (Springer 1989)

Rubini L, *The Definition of Subsidy and State Aid: WTO and EC Law in Comparative Perspective* (Oxford University Press 2009)

Rubini L, "Ain't Wastin' Time No More: Subsidies for Renewable Energy, The SCM Agreement, Policy Space, and Law Reform" (2012) 15 *Journal of International Economic Law* p. 525–79

Schill S and Briese R, "'If the State Considers': Self-Judging Clauses in International Dispute Settlement" (2009) 13 *Max Planck Yearbook of United Nations Law* p. 61–140

Schlag P, "Rules and Standards" (1985) 33 *UCLA Law Review* p. 379

Schropp S, *Trade Policy Flexibility and Enforcement in the WTO: A Law and Economic Analysis* (Cambridge International Trade and Economic Law, Cambridge University Press 2009)

Schwartz WF and Sykes AO, "The Economic Structure of Renegotiation and Dispute Resolution in the World Trade Organization" (2002) 31 *The Journal of Legal Studies* p. 179–204

Schorr DK, *Sustainability Criteria for Fisheries Subsidies: Options for the WTO and Beyond* (UNEP/Earthprint 2007)

Scott RE, "The Law and Economics of Incomplete Contracts" (2006) 2 *Annual Review of Law and Social Science* p. 279–97

Scott RE and Stephan PB, *The Limits of Leviathan: Contract Theory and the Enforcement of International Law* (1st edn, Cambridge Univiversity Press 2011)

Scott RE and Triantis GG, "Incomplete Contracts and the Theory of Contract Design" (2005) 56 *Case Western Reserve Law Review* p. 187–201

Scott RE and Triantis GG, "Anticipating Litigation in Contract Design" (2006) *The Yale Law Journal* p. 814–79

Shavell S, "Damage Measures for Breach of Contract" (1980) 11 *The Bell Journal of Economics* p. 466–90

Sinn H-W, "Germany's Economic Unification: An Assessment after Ten Years" (2002) 10 *Review of International Economics* p. 113–28

Slotboom M, *A Comparison of WTO and EC Law: Do Different Objects and Purposes Matter for Treaty Interpretation?* (London: Cameron May 2006)

Snidal D, "Coordination versus Prisoners' Dilemma: Implications for International Cooperation and Regimes" (1985) 79 *The American Political Science Review* p. 923–42

Staiger RW and Sykes AO, "Non-Violations" (2013) *16 Journal of International Economic Law* p. 741–75

Steger D, "The WTO Doha Round Negotiations on Subsidies and Countervailing Measures: Issues for Negotiators" (Symposium on Economic Restructuring in Korea in Light of the Doha Development Round Negotiations on Rules)

Steger D, "The Culture of the WTO: Why It Needs to Change" (2007) 10 *Journal of International Economic Law* p. 483–95

Stehmann O, "Export Subsidies in the Regional Aircraft Sector—The Impact of Two WTO Panel Rulings against Canada and Brazil" (1999) 33 *Journal of World Trade* p. 97–120

Stein A, "Coordination and Collaboration: Regimes in an Anarchic World" (1982) 36 *International Organization* p. 299–324

Stephenson S, *Addressing Local Content Requirements in a Sustainable Energy Trade Agreement* (2013)

Stille F and Teichmann D, "German Subsidisation Policy in the Wake of Unification" (1993) 29 *Economic Bulletin* p. 11–18

Sykes AO, "Countervailing Duty Law: An Economic Perspective" (1989) 89 *Columbia Law Review* p. 199–263

Sykes AO, "Subsidies and Countervailing Measures" in Macrory P and others (eds), *The World Trade Organization: Legal, Economic and Political Analysis* (The World Trade Organization: Legal, Economic and Political Analysis, Springer 2005)

Sykes AO, *The Limited Economic Case for Subsidies Regulation* (E15Initiative Think Piece 2015)

Thaler RH and Sunstein CR, *Nudge: Improving Decisions about Health, Wealth, and Happiness* (Yale University Press 2008)

Thirlwall AP, *Economics of Development: Theory and Evidence* (Palgrave Macmillan 2011)

Trachtman JP, "Regulatory Jurisdiction and the WTO" (2007) 10 *Journal of International Economic Law* p. 631–51

Trachtman JP, *The Economic Structure of International Law* (Cambridge University Press 2008)

Trachtman JP, "SCM and GATT Article XX – A Quick Question" (2014) World Trade Law <http://worldtradelaw.typepad.com/ielpblog/2014/11/scm-and-gatt-article-xx-a-quick-question.html> accessed 09.24.2016

Tran C, "Using GATT, Art XX to Justify Climate Change Measures in Claims under the WTO Agreements" (2010) 27 *Environmental and Planning Law Journal* p. 346

Trebilcock MJ, *Advanced Introduction to International Trade Law* (Edward Elgar Publishing 2015)

Trebilcock MJ and Howse R, *The Regulation of International Trade* (Psychology Press 2005)

Trofimov ID, "The Failure of the International Trade Organization (ITO): A Policy Entrepreneurship Perspective" (2012) 5 *Journal of Policy & Law* p. 56

UK OoFTot, *Public Subsidies* (UNCTAD's Seventh Session of the Intergovernmental Group of Experts on Competition Law and Policy, 2004)

van Aaken A, "Begrenzte Rationalität und Paternalismusgefahr. Das Prinzip des schonendsten Paternalismus" in Anderheiden M and others (eds), *Paternalismus und Recht : in memorian Angela Augustin (1968–2004)* (Paternalismus und Recht : in memorian Angela Augustin (1968–2004), Mohr Siebeck 2006)

van Aaken A, "Towards Behavioral International Law and Economics: A Comment on Enriching Rational Choice Institutionalism for the Study of International Law" (2008) *University of Illinois Law Review* p. 47–59

van Aaken A, "International Investment Law between Commitment and Flexibility: A Contract Theory Analysis" (2009) 12 *Journal of International Economic Law* p. 507–38

van Aaken A, "Opportunities and the Limits of an Economic Analysis in International Law" (2011) 3 *Transnational Corporations Review* p. 27–46

van Aaken A, "Control Mechanisms in International Investment Law" in Douglas Z and others (eds), *The Foundations of International Investment Law: Bringing Theory into Practice* (The Foundations of International Investment Law: Bringing Theory into Practice, Oxford University Press 2013)

van Aaken A, "Behavioral International Law and Economics" (2014) 55 *Harvard International Law Journal* p. 421–83

van Aaken A, "Delegating Interpretative Authority in Investment Treaties: The Case of Joint Commissions" (2014) 11 *Transnational Dispute Management* p. 21–47

van Aaken A, "Smart Flexibility Clauses in International Investment Treaties and Sustainable Development" (2014) 15 *The Journal of World Investment & Trade* p. 827–61

Wendt A, "Anarchy Is What States Make of It: The Social Construction of Power Politics" (1992) 46 *International Organization* p. 391–425

Whish R and Bailey D, *Competition Law* (Oxford University Press 2015)

Wouters J and Coppens D, "An Overview of the Agreement on Subsidies and Countervailing Measuress Including a Discussion on the Agreement on Agriculture" in Bagwell K and others (eds), *Law and Economics of Contingent Protection in International Trade* (Law and Economics of Contingent Protection in International Trade, Cambridge University Press 2010)

WTO, *Exploring the Links between Subsidies, Trade and the WTO* (World Trade Report 2006)

WTO, *Understanding the WTO* (WTO 2015)

WTO, "Dispute Settlement: Disputes by Agreement" (2016) <https://www.wto.org/english/tratop_e/dispu_e/dispu_agreements_index_e.htm?id=A20#> accessed 09.01.2018

WTO, "Multilateral Negotiation Rounds" (2016) <www.wto.org> accessed 08.16.2016

Zeiler TW, "The Expanding Mandate of the GATT: The First Seven Rounds" in Narlikar A and others (eds), *The Oxford Handbook on The World Trade Organization* (The Oxford Handbook on The World Trade Organization, Oxford University Press 2012)

INDEX

Actionable subsidies, 109, 119, 120, 126, 128, 129, 131, 132, 134, 135, 147, 151, 152, 154, 184, 185, 186, 190, 191, 208, 211, 216, 220, 222, 226, 227, 228, 229, 231

Adverse effects, 27, 74, 115, 120, 121, 129, 130, 131, 134, 147, 152, 185, 220, 222, 223

Appellate Body, xxii, xxiv, xxv, xxvi, xxvii, xxviii, xxix, 13, 47, 119, 127, 128, 131, 145, 146, 166, 167, 168, 169, 170, 171, 174, 175, 176, 177, 178, 179, 180, 181, 182, 183, 194, 195, 196, 197, 198, 204, 211, 214, 215, 218, 239

Article XVI, 108, 112, 113, 114, 163, 173, 205, 220

Article XX, 14, 48, 126, 186, 192, 194, 195, 196, 197, 198, 200, 202, 209, 210, 211, 212, 213, 214, 215, 216, 217, 218, 219, 220, 222, 225, 229, 230, 235, 242

Beggar thy neighbor, 78, 94, 105

Benefit, xii, 1, 2, 6, 7, 19, 20, 21, 24, 25, 26, 36, 53, 59, 62, 63, 64, 66, 70, 72, 73, 74, 75, 76, 77, 78, 79, 81, 82, 85, 86, 88, 91, 93, 94, 95, 96, 98, 102, 104, 118, 122, 124, 125, 131, 148, 158, 161, 172, 178, 179, 180, 181, 182, 183, 186, 193, 207, 223, 226

Benevolent governments, 71, 73, 80, 85, 94

Biases, 41

Bounded rationality, 40

Circumvention of commitments, 104

Committee on Subsidies and countervailing Measures, xxii, 150

Competitive advantage, 4, 61, 66, 72, 88, 91, 124

Complete contract, 15, 34, 35, 36, 37, 49, 51, 53, 57, 103, 225

Confer a benefit, 128, 177, 180

Contingencies, 9, 39, 42, 44, 50, 51, 57, 100, 144, 156, 157, 158, 159, 164, 166, 167, 207, 226

Contingent upon export performance, 91, 125

Contract theory, 43, 46, 62, 225

Contracting Parties, 110, 112, 114, 115, 116, 139, 140, 143, 144, 163

Contracts, 6, 15, 17, 19, 23, 31, 32, 33, 34, 35, 36, 37, 38, 39, 41, 42, 43, 44, 47, 48, 50, 51, 53, 55, 58, 100, 103, 104, 134, 156, 172, 222, 224, 225, 236, 239, 241

Contractual incompleteness, 38, 39, 42, 48, 50, 238

Coppens, xxi, 95, 100, 106, 107, 108, 114, 116, 118, 119, 120, 126, 127, 128, 130, 132, 138, 139, 148, 149, 150, 179, 183, 191, 193, 194, 216, 229, 230, 231, 235, 243

Countervailing duties, 11, 56, 89, 119, 135, 136, 139, 140, 141, 166, 174, 186, 188, 190, 205, 234

Cross-border effects, 15, 62

Customary international law, 29

CVDs, xii, xiii, 11, 12, 108, 112, 116, 135, 136, 137, 138, 139, 140, 141, 142, 163, 180, 194

De minimis, 193

Default rules, 57, 225

Disadvantaged regions, 120, 186, 188

Economic analysis, 18, 20, 33, 235

Effects test, 129, 130, 152, 208, 222